David Ricardo, Jacob Harry Hollander, James Bonar

Letters of David Ricardo to Hutches Trower and others

1811-1823

David Ricardo, Jacob Harry Hollander, James Bonar

Letters of David Ricardo to Hutches Trower and others
1811-1823

ISBN/EAN: 9783337134808

Printed in Europe, USA, Canada, Australia, Japan

Cover: Foto ©ninafisch / pixelio.de

More available books at **www.hansebooks.com**

LETTERS

OF

DAVID RICARDO

TO

HUTCHES TROWER

AND OTHERS

1811—1823

EDITED BY

JAMES BONAR
M.A. OXFORD, LL.D. GLASGOW

AND

J. H. HOLLANDER
PH.D.
ASSOCIATE PROFESSOR OF FINANCE, JOHNS HOPKINS UNIVERSITY, BALTIMORE

Oxford
AT THE CLARENDON PRESS
1899

INTRODUCTION

SINCE the publication by the Clarendon Press of the Letters of Ricardo to Malthus (1887), two collections of Ricardo's letters have appeared: (1) the privately printed 'Letters written by David Ricardo (1822) during a Tour on the Continent' (Gloucester, 1891); (2) the 'Letters of David Ricardo to John Ramsay McCulloch, 1816–1823; Edited, with introduction and annotations, by J. H. Hollander, Ph.D.', published for the American Economic Association by Macmillan and Co., New York, Sonnenschein and Co., London, 1896. This collection was presented to the British Museum by Mr. H. G. Reid, the last surviving executor of McCulloch, in April, 1894.

After the publication of the Letters to McCulloch, our attention was turned to the Letters of Ricardo to Hutches Trower, in the library of University College, London; and further inquiry led to the discovery of the earlier half of that correspondence. Hutches Trower (born July 2, 1777) was a member of the firm of Trower and Battye, Stockbrokers, 1 Bank Street, Cornhill; and it was on the Stock Exchange that he formed the acquaintance of Ricardo and discovered their common interest in economics and political philosophy (see Letter XVIII). Like Ricardo, he was a shareholder in the Bank of England, and attended the meetings of its Court (see VII). He was also concerned in the East India Company, spoke often at its meetings, and took a lively interest in its general policy (see II). In 1813 (Aug. 4) he married Penelope Frances, third daughter of Gilbert Slater or Sclater, a partner of his brother's in Eastcheap[1]; and his marriage was followed, at the end of 1814, by his purchase of Unsted Wood, Godalming, Surrey, and his retirement to a country life. He became Chairman of the Guildford bench of magistrates, and studied his law books carefully. He was Grand Sheriff of Surrey in 1820. He took an active part in county politics. He was a warm supporter of Savings Banks. He was an occasional contributor of articles to the Times, and he wrote letters to that paper and others on various public questions. It was probably his letters to the Morning Chronicle in 1809 on the Bullion controversy that led to his first acquaintance with another contributor of letters to the Chronicle, Ricardo, in whose career as an economist that controversy made an epoch. In Ricardo's first letter, or rather communication, of August 29, 1809, on 'The Price of Gold,' he had attributed 'all the evils of our currency' to the over-issues of the Bank,

'to the dangerous power with which it was entrusted of diminishing at its will the value of every monied man's property, and by enhancing the price of provisions and every necessary of life, injuring the public annuitant and all those persons whose incomes were fixed, and who were consequently not enabled to shift any part of the burden from their own shoulders.'

This letter provoked, among other replies, Trower's letter of Sept. 14, 1809. He thinks Ricardo has exaggerated the evils of the situation, and has misconceived the causes of the High Price of Gold, which are, in Trower's opinion, (1) the discredit brought by the French Assignats on all

---

[1] See Post Office Directory, 1817. His brother is mentioned in Letter XXVI, page 77, and XLVIII, 158.

paper money, and (2) the neediness of nations engaged in war. It is (he says) really to the high or low rate of Interest that we should look in order to ascertain the proportion which the circulation bears to the demands of the people. Ricardo's second letter is largely a refutation of this latter idea. So Trower's second letter contained the statement that 'Silver is the only measure of value,' and Bank Notes represent Silver,—an idea refuted by Ricardo in his third letter (Nov. 23), and in the paper given below (Appendix A (2)). We can therefore say with truth that Ricardo's famous pamphlet on the High Price of Bullion, being as it was a free version of the letters to the Chronicle, owes much of its shape to Trower.

Trower became an intimate friend of the whole family of Ricardo (see LXVI). He was a scholarly man of wide reading, interested not only in economics, politics, and social reform, but in theology, literature, geology, and tree-planting. He was 'aye stickin'-in a tree' and transforming the landscape (LXIV). In political economy, if not a match for Ricardo, he was often acute in his criticisms (XLVIII and Appendix). The following passage occurs in an undated fragment of his MSS.:—

'It must be confessed that Political Economists in their speculations "take no note of time." They point out the general rules which govern the subject of which they treat, but they forbear to designate the obstacles by which these rules are opposed in their operations, and the period that elapses before these obstacles are removed. And yet time is a mighty[1] ingredient in all human affairs. It is the great artificer which brings all things to perfection, and bears them onward[2] to their destination. These principles are not the less true because, in practice, circumstances may arise to interfere with their operations, and to obstruct their progress, their predictions are not the less infallible, nor their effects the less unerring.

[1] 'Grand' written under 'mighty.'   [2] 'Along' under 'onward.'

'Great injustice and great mischief have been done to the science of political economy, by attributing to its precepts a more unerring certainty than is claimed for them by their advocates. What is the object of that science? To discover a very difficult problem: What are the circumstances that constitute the wealth of nations,—which influence their commercial prosperity, assist or retard their progress in riches, and which improve or deteriorate the condition of the people. These, it must be confessed, are objects of sufficient importance to be well worthy the most serious attention of the philosopher.'

It may not be quite true that the element of time was altogether overlooked[1], but it certainly was not sufficiently regarded by the older economists. Trower himself sided with Ricardo against Malthus, and was of the 'New School' which had (says Samuel Turner, 'Considerations,' 1822, pp. 1, 2) converted Liverpool, Londonderry, Vansittart, and Huskisson.

Hutches Trower outlived Ricardo ten years, dying on June 5, 1833, from an injury to his spine. He left four daughters; and his widow survived till 1875. His daughter, Miss Frances Trower, of Twyning Manor, Tewkesbury, Gloucestershire, to whom we owe most of the above facts, wrote (on Nov. 12, 1895) nearly a year before her death:—

'I have frequently heard my mother speak of that correspondence, of which she was very proud, and state that, when (I should suppose about 50 years ago) a new edition of Ricardo's works was contemplated, she sent up to the Publisher all Ricardo's letters to her Husband. These letters unfortunately reached the publisher too late to be included in the book, which was already in the Press. That these letters were not returned,— probably remained with the then Publisher, is I imagine certain. as my mother looked forward to the possibility of another edition of Ricardo's works being printed in which the Editor would then include his letters to my Father.

[1] See Letters to Malthus, Pref. p. xvi; Letters to MacCulloch, Introd. p. xxi.

'Only lately, in looking over old papers I came upon a letter from my mother, in which she refers to this Correspondence, adding: "It does an honour to any man to have corresponded with Ricardo."'

It was McCulloch who edited the first collection of Ricardo's collected Works in 1846 (Preface dated April of that year), Murray being the publisher. The letters sent by Mrs. Trower for McCulloch could only have been the collection preserved for the last fifty years in University College, and consisting of the last twenty-two letters addressed to Trower in the present volume together with two letters of Anthony Austin (LXV, LXVI). They are carefully bound in full calf, lettered along the back 'Mr. Ricardo to Mr. Trower. MS. Letters 1820-23'; and on the fly-leaf is written: "'MS. Letters of Mr. D. Ricardo, 1 vol. 4to., *Donation of* Mrs. Trower through Mr. Greenough.' Copy of an entry in University College London Additions to Library, vol. 4, under date of Feb. 22, 1844. The words underlined are printed headings. A. Wheeler [librarian], Sept. 1895."

Mrs. Trower must have forgotten that she had presented the collection to University College library, where McCulloch could easily have used them if he had been so disposed, in good time for his edition of Ricardo's Works.

There was a collection of letters (the first thirty letters to Trower in the present volume) which were not sent in 1844, but remained unobserved among the MSS. of Hutches Trower till Miss Trower came upon them and kindly lent them to us at the end of 1895, giving us also an opportunity of looking through such miscellaneous papers of her father's as seemed to be of public interest. Among these papers were two in Ricardo's handwriting (Appendix A (2) and B (1)).

Through the kindness of Miss Trower's executors the whole Collection is now in the possession of University College, London, which has given its ready consent and help to the publication of it. We have included, with these Letters, some papers from the Trower MSS. that bore on the subjects of the Letters, and also some correspondence of Ricardo which, if previously published at all, was not now easily accessible, such as with Sinclair, Place, Wheatley, and Goldsmid. The judgement of economists on Ricardo is noticeably a more favourable one now than it was before the publication of the letters to Malthus [1]. The later collections should have a like effect. In view of the present series of letters to Trower, we should no longer speak of Ricardo as legislating for Saturn (Malthus and His Work, p. 212). In Letter XLI for example, in dealing with the positions of Malthus, he shows greater regard than that economist for the immediate effects of any change as compared with the ultimate; corn does not *at once* raise up its own consumers; the effect of high wages will not be *at first* more mouths but greater demand for workmen's luxuries. We must not argue on the assumption that land is held by one man, but, as it is held now, by many different owners, who produce for private gain under the stimulus of prices (XL). So he complains of Tooke: 'He will not allow you to reason with a view to practice from the observations of the produce for ten years,' but will look to results over half a century (LXII). In theory, Ricardo approved of a Sinking Fund raised from taxes, but as a practical politician he came to think it worse than useless from the inability of ministers to avoid tampering with it, and so, 'if we are to be taxed only for the purpose of creating a sinking fund, I for one dissent from it' (XXXI). Yet he had just been maintaining its theoretical justification against Francis Place (XXIX, XXX). In a somewhat similar spirit he supports the

---

[1] See for example Professor Gonner's Preface and Introduction to his edition of the Principles of Political Economy and Taxation (Bell, 1891).

Resumption of Cash Payments, although according to his own plan the currency could have been put on a solid basis without Resumption (XIV, XXV, XXXVI, XLIX). He is a Free Trader; but the Resolutions he laid before the Agricultural Committee strike even the cautious Trower as savouring of Protectionism (LVI). Ricardo says he despaired of doing any good now in the way of making better laws, but 'hoped to lay the foundation of a better system in the future.' He considers that a direct levy on property to buy out a great part of the National Debt would be better than a sinking Fund (XXXII), but (as has just been observed) he is not averse to all Sinking Funds. He admits that, like other Bullionists, he at first considered gold and silver to be less variable than they have turned out to be (VI). On the other hand, he was never shaken in his opinion that (1) the depression of Agriculture after the war was due to over-production, and (2) the distress of industry generally was due to want of the capital absorbed by the Debt, though in these letters we hear more of the first contention than the second. His political views are equally steadfast; he evidently enjoyed his hard fights in Parliament ('I like business,' LI); he does his best to convert Trower to the principles of the Radical Reformers, though with little success (XX, &c.).

Trower agrees with him to some small extent in politics, but most fully in love of economic studies. Ricardo would have wished him to throw himself even more unreservedly into economic work; 'men of education and liberal views' in Trower's position might help to introduce improvements in agriculture, and to break down the deep-rooted prejudices of agriculturists (XXXI). Under free trade, he thought, though a few individuals might suffer, political economy would be able to guard the mass of the people against every domestic revulsion, unless such were caused (*a*) by political revolutions outside; (*b*) by industrial improvement in other countries; or (c) by the caprices of fashion (XLI). Hence he deplored the slow advance and small influence of political economy (XXXIV, XXXVIII), and deplored the differences among economists that could not but hinder the good cause. When three or four economists meet together and discuss rising or falling values, they have three or four different measures of value by which to judge (LXII).

For himself his heart was in economic work. He could not judge well whether Mill's Elements were good for their purpose: 'I have thought so much on the subject myself that I can form a very inadequate idea of the impression which his work is calculated to make on one who is a learner' (LII). He would wish to devote all the talent he possessed to the clearer establishing of those doctrines on rent, profit, and wages, in regard to which he differs from Adam Smith and Malthus (V). There is need, at this time more especially, for a patient thinker (XXVIII) who will consider the question of taxation and the revenue of the State, because no doubt government does best to leave agriculture, commerce, and manufacture alone, but the State must still 'interfere' in order to get money for its proper functions (XXXI). He would willingly labour himself on this subject if he had any leisure left. Malthus had not touched it, and, if he had touched it, they might not have agreed. Their other points of difference are discussed with some warmth. One question between them is summed up neatly in Letter III: Do the profits of the farmer regulate the profits of all other trades? Does the production of food regulate the profits of all other production? — The possibility of a Measure of Value, discussed at such length in the correspondence with Malthus, comes up again for discussion here chiefly in Letters XXXVIII, XXXIX, LXIII, LXIV. They are hardly equal in vigour to the onslaught on Malthus and Trower in the earlier Letters, about the relation of the supply and demand to the price of corn. Ricardo, whose political economy may be said[1] to have 'entered the court as plaintiff and left as defendant,' has been held responsible for a more cruel view of wages than he actually held. We read in these letters that wages should be above the minimum of necessaries in order that saving may be made possible (XVIII), and the writer put that merciful principle into practice: 'I believe they have lowered the price of labour here, but I, as a gentleman I suppose, always pay the same' (XLII). Yet we know from Bentham[2], and from the 'Tour on the Continent,' that in the way of bargain Ricardo would cavil on the ninth part of a hair.

These letters cover a greater variety of topics than will be found in the letters to McCulloch or to Malthus. Ireland, Savings Banks, and Queen Caroline, take up almost as much room as pure economics and finance. The MSS. of Hutches Trower, kindly placed at our disposal by Mr. Walter Trower, sometimes enable us to see both sides of a dispute, and understand Trower's case as presented by himself. We have given no analysis of the economical arguments, which as a rule are those of the Letters to Malthus and to McCulloch. The spelling and punctuation of the original manuscripts have been preserved wherever possible.

With the present volume practically all of Ricardo's informal writings have been made accessible. The series of letters to Malthus, McCulloch, and Trower, and the privately printed correspondence of the continental tour have not only modified the common estimate of Ricardo's personal character, and of certain of his fundamental doctrines, but

---

[1] Cf. Letter XLVIII.
[2] Letters to Malthus, p. 55, Bentham, Works, x. 498.

have made possible, for the first time, an acquaintance with the details of his every-day activity. Two appreciable *desiderata* still remain,—literary evidence of his long and close intimacy with James Mill, and the important 'Notes on Malthus,' to which frequent reference is made in the following pages. Inquiry in various directions has failed to reveal the existence of either collection. Until some fortunate accident or more successful search brings to light the additional sources, it seems likely that our acquaintance both with Ricardo's personality and with his economic system will be based upon the material now in the hands of the public.

{ J. BONAR.
{ J. H. HOLLANDER.

LONDON, *July*, 1899.

The mother of Hutches Trower was Miss Smith, an aunt of Sydney Smith. He was born at Clapton and was adopted by a Mr. Palmer who made him his heir and left him a house in the city where it is said a quantity of diamonds were found, greatly contributing to Trower's fortune.

CONTENTS

	PAGE
INTRODUCTION	v

LETTERS.

I. RICARDO TO BENTHAM, *August* 13, 1811 1
   Regretting that he is unable to visit Bentham in the country to meet Mill.

II. RICARDO TO TROWER, *November* 8, 1813 2
   Acknowledging receipt of Trower's pamphlet on the proposed Church establishments in India, and expressing agreement with Trower's opinion on the subject.

   NOTE ON TROWER'S PAMPHLET 3

III. RICARDO TO TROWER, *March* 8, 1814 4
   Describing the nature of his dispute with Malthus in regard to the employment of capital in Agriculture, — whether its extension in agriculture is a condition precedent of its extension in other fields, Ricardo maintaining the invariable precedence and Malthus denying it.

IV. RICARDO TO SINCLAIR, *October* 31, 1814 6
   Describing the mental attitude of the average member of the Stock Exchange, and mentioning some superior men who might be of use to Sinclair in his inquiries into the currency.

V. RICARDO TO TROWER, *October* 29, 1815 7
   Telling of his labours on a new pamphlet [Economical & Secure Currency] and of his project of a more general treatise, —commenting also on the character and career of Napoleon.

Contents

		PAGE
VI. RICARDO TO TROWER, *December* 25, 1815		11

Describing his difficulties in public speaking, expressing his agreement with Trower on the Bullion question, and his hopes for a revival of Agriculture and Trade, in spite of the Debt.

VII. RICARDO TO TROWER, *February* 5, 1816 14

Remarking on the prospects of an attack on the policy and position of the Bank of England, discussing the position of Savings Banks, giving his views on English Agriculture, its misfortunes and its consolations, hoping for the maintenance of the Sinking Fund, and deploring the condition of his own house in Brook Street.

VIII. RICARDO TO TROWER, *March* 9, 1816 17

Expressing satisfaction at the favourable reception of his pamphlet [Economical & Secure Currency], discussing Savings Banks, and touching on the trials and labours of Malthus, the speeches of Western, and the proposed Property Tax.

NOTE ON SAMUEL TURNER 19

IX. RICARDO TO TROWER, *July* 15, 1816 20

Giving an account of his fortnight's holiday, criticizing the views of Weyland on Population, especially in regard to Ireland, defending the English people against Trower's charge that they had been degraded by the war, and giving some details of London Savings Banks.

NOTE: LETTER OF GREENOUGH TO TROWER ON THE STATE OF PUBLIC AFFAIRS AND THE CAUSE AND REMEDY OF THE PRESENT DISTRESS, *December* 14, 1816   23

X. RICARDO TO TROWER, *January* 27, 1817 24

Discussing the policy and administration of the Poor Laws, and disputing the wisdom of a certain clause in Rose's Saving Bank Bill [permitting Poor Law relief to be given to members of Provident Institutions].

XI. RICARDO TO TROWER, *February* 24, 1817 27

Continuing the discussion of the Poor Laws and Rose's Bill.

XII. RICARDO TO TROWER, *March* 30, 1817 29

Describing the difficulty he has found in getting parliamentary papers for Trower, and asking his candid opinion of 'Political Economy and Taxation,' now being published.

XIII. RICARDO TO TROWER, *May* 9, 1817 31

Discussing the privileges of Depositors in the Savings Banks as regards Government Debentures.

Contents

	PAGE
XIV. RICARDO TO SINCLAIR, *May* 4, 1817	33

Defending the return to Cash Payments, while allowing the wisdom of a properly secured paper currency.

XV. RICARDO TO TROWER, Antwerp, *June* 15, 1817 . . . 34

Giving an account of his tour on the Continent, and his impressions of the condition of Manufacture, Trade, and Agriculture there and in England.

XVI. RICARDO TO TROWER, *August* 23, 1817 37

Jocularly referring to Owen, describing interviews with Say in Paris, quoting a criticism of Malthus on the 'Political Economy and Taxation,' mentioning his own relations with Torrens, and alluding to a financial scheme of Trower.

NOTE: ROBERT OWEN IN LONDON, 1817 . . . 41

XVII. RICARDO TO TROWER, *December* 10, 1817 . . . 41

Regretting the death of Princess Charlotte, and speaking of the Report of the Commons Committee on the Poor Laws, the success of his book, the struggles of Savings Banks against the prejudices of the workmen, and the new works of Mill and Malthus.

XVIII. RICARDO TO TROWER, *January* 26, 1818 . . . 45

Recalling his first meetings with Trower, and the good effect on him of conversations with his friends generally, alluding to various reviews and singling out Sumner's for special praise, recurring to the Poor Laws and Savings Banks, and eulogizing Mill's 'British India' now about to appear.

XIX. RICARDO TO TROWER, *March* 22, 1818 . . . 49

Thanking him for congratulations on his elevation to the Sheriffship, and for praise of his book,—making some remarks on Birkbeck's 'Journey in America,' Vansittart's Stock Notes, Bentham's 'Parliamentary Reform,' and Llandaff's 'Life.'

XX. RICARDO TO TROWER, *June* 27, 1818 53

Commenting on the General Election and parliamentary representation in general, with some strictures on Brougham.

XXI. RICARDO TO TROWER, *September* 18, 1818 . . . 56

Mentioning his recall to London through his brother's illness, discussing the reviews of his book, especially in regard to price and rent, and giving his views on parliamentary reform.

XXII. RICARDO TO TROWER, *November* 2, 1818 . . . 60

Arguing on behalf of parliamentary reform, on Utilitarian principles, and telling of his own approaching election.

Contents

	PAGE
XXIII. RICARDO TO TROWER, *December* 20, 1818 . . .	66

Dealing with Trower's objections to reform, especially those founded on a desire to preserve the alleged present balance of powers and present checks with only an indirect representation of the mass of the people,—mentioning a French translation of his 'Political Economy,' and alluding to a visit of Malthus.

XXIV. RICARDO TO TROWER, *February* 28, 1819 . . . 71

Announcing his election to a seat in Parliament, and alluding to conversations with members of the Committees on Currency.

XXV. RICARDO TO TROWER, *May* 28, 1819 73

Recording the decision of the House in favour of Resumption, and describing his own part in the deliberations, as well as his views on various other topics before Parliament.

XXVI. RICARDO TO TROWER, *June* 1, 1819 75

Advising him as to investment in Bank of England Stock, and giving reasons for caution.

XXVII. RICARDO TO TROWER, *July* 8, 1819 77

Saying that he is satisfied on the whole with the work of the Session and the financial prospects of the country, explaining his attitude to Robert Owen, and describing what happened at the meeting in London.

NOTE ON OWEN'S COMMITTEE 81

XXVIII. RICARDO TO TROWER, *September* 25, 1819 . . 81

Telling of his attempt amidst the distractions of a country life to write on the Sinking Fund, praising Hamilton's book on the Debt, admitting the need of a good work on Taxation, estimating the extent of the popular education in economics, and giving his views of the Manchester Massacre.

XXIX. RICARDO TO FRANCIS PLACE, *November* 1, 1819 . . 85

Refusing to join him in condemnation of all Sinking Funds, distinguishing between a Sinking Fund raised by loans and one raised by taxes, and maintaining that the latter kind is no delusion, apart from the bad faith of Ministers.

XXX. RICARDO TO PLACE, *November* 3, 1819 90

Contending that Hamilton would not have denied that there could be a Sinking Fund from taxes which would diminish the Debt by compound interest.

Contents

	PAGE
XXXI. RICARDO TO TROWER, *November* 12, 1819	92

Wishing he had time to study the best way for the State to raise funds, and regretting that Malthus does not deal with it in his new book,—vindicating the right of the people to hold meetings [to protest against the Manchester Massacre], — and deploring the alleged intention of Government to defer Resumption and to impose an Income Tax.

XXXII. RICARDO TO RICHARD HEATHFIELD, *December* 19, 1819 96

Expressing general agreement with Heathfield's plan, which is in fact his own, for the extinguishing of the National Debt, but pointing out details in which he cannot follow Heathfield.

NOTE (1): HEATHFIELD'S PLAN 98
NOTE (2): DAVID HUME ON HUTCHESON'S PLAN . . 99

XXXIII. RICARDO TO TROWER, *December* 28, 1819 . . . 100

Criticizing the policy of the Six Acts, defending his proposal for a direct contribution towards payment of the Debt, and commenting on the Debates in the House of Commons.

XXXIV. RICARDO TO TROWER, *January* 28, 1820 . . . 103

Discussing the effect on prices of an Income Tax as compared with a Tax on Goods, and remarking on the effects of Taxation in general.

XXXV. RICARDO TO TROWER, *March* 13, 1820 . . . 107

Agreeing to visit him with Mill, denying any intention of changing his seat, making remarks on the Election, on the present position and influence of Political Economy, and on the Petition of London Merchants in favour of Free Trade.

XXXVI. RICARDO TO SINCLAIR, *May* 11, 1820. . . . 110

Maintaining the rightness of Resumption without prejudice to his own plan of a purely paper currency, insisting on the desirability of not only paying off the Debt, but forbidding any new Debt, and contrasting point by point his own views with Sinclair's.

XXXVII. RICARDO TO MACVEY NAPIER, London, *May* 15, 1820   111

Returning (with remarks) the proof of his article on the Sinking Fund.

XXXVIII. RICARDO TO TROWER, Brighton, *July* 21, 1820 . 112

Regretting the proceedings against the Queen, discussing the views of Malthus on price, cost, and rent, pointing out his misrepresentations of Ricardo, and singing the praises of Joseph Hume.

	PAGE

XXXIX. RICARDO TO TROWER, *September* 15, 1820 . . . 117
    Describing an excursion on the Wye with Mill, giving comments on various passages in Malthus' 'Political Economy,' especially in regard to Measure of Value, and the paradox that corn raises up its own demanders.

XL. RICARDO TO TROWER, *September* 26, 1820 . . . 124
    Arguing at some length against Trower that the supply of corn follows and does not precede the demand for it, concluding with a defence of Say's view that demand is only limited by production.

XLI. RICARDO TO TROWER, *October* 3, 1820 . . . 128
    Pointing out that an equally increased production of all articles may not leave their value unaffected, necessaries having a limited demand and luxuries an unlimited, contending that apart from miscalculation production follows demand, and that it is best to leave trade free.

XLII. RICARDO TO TROWER, *November* 26, 1820 . . . 134
    Expressing his indignation at the treatment of the Queen, and despondency about politics,—quoting some specimens of his own unpublished Notes on Malthus in regard to the Nature and Measure of Value.

XLIII. RICARDO TO TROWER, *January* 14, 1821 . . . 139
    Disapproving of Mr. Vansittart's treatment of the Sinking Fund, doubting whether Five Per Cents can have the popularity of Three Per Cents, and asking Trower's opinion about his Notes on Malthus, now with McCulloch. [Letter imperfect.]

XLIV. RICARDO TO TROWER, *March* 2, 1821 . . . 143
    Referring to the Surrey (County) Meeting to protest against the persecution of the Queen, mentioning his controversy with Malthus on the alleged good effects of expenditure, describing his dispute in the House with Baring on the Currency, and giving his views on the Agricultural interest and the Catholic claims.

    NOTE: COUNTY MEETING AT EPSOM 146

XLV. RICARDO TO TROWER, *April* 21, 1821 . . . 146
    Touching on Godwin's book against Malthus, Mill's 'Political Economy,' the claims of Ireland, and at greater length on the Agricultural Committee.

XLVI. RICARDO TO SINCLAIR, *June* 15, 1821 . . . 150
    Refusing to approve Sinclair's proposals for an increase of paper currency.

Contents

                                                                                                 PAGE

XLVII. RICARDO TO TROWER, *July* 4, 1821 150
    Vindicating some of his positions in regard to the Measure of Value in the Notes on Malthus, and remarking on the political situation.

XLVIII. RICARDO TO TROWER, *August* 22, 1821 . . . 154
    Describing his share in the proceedings and report of the Agricultural Committee, continuing the discussion on Value, and adding remarks on the Queen, the prospects of Peace, Mushet's Tables, and the valuation of Tithes.

XLIX. RICARDO TO JOHN WHEATLEY, *September* 18, 1821 . 159
    Maintaining that the price of corn must be referred not only to supply and demand, but to cost of production,—that the nation have not been losers by Resumption of Cash Payments, the farmers and manufacturers having as much less to give as they have to receive, but admitting there have been inequalities, and there has been real increase of Taxation,—denying that he recommended Resumption at a time when depreciation was 30 per cent.

L. RICARDO TO TROWER, *October* 4, 1821 161
    Touching on the Agricultural Committee, believing in spite of Tooke that England will always be an importing country, hoping with Trower that statesmen will be more guided by principles of Political Economy than they now are, discussing whether tithes are or are not a good investment as compared with land, and referring to articles in the Edinburgh Review by Sydney Smith and Malthus.

LI. RICARDO TO TROWER, *December* 11, 1821 166
    Describing his visit to Hereford and the Dinner in honour of Joseph Hume there, mentioning various signs of progress in the diffusion of sound doctrine, defending himself against the charge of responsibility for Resumption as actually effected, and making remarks on the political situation.

LII. RICARDO TO TROWER, *January* 25, 1822 170
    Insisting that Agricultural Distress must not be ascribed to taxation, but mainly to the low prices caused by over-supply, for Resumption accounted at most for 10 per cent. of the fall,—and giving his views on the condition and prospects of Ireland, and on the writings of Mill, Godwin, and McCulloch.

LIII. RICARDO TO SINCLAIR, *January* 29, 1822 . . . 174
    Reminding him that they do not agree on the causes of the Agricultural Distress, and finding a flaw in his criticism of Attwood's view of the relation of the exchanges to the price of corn.

	PAGE
LIV. RICARDO TO TROWER, *February*, 20, 1822 . . .	175
Condoling with him on his misfortunes at a Surrey (County) Meeting to consider Agricultural Distress, contrasting his own better fortune in the House, and dilating on the fallacies of Cobbett.	
NOTE (1): MEETING AT EPSOM	177
NOTE (2): LETTER OF GRENSIDE TO TROWER . . .	178
NOTE (3): BROUGHAM AND RICARDO	179
LV. RICARDO TO TROWER, *March* 5, 1822	180
Criticizing Trower's proposal to allow compounding for assessed taxes as a rival scheme to the Sinking Fund, mentioning a suggestion of Parnell's for the better control of the latter by the conversion of perpetual into terminable annuities, deploring the imperfections of parliamentary reporters, and making general remarks on the position of affairs in parliament.	
NOTE: TROWER ON ASSESSED TAXES	183
LVI. RICARDO TO TROWER, *March* 25, 1822 . . .	185
Explaining why he and Mill cannot visit Trower at present, complaining of the uselessness of the Sinking Fund as at present administered, and giving his views and his hopes about the Agricultural Committee.	
NOTE: RICARDO'S RESOLUTIONS ON THE CORN DUTIES .	187
LVII. RICARDO TO TROWER, *May* 20, 1822	189
Telling of his project of another tour on the Continent, and discussing Samuel Turner's pamphlet and other matters connected with the Corn Laws and public affairs generally.	
LVIII. RICARDO TO TROWER, *June* 9, 1822	191
Reporting that he is trying through Mill to procure insertion in the Chronicle for a letter of Trower on the monetary situation, and discussing the said letter.	
LIX. RICARDO TO TROWER, *December* 14, 1822 . . .	193
Describing his visit to Holland, Switzerland, and France, and his conversations with Dumont, De Broglie, Sismondi, Say, and Garnier,—and remarking on the œconomical and financial situation.	
LX. RICARDO TO TROWER, *January* 30, 1823 . . .	199
Explaining his political position as an advocate of reform who is unable to attribute the present distress to taxation and misgovernment,—touching on public events, on a pamphlet in	

defence of the Government, and on the prospects of changes in Currency.	
NOTE: COUNTY MEETING AT HEREFORD	202
LXI. RICARDO TO ISAAC LYON GOLDSMID, *April* 4, 1823	204
Expressing his views on religious toleration.	
LXII. RICARDO TO TROWER, *July* 24, 1823	205
Regretting that Trower is so little in London, the meeting-place of all the talents,—regretting also that economists differ so much about value, and giving his views on the proposals of Owen and others for the relief of Ireland, and on the theories of Tooke in regard to Agricultural Depression.	
LXIII. RICARDO TO TROWER, *July* 24, 1823	209
Responding to his questions about Parliament, and criticizing Malthus' 'Measure of Value.'	
LXIV. RICARDO TO TROWER, *August* 31, 1823	211
Hoping to have a visit from Trower, to meet Mill, in September,—and touching on his difference from Malthus and McCulloch in regard to a Measure of Value, on the good harvest, the Spanish War, and on the growth of trees at Unsted Wood and Gatcomb.	
LXV. AUSTIN TO TROWER, *September* 6, 1823	214
Telling of Ricardo's illness, which was not considered serious.	
LXVI. AUSTIN TO TROWER, *September* 12, 1823	214
Telling of Ricardo's death.	

APPENDIX—

A. Hutches Trower on Silver Bullion and Depreciation of Bank Notes	217
Ricardo in reply to Trower and Trotter	222
B. Ricardo on Taxation of Corn, and its alleged effect on the Currency	234
Trower on the same	235
INDEX	237

LETTERS OF DAVID RICARDO

TO

HUTCHES TROWER

AND OTHERS

I[1].

[TO BENTHAM.]

DEAR SIR, MILE END, 13 *Aug.*, 1811.

I BEG you to accept my thanks for your kind communication. I should have been most happy to have passed a few weeks in your neighbourhood, as besides the pleasure of Mr. Mill's society it would have afforded me the opportunity which I have long desired of procuring the gratification of your acquaintance [2], but there are obstacles in the way of my wishes which cannot be surmounted. My family is large, and for Mrs. Ricardo's comfort it would be necessary to have the whole of it with us. She would not be happy if one child were absent. At the present time this would be unattainable unless we were to withdraw the greatest part of our children from school, to

---

[1] The original is in the British Museum, Bentham Papers, Correspondence, vol. viii. 1803–1812, Add. MSS. 33, 544, f. 549.

[2] It thus appears that Ricardo became acquainted with Bentham through Mill, instead of with Mill through Bentham, as suggested by Professor Bain ('James Mill,' p. 74). For his later relations with Ricardo, see Letters to Malthus, p. 55, and article Bentham in Palgrave's Dictionary of Pol. Ec. vol. i. (1894), especially p. 132. Mill became acquainted with Ricardo on the appearance of Mill's 'Commerce Defended' (1807). See J. S. Mill, Pol. E. III. xiv. § 4.

B

which they have, after a long vacation, but just returned. I regret that I have been the occasion of so much trouble to you. I trust that on your return to London, to compensate me for my present disappointment, you will give me your company at Mile end,—a pleasure which Mr. Mill has often flattered me with and to which your obliging letter appears to have given me a new claim.

I am, Dear Sir, with great esteem,

Your obed^t. Servt.,

DAVID RICARDO [1].

J. BENTHAM, Esqr.

II [2].

DEAR TROWER,   UPPER BROOK STREET, 8th *Nov.*, 1813.

After reading the Pamphlet [3] which you were so kind as to send me, I fully intended calling on you [4], to thank you for the pleasure and information which I had received from it,—but I am so circumstanced at present that I am seldom at this part of the town at an hour when I am likely to meet you. Even yesterday,—a day generally at my disposal, I was obliged to leave home immediately after breakfast, and I did not return till this evening. In about a fortnight my family will return from Ramsgate, when I shall live more like a rational being. I shall then hope to see you both at your house and at mine.

I have read the letters written by you and Laicus (for the first time) with very great interest. All that can be said on the subject has, I think, been ably said on both sides. My opinion coincided with yours before I read your

---

[1] On the reverse of the last sheet are memoranda, probably by Bentham himself: '1811, Aug. 14, Ricardo (David) of Mile End, [to] J. B. Q. S. P. [Queen's Square Place], declines the house [?] at Bletchingley.'

[2] No cover or address.   [3] See Note.

[4] Trower was then living in Harley Street close by.

letters, and it is now very much strengthened by the facts and reasoning which you have brought forward. I quite rejoice that your time is so usefully employed.

Yours very truly,
DAVID RICARDO.

NOTE.—The family papers now in possession of Mr. Walter Trower enable us to assign to Hutches Trower the editorship of the pamphlet: 'Christianity in India. Letters between Laicus and an East India Proprietor, as they appeared in the *Times* newspaper in the months of August, September, and October, 1813.' London, Rivington, &c., N.D. The correspondence attracted some notice: see Gentleman's Magazine, Nov. 1813, Critical Review, Nov. 1813. The exciting cause of the whole was a remark by the Times in August on the renewal of the Charter of the East India Company: 'The conversion of the Hindoos, however, is a measure pregnant with danger; nay, the mere discussion of it may tend to excite those apprehensions, which it is of so much importance to calm, or to keep dormant.' 'Laicus' wrote on August 7th questioning this statement; 'East India Proprietor' (Hutches Trower), on August 26th, defended it; we must (he said) avoid the remotest appearance of an intention to effect compulsory conversion, or else we shall rouse a rebellion that will drive us from the Peninsula (p. 22 of the pamphlet). The establishment of bishops now conceded by charter might produce that appearance. Laicus (who declares himself also an East India Proprietor) returns to the charge in a second letter, and the correspondence goes on over seven letters, filling 102 pages of an 8vo pamphlet. Laicus is allowed to have the last word (Oct. 7). Though Trower is orthodox, devout, and politically a very moderate Whig, he goes so far as to say that the conversion of the Hindoos, even if expedient, is impossible; and he has the assent not only of Ricardo (in the above letter), but of G. B. Greenough, who says: 'In reading the letters of the East India Proprietor, I could not fail to derive great pleasure from seeing you support so good a cause with so much good temper and good sense' (letter in Trower MSS., dated 'Parliament Street, Nov. 6, 1813'). Hutches Trower's eldest brother, John, seems to have differed from him, and to have prepared a pamphlet on the other side (mentioned in the Trower MSS.). Hutches Trower had frequently spoken his mind on the matter in the Court of East India Proprietors, e.g. June 24, 1813, on the motion of Mr. John Bebb, afterwards Deputy-Chairman of the Company. For previous discussion of the subject, see Edin. Rev., April 1808 (p. 151), and April 1809 (p 40); Annual Register, 1813 [p. 58], cf. 315 (Debate and Bill).

III[1].

DEAR TROWER,   UPPER BROOK STREET, 8th *March*, 1814.

I called at your house yesterday; I wished to tell you that though well disposed to enter into the defence of my opinions, I was now so much occupied by business, that I could not devote the necessary time to it. Not having found you at home, I must tell you so by 'these present' [*sic*]. At the same time I must observe that what I feared, I believe has happened. To one not aware of the whole difference between Mr. Malthus and me, the papers[2] you read were not clear, and I think you have not entirely made out the subject in dispute.

Without entering further into the question, I will endeavour to state the question itself. When Capital increases in a country, and the means of employing Capital already exists, or increases, in the same proportion, the rate of interest and of profits will not fall.

Interest rises only when the means of employment for Capital bears a greater proportion than before to the Capital itself, and falls when the Capital bears a greater proportion to the arena, as Mr. Malthus has called it[3],

---

[1] The last sheet of the letter is used as the cover, and addressed, 'Hutches Trower, Esq., 33 Harley Street.'

[2] See following note.

[3] 'This country, from the extent of its lands, and its rich colonial possessions, has a large *arena* for the employment of an increasing capital.' 'Essay on Population,' 5th ed. (1817) vol. ii. p. 406. 'Of the Commercial

for its employment. On these points I believe we are all agreed, but I contend that the arena for the employment of new Capital cannot increase in any country in the same or greater proportion than the Capital itself[1], unless there be improvements in husbandry,—or new facilities be offered for the introduction of food from foreign countries; that in short it is the profits of the farmer which regulate the profits of all other trades,— and as the profits of the farmer must necessarily decrease with every augmentation of Capital employed on the land, provided no improvements be at the same time made in husbandry, all other profits must diminish, and therefore the rate of interest must fall. To this proposition Mr. Malthus does not agree. He thinks that the arena for the employment of Capital may increase, and consequently profits and interest may rise, altho' there should be no new facilities, either by importation, or improved tillage, for the production of food;—that the profits of the farmer no more regulate the profits of other trades, than the profits of other trades regulate the profits of the farmer, and consequently, if new markets are discovered in which we can obtain a greater quantity of foreign commodities in exchange for our commodities, than before the discovery of [such][2] markets, profits will increase and interest will rise. In such a state of things the rate of interest would rise as well as the profits of the farmer,

---

System,' Book III. ch. ix. As the phrase first appears in the fifth edition, we may suppose that Malthus had communicated to Ricardo his draft of the rewritten chapter (ix.) containing it (see also Preface to fifth edition). They may have exchanged their views in letters now lost. Reference to the Letters of Ricardo to Malthus (Clar. Pr. 1886) will show a gap between January 1 and June 26, 1814. But Ricardo's expression 'papers' would better apply to a draft.

[1] Ricardo adds in a footnote, at this point, 'the following to be inserted : unless Capital be withdrawn from the land;' and Trower adds in pencil, 'because the employment of capital depends upon the existence of capital.'

[2] Covered almost entirely by the seal.

he thinks, even if more Capital were employed on the land. Do you understand? Nothing, I say, can increase the profits permanently on trade, with the same or an increased Capital, but a really cheaper mode of obtaining food. A cheaper mode of obtaining food will undoubtedly increase profits, says Mr. Malthus, but there are many other circumstances which may also increase profits with an increase of Capital. The discovery of a new market where there will be a great demand for our manufactures is one [1].

Believe me, yours very faithfully,

DAVID RICARDO.

I have written this in great haste after devoting the necessary time to my accounts. You must excuse the scrawl and corrections.

IV.

[TO SIR JOHN SINCLAIR [2].]

GATCOMB PARK, MINCHINHAMPTON,
31st *October*, 1814.

DEAR SIR,

I have not quite given up the Stock Exchange; but for a few months in the year, I mean to enjoy the calm repose of a country life.

Though I have a few acres of land in hand, I am not yet become a farmer. I leave the management of them wholly to others, and hardly take sufficient interest in

---

[1] For a statement of the theory here advanced, see Ricardo's 'Essay on the Influence of a Low Price of Corn on the Profits of Stock, &c.,' in 'Works' (ed. McCulloch), pp. 371 et seq.

[2] Sir John Sinclair's Correspondence (1831), vol. i. 371. Sinclair says: 'I had conceived the idea that much information on the subject of circulation might be obtained from the members of the Stock Exchange, and had requested Mr. Ricardo to inform me who were the proper persons to apply to.'

what is going on, to make it probable that I shall ever be conversant with agricultural subjects.

The Stock Exchange is chiefly attended by persons who are unremittingly attentive to their business, and are well acquainted with its details; but there are very few in number who have much knowledge of political economy, and consequently they pay little attention to finance, as a subject of science. They consider more, the immediate effect of passing events, rather than their distant consequences. Amongst the most enlightened, I should name Mr. —— [1], Mr. —— [1], Mr. —— [1], and Mr. —— [1]; but I cannot answer that they will be able to afford time, or feel sufficient zeal, to engage in financial discussions. I am going to write to my brother, Ralph Ricardo, who is a member of the Stock Exchange, and I will request him to mention your wish to the above gentlemen, so that they will be prepared for any application you make to them.

I am, Dear Sir,
your obedient and humble servant,
DAVID RICARDO.

V [2].

GATCOMB PARK, MINCHINHAMPTON,
29th *Oct.*, 1815.

DEAR TROWER,

I sincerely congratulate Mrs. Trower and you on the increase of your family, which I hope will be attended with an increase of happiness.

You observe justly that having friends staying with us unsettles our regular habits. I find it very materially to interfere with my pursuits. Reading or writing, when

---

[1] Left blank in the letter as printed by Sinclair.
[2] The last sheet of the letter is used as the cover, and addressed, 'Hutches Trower, Esq., Unsted Wood, Godalming, Surry' [*sic*].

one has an object in view, should be followed systematically, and at no distant intervals, for after a time our thoughts are turned into new channels, and we cannot easily recal [*sic*] the ideas which were only beginning to be indistinctly formed in our minds. I have scarcely been a week without visitors since I have been in the country, and to that I ascribe the imperfection of the little that I have done in the writing way. So far from imitating the illustrious example that you set before me, and improving as I go on, each successive attempt is attended with less success than the former, and it invariably happens that my last performance is the worst. I have hitherto done nothing than write what would make a very small pamphlet on Bank affairs, which I took with me to town, where I was obliged to go for a few days, a fortnight ago[1]. I had very little intention of publishing it, but I thought I might as well ask my friend Malthus' opinion of it. That opinion was not unfavourable to the matter, but was decidedly expressed respecting its inferiority in style and arrangement to my two first pamphlets[2]. Thus you see that I have no other encouragement to pursue the study of Political Economy than the pleasure which the study itself affords me, for never shall I be so fortunate however correct my opinions may become as to produce a work which shall procure me fame and distinction. I am determined, however, not to be daunted by common difficulties. I shall again set to work to endeavor to improve the style and arrangement of what I have just written, not that I am quite sure that I shall publish it if I succeed,

---

[1] 'Proposals for an Economical and Secure Currency; with observations on the Profits of the Bank of England, as they regard the public and the proprietors of Bank Stock.' The pamphlet was not actually published until the following year. See Letters of Ricardo to Malthus, pp. 96, 100, 109.

[2] At this time Ricardo had already written his three most important pamphlets: 'High Price of Bullion' (1810); 'Reply to Bosanquet' (1811); 'Influence of a Low Price of Corn on the Profits of Stock' (1815).

but at least it will afford me an opportunity of exercising the limited powers which I possess. Mr. Malthus and I continue to differ in our views of the principles of Rent, Profit, and Wages. These principles are so linked and connected with everything belonging to the science of Political Economy, that I consider the just view of them as of the first importance. It is on this subject, where my opinions differ from the great authority of Adam Smith, Malthus, etc., that I should wish to concentrate all the talent I possess, not only for the purpose of establishing what I think correct principles, but of drawing important deductions from them. For my own satisfaction I shall certainly make the attempt, and perhaps with repeated revisions during a year or two I shall at last produce something that may be understood.

The anecdote you gave me respecting an article [1] intended to have been inserted in the last number of the Edinburgh Review is very amusing. It shows that nothing is more dangerous than to set up for a prophet, unless we use such ambiguous language that with a little stretch of the imagination may suit all occurrences. Our politicians are not so wary in this particular as I should have expected, witness their prognostics concerning the war in Spain, the utter impossibility of beating Bonaparte, not to mention the Bank restriction bill, &c. &c.

Respecting this last-named personage, I quite agree with [you that] [2] a man's character and renown must be estimated upon a reference to the whole of his conduct. 'We must cast up the account of the good and bad qualities and strike a balance.' It is by this rule that I would try Bonaparte, and by this rule he will be tried by the future historian. I thought you departed from it, when after his brilliant career for twenty years, you pronounced

---

[1] Prepared on the assumption that Napoleon was victorious.
[2] MS. torn.

his glory wholly effaced by being obliged in consequence of an unsuccessful battle, bravely contested, to surrender himself a prisoner. It was the balance only that I was contending for, which I still think is on the credit side of the account.

Having given you so particular an account of my employments, allow me to ask what are yours? Are you amusing yourself with desultory reading, or is your attention engaged by some particular subject? If the latter, I should hope that your thoughts are turned towards the press, for one who can stimulate others to exertion and perseverance so well, ought himself to be animated with a desire to shine, and where every advantage of leisure and qualifications are given, it would be unpardonable to preach a doctrine which you did not yourself practise.

Mr. Mill writes to me that he has nearly finished his 'Indian History [1].' He is this Autumn where he was last, with Mr. Bentham at Ford Abbey, Somersetshire, where they have both ample leisure for their literary pursuits [2]. Mr. Malthus is, I believe, engaged in preparing a new Edition of his Essay on Population for publication [3]. Some of the doctrines on Political Economy in that work required revision. I hope they will receive a radical amendment. Mrs. Ricardo and my daughter join with me in kind regards to Mrs. Trower, whose health we hope is quite restored.

Yours very truly,
DAVID RICARDO.

---

[1] Not actually published until early in 1818.

[2] See Bain, 'James Mill,' p. 146, and for a letter of Ricardo to Bentham, see above, p. 1.

[3] See above, p. 5 n.

VI[1].

Dear Trower,
     Gatcomb Park, Minchinhampton,
     25th *Dec.*, 1815.

  Since I received your letter, I have been in London. I attended the Bank Court, and even ventured to give my opinion on the subject under discussion, which I did with considerable agitation to myself, but which I believe was not apparent to those whom I was addressing[2]. You appear to me to have got over the first difficulties of public speaking[3]. I have them all to encounter, and they really assume too formidable an array for me to dare to wrestle with them. As I am busily employed on my MS.[4] with a view to publication, and as you will there see my sentiments on Bank affairs, I shall not make them the subject of my letter. So much has already been said on the Bullion question that I have thought it better to say very little on that subject. I may therefore be permitted to express here my entire assent[5] with your opinions on the prices of bullion and other things.

  I have very little doubt but that there has been a considerable rise in the value of money, which I think has been effected by the many failures of country Banks, which has increased the use of Bank of England notes

---

[1] The last sheet of the letter is used as the cover, and addressed, 'Hutches Trower, Esqr., Unsted Wood, Godalming, Surry.'

[2] 'I spoke for five or ten minutes with considerable inward agitation.' Letters to Malthus, XL. (Dec. 24, 1815), p. 104, where Ricardo gives the drift of his speech.

[3] Hutches Trower had, for example, spoken at the Court of East India Proprietors, 1813, on the question of Missions, the opening of the Indian trade, and, generally, the topics connected with the renewal of the Charter in that year.

[4] See above, p. 8, note 1.

[5] They did not always agree. See Appendix.

in the country, both as a circulating medium, and as a deposit against the alarm which always attends extensive failures in the country. I believe too that bullion has had a real fall, which has also contributed to bring it nearer to the value of paper. The bullionists, and I among the number, considered gold and silver as less variable commodities than they really are, and the effect of war on the prices of these metals were certainly very much underrated by them. The fall in the price of bullion on the peace in 1814, and its rise again on the renewal of the war on Bonaparte's entry into Paris are remarkable facts, and should never be neglected in any future discussion on this subject[1]. But granting all this it does not affect the theory of the bullionists.

The description you give me of the mode in which you pass your time leaves me nothing to regret on your account. You have exercise both of the body and of the mind; you are living in a healthful country, do not know what ennui is,—are surrounded by a charming family, and must necessarily be a happy man. Do not however imagine that emulation and ambition are extinct in you, they are only dormant for a time, or perhaps they may have only changed their field of exercise. The love of distinction is so natural to man that he never relinquishes his title to it if he sees it clearly within his grasp, and notwithstanding your present humble system of philosophy you have yourself been stimulated, and do not fail on every occasion still to stimulate others, by the rewards which are held out to successful exertion.

---

[1] The price of standard gold bars per ounce fell from £5 3s. on May 31, 1814, to £5 on June 7, to £4 17s. on June 14, to £4 10s. on June 28. It rose sharply from £4 9s. on February 28, 1815, to £5 7s. on April 4. See 'House of Commons Reports from the Secret Committee on the Expediency of the Bank resuming Cash Payments,' London, 1819, Appendix, pp. 307-308. The first Peace of Paris was concluded on May 30, 1814, and Napoleon entered Paris on March 20, 1815.

I am glad not to hear any complaints from you of the low price of produce, though you must suffer from such low price in common with all other land-holders. Those who have their property in land will not I think for a considerable time regain the advantageous position in which they stood during the war in relation to the rest of the community,—yet the price of corn appears to me unnaturally low and their situation will on the whole improve from the present state of depression. In every change from peace to war, and from war to peace, there must be great changes in the distribution of capital, and much individual distress. In the present case I fully expect that it will be followed by a rapid and brilliant course of prosperity, notwithstanding the disadvantages we labour under from the pressure of our enormous debt[1]. I am every day becoming a greater enemy to the funding system. Besides its other evils it disturbs so cruelly the prices of commodities as to give us a serious disadvantage in all foreign markets. If the supplies were always raised within the year, and if in consequence one class of the people were obliged to borrow from another in order to discharge their quota of the taxes,—a debt as large as the present might exist, but the effects would in my opinion be beyond all comparison less injurious.

But I am getting on high matters at the fag-end of my letter, and have barely left myself room to request you to give the united regards of Mrs. Ricardo and myself to Mrs. Trower.

Ever truly yours
DAVID RICARDO.

---

[1] Compare Letters of Ricardo to McCulloch, Introduction, xvi.

VII[1].

DEAR TROWER, [LONDON, *February* 5, 1816.]

I ought to have answered your kind letter before, but I have been much engaged and perplexed by sundry domestic affairs, as well as with the printing of my pamphlet[2]—besides which, I have been staying some time at Bath with my eldest daughter[3].

The Bank Directors have, I fear, too much influence to give us any hope of outvoting them in a general Court. They would however be very much discomposed by repeated attacks, particularly as reason and justice are so evidently against them. I wish some of the independent proprietors would try the question in a court of justice, for to my plain understanding the law also is against the directors. I wish you *would* fight side by side with me, and would infuse a little of your energy into some of the proprietors who think correctly, but are lukewarm from natural timidity. Mr. Bouverie[4] is not a good speaker—he makes but little impression on his hearers from want of animation and warmth.

My pamphlet will be out on monday. I have directed Mr. Murray to send you a copy immediately after it is published.

You ask my opinion of the saving Banks. I think them excellent institutions and calculated to improve the

---

[1] The last sheet of the letter is used as the cover, and addressed, 'Hutches Trower, Esq., Unsted Wood, Godalming, Surry.' The writer gives no date; but the (London) postmark is of February 5, 1816. Cf. Letters of Ricardo to Malthus, p. 110, as to the Bank.

[2] See above, p. 8, note 1.

[3] Mrs. Thomas Clutterbuck, of Widcomb, Bath, later of Hardenhuish Park, near Chippenham, Wiltshire.

[4] Probably William Pleydell Bouverie, later third Earl Radnor, the Whig politician.

condition and morals of the poor, provided they are properly managed. My fear is that though they will at first be established by gentlemen of great respectability and fortune,—as they spread they will at last be undertaken by speculative tradesmen, as a business from which to derive profit. The poor should have some check on the employment of the funds, or the same evils will arise as from the indefinite multiplication of country Banks.

This check should be afforded by the legislature, or there will be no security against the failure of the undertakers. The poor have no means of discovering the wealth and respectability of the parties who open these Banks.

The low price of corn is an evil to the landed gentlemen, which no decrease of charges can wholly compensate—they must submit to a fall of rents and they ought to rejoice in the evidence which the low price of produce affords of the yet unexhausted state of the resources of the country. High rents are always a symptom of an approach to the stationary state—we are happily yet in the progressive state, and may look forward with confidence to a long course of prosperity. It is difficult to persuade the country gentlemen that the fall of rents, unaccompanied by loss of capital and population, will essentially contribute to the general welfare, and that their interest and that of the public are frequently in direct opposition.

I hope the minister will not now touch the sinking fund—I hope he will never touch it. It is the general saving bank of the Nation, and should be encouraged on the same principles as encouragement is given to those institutions. I am sorry to observe that amongst those who have the power to decide on these matters, there does not appear any reluctance to meddle with the sinking fund. I am told that Lord Grenville is not averse to such a measure.

It is true that I am going to lose another daughter[1]. If she be happy, I must not repine—yet both Mrs. Ricardo and myself have felt, and do still feel, that in losing the society of these dear girls we have lost a portion of our happiness.

Report has spoken truth concerning my house in Brook Street. We observed a large crack in the ceiling of the drawing room last winter. I sent for Mr. Cockerell, he said it must be looked to when we left it for the summer, but that it was perfectly safe then. We have since found that we were in the utmost hazard—that Mayor[2] of whom I bought the house was a complete knave, and from the holes in the chimnies and the communication between them and the beams, he perhaps intended that it should be destroyed by fire, so that no one might ever find out the total insufficiency of the materials to support the house. What must I think of Mr. Cockerell, whom I paid to examine it? What compensation can he make me for his shameful neglect? I have not seen him since the discovery. The workmen have been in it ever since July, and it will cost me several thousand Pounds. We go into it on tuesday next but are obliged to be satisfied with the newly plaistered walls, unpapered and unpainted, or we must not have gone into it this season.

I am glad to hear that you will probably pass some time in London after Easter. I hope I shall see more of you than I did last year. Mrs. Ricardo and my family unite with me in kind regards to Mrs. Trower.

Very truly yours
DAVID RICARDO.

---

[1] Probably Priscilla (the S— (Sylla) of the Letters to Malthus), who married Anthony Austin, of Bradley, Wotton-under-Edge. There is a tablet to their memory, in Hardenhuish Church, as also to the Clutterbucks'. See also the last two letters of this collection.

[2] Name not clear.

VIII [1].

DEAR TROWER,   LONDON, 9th *March*, 1816.

The approbation which you express of the general subject of my pamphlet [2] could not fail to give me much pleasure, but I should have been equally obliged to you for your opinion if it had not been favourable. Truth is my object, and if I can succeed in promoting the establishment of right principles, it cannot fail to give me satisfaction. Yet I hope I shall not be unwilling to profit from the just criticism of those who differ from me, and to adopt more correct views when they are fairly set before me.

I have been agreeably disappointed in the interest which my book [2] has excited. It has very unexpectedly to me gone to a second edition, and is much better understood than [that on] the more difficult subject on which I before attempted to give my opinion. Mr. Grenfell has published his speech which I heard him deliver [3]. It is very clear and satisfactory, but our joint efforts will I fear be of little use. The accumulated treasure of the Bank must however one day be divided, and so confident are some that a bonus, or increase of dividend will be paid next April, that they

---

[1] The last sheet of the letter is used as the cover, and addressed, 'Hutches Trower, Esq., Unsted Wood, Godalming, Surry.'

[2] See above, p. 8, note 1.

[3] Pascoe Grenfell (1761-1838), member of the House of Commons, 1802-1826, was a zealous supporter of Wilberforce in debates upon negro emancipation, and a watchful critic of the actions of the Bank of England. It is said to have been chiefly through his efforts that the Bank undertook a periodic publication of its accounts. Compare Letters of Ricardo to Malthus, p. 89; Works of Ricardo (ed. McCulloch), pp. 395, 451.

The speech here referred to was delivered in the House of Commons on February 13, 1816, upon Grenfell's own motion for a select committee 'to inquire into the engagements now subsisting between the public and the Bank of England.' The speech appears in full in Hansard, Parliamentary Debates, vol. xxxii (1816), 458.

venture to make even bets on the subject. I shall however not be satisfied without a statement of accounts,—and I can see no good reason why they should be withheld.—

I hope your efforts will succeed in establishing a saving bank in your neighbourhood [1]. Their general diffusion in all parts of the kingdom will be of great service, if the rich and well informed will continue to bestow some attention on them. They will tend to introduce economy and forethought amongst the poor, which may in time check the propensity to a too abundant population, the great source from whence all the miseries of the poor flow in so profuse a stream. The quakers, who are a very benevolent people, are about to open a saving bank in the populous borough of Southwark, from which they anticipate the happiest effects. On my return to the country we shall attempt a similar establishment in our district. I hope you will have a perfect model to offer me.

Mr. Malthus has been staying a few days with me. The disgraceful disturbances at the College [2] have very much interfered with his leisure, which I very much regret, as he has been prevented from proceeding with the work which he has in hand. He is yet doubtful whether he shall add an additional volume to his Essay on Population, or whether he shall publish a separate and independent work, containing his present views on the interesting subjects of Agriculture and Manufactures, and the encouragement which is afforded them by natural and artificial causes [3].

---

[1] See 'An Account of the Provident Institution for Savings established in the Western Part of the Metropolis,' by Joseph Hume, London, 1816 (May). Ricardo, Malthus, Trower, and Elwin, are among the Managers (pp. 7, 8), as are also Torrens, Edward Wakefield, Hume, Rose, Baring, Colquhoun, and Wilberforce. It was founded by the Society for bettering the condition of the Poor, on the model of the Bath Provident Institution.

[2] See Bonar, 'Malthus and his Work,' p. 422, Ricardo to Malthus, p. 104.

[3] The fifth edition of 1817 was in three volumes, the third and fourth having been in two. Malthus expressed his views on Agriculture and

Mr. Western appears to me to hold very incorrect opinions, yet they are applauded by many in the House of Commons [1].

I am glad to hear from Mr. Turner [2] that we shall soon see you in London. I hope you will bring up a petition with you against the property tax. It is more objectionable I think as a 5 p.c. than as a 10 p.c. tax, yet I would willingly submit to it if I thought that it would really end in two years. The machinery of it is too easily worked to allow it to be at the disposal of our extravagant ministers during a period of peace. Mrs. Ricardo unites with me in kind remembrances to Mrs. Trower.

Ever truly yours,
DAVID RICARDO.

NOTE.—Samuel Turner, F.R.S., Trower's brother-in-law, was the author of 'A Letter Addressed to the Right Hon. Robert Peel, &c., late Chairman of the Committee of Secrecy appointed to consider of the state of the Bank of England with reference to the expediency of the Resumption of Cash Payments at the period fixed by law' (Asperne, Richardson, Hatchard), 1819. The letter is dated 31st May, 1819. He describes himself (p. 4) as having been for thirteen years a Director of the Bank, though now retiring by rotation. He is opposed to the principles of the Bullion Committee's report, believing as he does that 'wherever the precious metals and paper circulate together, although one may be constantly exchangeable for the other, yet every article is

Manufactures at considerable length in this fifth edition, though they found expression again in 'a separate and independent work,' the 'Political Economy,' 1820.

[1] On March 7, 1816, Mr. Western, member for Essex, moved for a Committee to inquire into the distressed state of Agriculture, and brought forward fourteen resolutions in favour of the reduction of the duties on malt, beer, and spirits, the warehousing of home corn and the exclusion of foreign, the further protection of home industries by duties on imports and, in view of the heavy tithes and poor rates, the exemption of agriculturists from other burdens.

[2] See Note.

measured by a standard bearing a higher nominal value than it would be possible to obtain, if the precious metals were the real measure' (p. 18). There is a reference (p. 69) to Ricardo's speeches in the House, with a criticism of his 'Plan' of bullion payments instead of payments in coin (pp. 69–80). For Turner's later pamphlet, see below, letter of 20th May, 1822. It was probably the same 'Mr. Turner of the Bank of England' that showed Miss Edgeworth over the building. See 'Memoirs' (for priv. circ.) iii. 39. See also Ricardo to Malthus, p. 164, and Mr. Macleod's 'Theory and Practice of Banking,' vol. i. (1855) § 46, p. 227.

IX [1].

DEAR TROWER,   LONDON, 15th *July*, 1816.

    Mrs. Ricardo has already left London and I am preparing to follow her, so that your next letter must be directed to me at Gatcomb. You must not suppose that I have been closely confined to London since your absence from it, for I have been to Bath for a week, and to Gatcomb for another week. Hitherto however the weather has been so unsettled that we have had no great reason to envy you country gentlemen. During my fortnight's holidays, I was not only drenched to the skin by the rain, but was often precluded from leaving the house for a whole day together. At Bath I met Mr. Elwin [2] twice at dinner, once at his own house. He is equally warm as when you saw him in the encouragement of Provident Institutions, and from the little I have seen of him I have formed a very favourable opinion both of his head and heart. Mr. Malthus, who was also on a visit near Bath, dined with Mr. Elwin at Mr. Clutter-

---

    [1] The last sheet of the letter is used as the cover, and addressed, 'Hutches Trower, Esq., Unsted Wood, Godalming, Surry.'

    [2] 'H. Elwin, Esq.,' is among the Managers of the Provident Institution for Savings, mentioned in Joseph Hume's Account of it (1816), p. 7. See above, p. 18.

buck['s][1]. We passed a very agreeable day, and I have reason to believe these two gentlemen were mutually pleased with each other.

When I tell you that Mr. Malthus accompanied me for a couple of days to Gatcomb, and that we were held prisoners by the weather, you will naturally conclude that we had ample opportunity to discuss our different views on some of the questions in Political Economy, and although we have approached a little in opinion, we have left ourselves sufficient matter for further controversy.

I think it very doubtful whether Mr. Malthus will notice Mr. Weyland's book[2], although Mr. Weyland treats him with the greatest possible courtesy. He has, I think, not in the least succeeded in establishing his own doctrines in opposition to those of Malthus on the principle of population, but he has shewn that in the early stages of society when the population presses against food, no remedy would be afforded by lessening the number of the people, because the evil they then experience proceeds from the indolence and vice of the people, and not in [sic] their inability to procure necessaries. By reducing the population you reduce food in perhaps a larger proportion, and rather aggravate than remove their misery. He is singularly inconsistent in denying the truth of this principle when applied to Ireland and really recommends means by which the population of that country should be reduced, whereas the remedy required in Ireland is a taste for other objects besides mere food. Any stimulus which should rouse the Irish to activity, which should induce them to dispose of their surplus time in procuring luxuries for themselves, instead of employing it in the most brutal

---

[1] A son-in-law of Ricardo; see above, p. 14, note 3.
[2] 'The Principles of Population and Production, as they are affected by the Progress of Society; with a view to Moral and Political Consequences.' By John Weyland, F.R.S. London, 1816. Malthus answered him at great length in an Appendix to Essay, fifth ed., 1817.

pursuits, would tend more to the civilization and prosperity of their country than any other measures which could be recommended.

I cannot agree with you in thinking that the war has had much effect in degrading the morals of the people. The outrages of which they are at present guilty may be sufficiently accounted for from the stagnation in trade which has never failed to produce similar consequences. I am disposed to think that the people are both improved in morals and in knowledge, and therefore, that they are less outrageous under these unavoidable reverses than they formerly used to be. I am in hopes too that as they increase in knowledge they will more clearly perceive that the destruction of property aggrav[a]tes and never relieves their difficulties. Sure[ly the][1] disastrous effects which always attend an important change in the employments of capital cannot much longer continue and we shall soon witness a renovation of commercial activity and credit. I have not in the least abated in my confidence of the real stability of the finances of the country, although I do not look with much satisfaction on the defalcation of the revenue at a time when it was already so many millions less than the expenditure. We have ample resources, but we want able ministers and a disinterested House of Commons. In our assembly the landed interest is too prevalent, and under very trying difficulties I should not have much reliance on their virtue.

If your Provident Institution is progressive you have no reason to complain, it will ultimately be productive of much good. Our receipts in Westminster are about £350 pr. week. We have realized £3,000 *money*, and find no difficulty in managing the business. In the City of London we shall commence business on Monday next. We have been hitherto prevented from receiving deposits from the

[1] MS. torn.

want of a proper office, which has at length been supplied—though not I think in the most eligible situation—being in Bishopsgate Church Yard. I am sorry that I cannot give my assistance at the first opening as no other manager has taken the least trouble to acquire the necessary information. Pray make my kind regards to Mrs. Trower and believe me,

Very truly yours,
DAVID RICARDO.

I wish Mrs. Trower and you would take a trip to Gatcomb this Autumn.

NOTE.—An extract from a letter of G. B. Greenough, the geologist, to Hutches Trower, 14th Dec., 1816, is given here as showing the opinions of another thoughtful man of the time, on the subjects of the above and following letter (X). Greenough writes:—

'Your opinions and mine square very well on the state of public affairs. It would be melancholy indeed to suppose our distresses more than temporary, for they are universal;—on that account among others it seems reasonable to refer them to some cause which operates on the rest of Europe as well as on Great Britain. The greatness and suddenness of the change which has taken place in the political situation of the whole civilized world is I have no doubt the main evil—and this will get less and less every day. Time is the only remedy for it, but it is a certain remedy. Then comes a bad harvest all over Europe—to be cured only by having a good one next time and diminishing waste in our families till the good one comes.

'In addition to these evils, the latter of which was inevitable since we cannot control the seasons, and the former accompanied with so much good that it would have been madness to think of avoiding it, evils under which we suffer in common with both continents, there are others I think peculiar to this country, to which the attention of parliament may properly be directed with a view to discover whether the people groaning under temporary burthens which you cannot remove may not be relieved from permanent ones which you can. The state of the poor is the subject to which I more particularly allude. I have long since doubted whether we had any right to plume ourselves on exercising charity so much more extensively than other countries, and whether this was not rather a proof of the badness of our system than the goodness of our hearts. The more I reflect on the subject the more do I feel inclined to embrace that opinion. I dare not rail against a virtue so pre-eminently Christian; else I should say that, as hospitality exercised as it was among feudal barons showed a backwardness in civilization, so the outrageous extent to which charity is carried renders it probable that there is some lack of justice.

'I would rather the poor were ensured against necessary distress by a rise of wages than relieved from their distress by a rise of poor rates, and I think I could prove that this rise of wages would not be so incompatible with the interest of their employers as at first sight would appear—if instead of a letter I were to send you a dissertation.

'In regard to distress occasioned by their own imprudence the best mode of exercising charity is not the expenditure of money but the diffusion of education—in which last I know not whether you will be pleased or vexed to hear this country is behind almost all the others in Europe.'

Greenough was a well-known geologist (see Letters to Malthus, p. 75, and Miss Edgeworth's Memoirs vol. i). Miss Frances Trower wrote to one of the present Editors (on Dec. 30, 1895): 'I well remember Mr. Greenough staying at Unsted Wood, and myself as a "little thing" being led by hand by the great man, when deputed to show him the paths through the woods which led to the top of our hills, where the views of the country around are beautiful.'

X [1].

DEAR TROWER, LONDON, 27 *Jany.*, 1817.

Is it not desirable that the poor laws should be done away, and that the labouring classes should receive the recompense for their labour rather in the shape of wages than in that of bounty? If you answer in the affirmative then there is no way of preventing the single man from

[1] Last page of letter used as cover, and addressed as before.

receiving more than is sufficient for his support, and I can see no reason to regret it. When the wages of a married man with a family are barely adequate to his own and his family's maintenance, the wages of the single man may be ample. All this I admit, but if it is a necessary consequence of the abolition of the poor laws it must be acquiesced in under the circumstances of an abolition. Even if it were an evil, which I think it is not, it must be endured for the sake of the good which would accompany it. The ill effects of the poor laws then I suppose to be admitted and their abolition to be desirable[;] the question then is how is it to be effected? Can it be by any other means than by gradually limiting their application, by encouraging the poor man to depend on his own exertions only? Is not this to be done by refusing all relief in the first instance to any but those whose necessities absolutely require it—to administer it to them in the most sparing manner, and lastly to abolish the poor laws altogether? If the poor rates are to be resorted to not only by those who have no other means of subsisting, but by those who are possessed of property, instead of limiting their application you would extend it; instead of repressing population you would still further encourage it, and would place at a greater distance the ultimate effect which we have in view. It is a painful reflection but not less true on that account, that we can never get into a good system, after so long persevering in a bad one, but by much previous suffering of the poor. The population can only be repressed by diminishing the encouragement to its *excessive* increase,—by leaving contracts between the poor and their employers perfectly free, which would limit the quantity of labour in the market to the effective demand for it. By engaging to feed all who may require food you in some measure create an unlimited demand for human beings, and if it were not for the bad administration of the poor laws, for the occasional hard heartedness of overseers and the avarice of parishes, which in a degree checks their evil effects, the population and the rates would go on increasing in a regular progression till the rich were reduced to poverty, and till there would no longer be any distinction of ranks. The particular clause then in the Savings Bank Bill must be examined in reference to its effects on the poor rates[1]. By omitting the clause you narrow the application of the rates; you encourage a part of the population to maintain themselves and to afford a good moral example to others, and you gradually prepare the way for the adoption of a better system. The only argument of weight in favour of the clause is that without it saving will be discouraged. I cannot believe that this would be found to be the case; no man saves with the poor house in perspective. Poor and rich all have confidence in their good fortune, and whilst their affairs are prosperous never dream of a reverse.

I have scarcely left myself room to thank you and Mrs. Trower for your kind congratulations to Mrs. Ricardo and me, on the birth of our grandchild. I hope you are right and that these numerous ties are calculated to increase our happiness.

I suppose I must not expect you in London for two or three months; you generally come in the gayest time. I am sorry to see our finances in so bad a state, and so turbulent a spirit abroad. We want an energetic minister possessing and meriting the confidence of the people in his talents and integrity.

I am, dear Trower, very truly yours,

DAVID RICARDO.

---

[1] Probably the twenty-first clause of Mr. Rose's Bill,—enacting that the members of Provident Institutions should not be debarred from parish relief. See Quarterly Review, Oct. 1816, p. 113.

XI[1].

DEAR TROWER, LONDON, 24 Feb., 1817.

Mr. Rose[2] you will have seen has himself answered your questions concerning his proposed measures for regulating Provident Institutions, by the introduction of his bill into the House of Commons[3], which I believe does not in any material point differ from that of last year. It retains the clause respecting giving parish relief to contributors, notwithstanding they may have funds in the Bank, which I apprehend will not be suffered to pass without opposition. I am glad to find that we do not differ with respect to the pernicious tendency of the poor laws; we both wish to see them amended or abolished, but I believe are not quite agreed on the means of obtaining so salutary an end. If I thought with you that the clause in question was calculated to afford great encouragement to the poor to become depositors in these Institutions, I should be friendly to it. My apprehension from its continuing is more that it will not diminish the poor rates than that it will cause any addition to them. There are as you observe two classes of labourers, the single and the married. Notwithstanding that the tendency of the poor laws is to reduce the wages of these classes to the least possible amount on which single men can live, yet this effect is not probably fully accomplished. If it were, neither the single man, who receives no relief from the parish, nor the married man who does, could possibly become depositors, for they would have nothing to deposit. We must

---

[1] Addressed on last sheet, as before.

[2] George Rose (1744-1818), the close friend and supporter of Pitt, was the author of 'Observations on Banks for Savings,' London, 1816, and brought in a Bill for the Protection and Encouragement of Provident Institutions or Banks for Savings, May 15, 1816,—withdrawn in that year and reintroduced 1817.

[3] Hansard, Parliamentary Debates, vol. xxxv, 222, 348.

suppose then that the single men receive more than their wants require. Our object is to encourage them to accumulate what they can save from their wages, and the question is, what effect the insertion or omission of this clause will have on their minds. You think that the chances of poverty are so constantly before their eyes, and that it appears so probable that they may themselves fall into that state, that they would have no motive to acquire property if the possession of property precluded them from receiving relief. I on the contrary maintain that after expending on their own wants the property they had acquired they would be in no worse situation for having acquired it. This of course you would allow, but I am of opinion that the chances of a reverse of fortune are always considerably undervalued by all of us, and therefore that the fear of falling into poverty can have very little influence on the mind of any man whose wages are such as to enable him to save a part of his earnings. The only good that the most sanguine can expect from these Institutions is the withdrawing of this class from the influence of the poor rates, and thus by diminishing the number of paupers introduce more independent feelings.

You will accomplish this object most surely if you take security for the permanence of a man's good habits. Exclude the clause, he will know that to preserve his treasure he must be saving and prudent; insert it, he will as surely know that he may indulge in a week or month's dissipation without infringing on it. I am not so sanguine as many as to the excellent effects which are to follow from these Banks, unless we at the same time raise the general rate of wages by confining the operation of the poor laws to cases of extreme necessity. We are I think beginning at the wrong end. Every thing would go on well if we could rescue the lowest labourers with families from an habitual reliance on the rates. By so doing we should better the condition of all above that class and then these Institutions would become powerful auxiliaries. As it is, they may introduce better habits amongst a few who[1] now lavish their money away in idleness and extravagance; but in the other case, the field would be extended, and the result gratifying to every friend of the poor and to the cause of good government. These rates are a yawning gulph in which all that is valuable will be ultimately swallowed. I hope Mrs. Trower continues in good health. Pray make Mrs. Ricardo's and my compliments to her.

Ever yours

DAVID RICARDO.

[On the last sheet of the letter is written in Trower's handwriting: 'The answer to this argument is that the poor man is liable to difficulties independent of his own foresight and prudence, and that he ought to be secured against them by relief if distress should come upon him.']

XII [2].

DEAR TROWER,   LONDON, 30 *March*, 1817.

Before I leave London, for a very few days, I am desirous that you should know that I applied the morning after I saw you to the proper officer in the Vote Office of the House of Commons, to get you a set of Parliamentary papers, but I am sorry to say without success. It seems that a very limited number of copies are printed besides those distributed to the members; these are the perquisite of two gentlemen in the office, but they are all disposed of, and at no price can a single copy now be obtained there. To console you under your disappointment, I can assure you that it will give me great pleasure to lend you, whenever you may want them, any of my papers or reports.

---

[1] 'Who' is repeated by oversight, in original.
[2] Addressed on last page, as before.

The report of last year respecting the employment of children in Manufactures[1] should have been sent to you in town the other day, but I did not know your direction. I heard you say something about Montague Place, but I knew not at whose house you were to be found there. This year there have been very few reports,—the only one of importance is a very thick one containing the laws in reference to Roman catholics in the different protestant countries of Europe[2]. If you would like to have this, as well as the one before named, I will send them to you by the coach, and you may keep them for a twelvemonth if you please.

I called yesterday on my printer, and he appeared more inclined, than on the day you were with me, to promise that my book should be out on the Monday following the next[3]. When you read it remember that I want from you the candid opinion of a friend, both respecting the matter and manner. Independently of the desire which I have to form a correct judgment of the merits and demerits of the work, the opinions of those, whose opinions are worth having, will enable me to make such alterations in it as may render it more fit for the public eye if a second edition should be required. Therefore I request you not [to be][4] sparing in your criticism.

I hope that on your return home you found Mrs. Trower

---

[1] Report on the Minutes of Evidence taken before the Select Committee on the state of the children employed in the Manufactures of the United Kingdom, April 25 and June 18, 1816.

[2] Abstract of the Report of the Committee on the Laws and Ordinances existing in Foreign States, respecting the regulation of their Roman Catholic subjects in Ecclesiastical matters. Dated 1816. The document ends curiously with a quotation from the 'Wealth of Nations' on the Primitive and Medieval Constitution of the Church. See Annual Register. 1816, State Papers, pp. 436-9. In 1817 there was a very long report on the Poor Laws.

[3] 'On the Principles of Political Economy and Taxation.' By David Ricardo, Esq. London: John Murray, Albemarle Street. 1817.

[4] MS. torn.

and your children well, and that the former approved of the manner in which you executed your various commissions in London. If any were omitted I fear I must share the blame; the incessant talk which I kept up during our walk was well calculated to drive more important matters from your mind. I hope too that you will reconsider your resolution of not visiting London this spring. Living so near town it is a duty which you owe to yourself and to your friends, to meet them at least once in the year.

With best wishes to Mrs. Trower, in which Mrs. Ricardo most cordially unites, I am

      Dear Trower

        Very sincerely yours

          DAVID RICARDO.

XIII[1].

DEAR TROWER,   LONDON, 9 *May*, 1817.

I write although I can give you little information on the subject of your inquiry. I understand it is proposed that the managers of the three Provident Institutions in London shall meet for the purpose of agreeing on some general regulations, at which [meeting] it will no doubt be discussed whether it will be expedient to alter the rules, to enable us to avail ourselves of the privilege about to be granted of obtaining debentures at a fixed rate of interest, with a return of the money at the will of the trustees. It appears to me so desireable that the depositor should be secured in the receipt of the precise sum of money which he may originally deposit, that notwithstanding there are great objections against the limiting each man's deposit to £50, it should be agreed to, if on no other condition this advantage is to be obtained. This point has

---

[1] Addressed on last page, as before.

not yet been discussed, nor offered for discussion in our particular establishment, and probably will not be till the clause has been approved by Parliament.

I am very much surprised at Ministers sanctioning such a clause, for it cannot be doubted that if the amount of deposits should become very large, it will not only subject the country to a considerable tax, but may on the breaking out of a war very much embarrass the financial operations. Suppose that a sum as large as 3 millions of debentures should be issued by the Bank in return for deposits made by trustees, when 3 per cents.[1] are at 85, Government would by purchasing 3 per cents. obtain only $3\frac{1}{2}$ per cent. on 3 millions for which they would be paying to the holders of debentures more than $4\frac{1}{2}$ per cent., thus losing £30,000 per ann., and when 3 per cents. fell to 60 they would be called upon for the payment of this sum of 3 millions at a very inconvenient time, as to obtain it they would lose the difference between 85 at which they bought, and 60 at which they would be forced to sell or £750,000. Now though I am a friend to these Institutions I do not think that they are deserving of these extraordinary bonuses, particularly as I am persuaded that this loss to the public would not act as any great encouragement to savings. The depositors whether they received 5, 4 or 3 per cent. for their money, would be of little importance in determining them to economical habits [*sic*].

With respect to the moral influence on the[m of][2] these Institutions, do you think that a depositor will feel that he has an equal stake in the country and is therefore interested in its peace and good government, whether he have £5 in the funds or in a government debenture? In that respect I can see no difference.

Mr. Elwin is engaged to dine with me on monday next

---

[1] Written, as almost always, 'p. cts.'
[2] MS. torn.

when I shall give him your message. I shall not I think see him before.

Mrs. Ricardo joins with me in kind regards to Mrs. Trower.

Very truly yours,

DAVID RICARDO.

XIV [1].

[To Sir John Sinclair.]

UPPER BROOK STREET,
4th *May*, 1817.

SIR,

I thank you for your pamphlet [2], which I have read with attention. I agree with you that a part of our distress has been occasioned by the reduction of the circulation; but I consider it as a necessary price for the establishment of a better system, than that of encouraging an indefinite amount of paper circulation. I cannot think that any but a very small further reduction will be necessary to enable the Bank to meet any demands that may be made on them for specie. The remedy, grievous as it is, is the necessary consequence of former error. I hope we shall never try an unchecked paper circulation again, though I have no objection to a paper circulation, and nothing but a paper circulation. It is obvious that, if we have forty millions, or any other given amount of taxes to pay, they will fall heavier on those who are to pay them, if money, by the diminution of its quantity, is raised in value. I have not seen Mr. Attwood's publication [3].

I am, Sir, your obedient and humble servant,

DAVID RICARDO.

---

[1] 'Correspondence of Sir John Sinclair,' vol. i. p. 321.

[2] 'On the approaching Crisis or on the Impracticability and Injustice of resuming Cash Payments at the Bank in July, 1818' (1817).

[3] Letter to N. Vansittart, Esq., on the Creation of Money and on

XV[1].

DEAR TROWER,   ANTWERP, 15 *June*, 1817[2].

You will be very much surprised at receiving an answer to your letter dated from this place, but here I am, enjoying in the most delightful weather, one of the most agreeable journeys I have ever taken. My brother Ralph only is with me. We landed on tuesday last at Calais, and have already been through the towns of Cassel[3], Lisle and Ghent. Each place appears to improve on the last, and Antwerp, where we now are, is certainly the grandest. I am quite astonished at the magnificence and splendour of the Cathedrals and Churches in this country,—they far surpass any thing that I have seen in our own country, and the pictures which are to be found in them are the chefs d'œuvres [*sic*] of the masters by whom they are painted. To see the descent from the Cross by Rubens, which is in the Cathedral here, is alone worth all the trouble of a journey from London. There are others nearly as good in this and in the other churches, besides innumerable beautiful specimens of the delightful art of painting in the public and private collections. We intend leaving this place tomorrow for Brussels, from which place we propose going by Namur to Liege and thence to Cologne. From Cologne we shall proceed up the Rhine to Franckfort and

---

its Action upon National Prosperity: Birmingham, 1817. See below, p. 149. Thomas Attwood, banker in Birmingham, was the founder of the 'Birmingham School' of theorists on the Currency, and (1830) of the Birmingham Political Union (see Wallas, 'Life of Place,' p. 251).

[1] Addressed on last page: 'Hutches Trower, Esq., Godalming, Surrey, England.' English post-mark dated 20th.

[2] In 1822 he was struck by the diminution in the number of beggars in France since 1817, but 'that [1817] was a year of famine over Europe, and it is the producer who is now complaining' [1822]. 'Tour on the Continent,' p. 4.

[3] The small town of that name between St. Omer and the present French frontier.

Heidelberg, and then we shall make the best of our way to Paris, and after seeing the beauties of that luxurious capital we shall return home. I have long had a desire to make a tour on the continent, but one week before setting out I had not any idea that it was so near its accomplishment. Our pleasure is damped by witnessing every where the greatest distress and poverty, proceeding in a great degree from the last bad harvest. We are told that bread is more than three times its ordinary price, and would be higher if other causes did not abridge the ability of the purchasers to pay for it. The poor are obliged to have recourse to food which is never eaten by human beings but on the greatest emergencies. It is some consolation however to see every where around us in this fertile country abundant fields of corn, looking beautifully, and holding out the fairest prospects of an abundant harvest. Besides the evils resulting from dear food the people have to struggle as well as ourselves with a stagnation in trade. At the table d'hote yesterday in conversation with an intelligent man he ascribed much of this to the disadvantage of their trade with England, although he was abundantly inconsistent on this subject. First he complained of the goods which were imported from England, they were totally unlike what were formerly obtained from that country, and were made only to please the eye. Secondly he insisted on the necessity of rigourous [sic] enactments against the introduction of British manufactures on the continent while England continued her prohibitory system —they were now obliged, he said, to buy every thing, and were not allowed to sell any thing, and therefore were under the necessity of paying the balance in gold and silver. As well as I could, in my bad French, I endeavoured to set him right, and to correct his erroneous theory, but I fear I have not satisfied him that retaliation in such a case only aggravates the evil sought to be removed. I cannot but lament however that England, who ought to be the example to other nations for liberal and correct principles, should be justly accused of being the foremost in departing from the maxims of free trade, and shackling the most advantageous distribution of the general commerce of the world. You will conceive my surprise when I tell you that while I was present at the celebration of Mass today, in the great Cathedral, with all my attention fixed on the mummery by which I was surrounded, I was tapped on the shoulder by our friend Elwin[1], who had the evening before arrived from Bruxelles, in his way to Douay, where he is going to see a nephew whom he had a week before left at that place, after which he will immediately return to England. I experienced from him his usual kindness, for he insisted on our dining with him and his companion, Mr. Oxley I believe his name, at his hotel. We accepted his invitation, and after very much enjoying his company we went together to the Play, from which we are just returned. He will, I have no doubt, soon write to you himself.

I have scarcely left myself room to say how very much pleased I was with your observations on my book[2]. I shall take it very kind of you indeed to furnish me with every observation which you may think of importance to enable me either to explain what is obscure, or to correct what is faulty, previously to my publishing a second edition. Murray tells me that a second edition will most assuredly be required and you will of course conclude that I shall be most anxious to give it every improvement in my power, you cannot therefore oblige me more than freely to animadvert on every part of it[3].

Pray make my compliments to Mrs. Trower. I hope

---

[1] See above, p. 20.
[2] See above, p. 30.
[3] The second edition did not actually appear until early in 1819.

that she and your children are well, and believe me with the greatest regard,

Yrs very sincerely
DAVID RICARDO.

XVI [1].

MY DEAR TROWER

GATCOMB PARK, MINCHINHAMPTON,
23rd *Aug.* 1817.

I congratulate Mrs. Trower and you on the birth of (I believe) your third daughter, and sincerely wish that she may grow up to be all that fond parents can wish, and that she may long add to the happiness of your domestic circle. True, I am a much older parent than you, and now that I am a grandfather, I should be puzzled, even with the assistance of Mr. Malthus and Major Torrens, to calculate the accelerated ratio at which my progeny is increasing. I am sure that it is neither arithmetical or geometrical. I have some notion of consulting with Mr. Owen [2] on the best plan of establishing one of his villages for me and my descendants, admitting only in addition a sufficient number of families to prevent the necessity of celibacy. Now that the poor man is deserted by the world, and even by the editor of the Times, who had so ridiculously puffed him forward, he will be at leisure to devote all his talents, and all his enthusiasm to so hopeful a scheme.

I have been returned [*sic*] from the Continent about a month, after an absence from home of little more than six weeks. I assure you that they were six weeks of active exertion which was amply rewarded by the gratification which I had in viewing the different objects which came under my notice. The towns, Cathedrals, and pictures of Flanders; the country about the Rhine and Heidelberg [3]; Franckfort, Coblentz, and some other towns in Germany,

---

[1] Addressed on last page, as before, 'Surrey' now taking the place of 'Surry.'
[2] See Note below.   [3] Written 'Hiedelberg.'

have all afforded me very great pleasure, and my fortnight's stay in Paris was not the least agreeable of my journey. An excursion to Paris merely, is so very easily accomplished, that I shall be tempted to go there again with my family. Every body should see the Louvre and Versailles who lives within a week's journey of them.

I can give you but little information respecting the criticisms on my book; indeed I have heard of none but from M. Say and Mr. Malthus for some months past. The former I saw several times at Paris,—he was very friendly and agreeable—spoke favourably of my book—was quite sure that in a very few years there would not be a shadow of difference between us, but he complained that I had made demands too great on the continued exercise of thought on the part of my reader, and had not sufficiently relieved him or assisted him by a few occasional examples, and illustrations in support of my theory. He said that he was reading me with a pen in his hand, making notes to be employed in the next edition of his work, and he found it required all his attention to follow me. In the last edition of his work, published before my book appeared, he has spoken of me in very flattering terms, far exceeding my deserts[1].

In a letter which I lately received from Mr. Malthus he mentions my book in the following manner: 'I have read your book again with much gratification. There is much

---

[1] 'Traité d'économie politique, ou simple exposition de la manière dont se forment, se distribuent et se consomment les richesses'; troisième édition, à laquelle se trouve joint un épitome des principes fondamentaux de l'économie politique.' Paris, 1817.

In this edition Say described and commended Ricardo's 'Proposals for an Economical and Secure Currency,' and referred (ii. p. 29, note) to Ricardo himself as 'l'homme de l'Europe qui entend le mieux la théorie et la pratique des Monnaies.' In the fourth edition of the 'Traité' (Paris, 1819), Say inserted repeated references to Ricardo's 'Principles'; but the running commentary on Ricardo's exposition, as suggested above, was made by Say only in his annotations to Constancio's translation of Ricardo's 'Principles,' published in Paris in 1819.

collateral matter in which I quite agree with you. I also quite agree with you that the difficulty of procuring subsistence is the necessarily limiting cause with regard to profits, but still I cannot agree with you that labour done in the sense you understand it is either in theory or fact the best measure of exchangeable value ; or that the state of the land practically determines the existing rate of profit in different countries. Pray do you allow that in different countries where profits are different your theory of value does not hold good? I don't feel quite sure.' On the whole I have reason to be satisfied with the opinions of these distinguished professors. I was told by Mill that Major Torrens had applied to the editor of the Edinburgh Review for permission to review my book in that journal, and the answer returned was that they must first know from Malthus whether he meant to undertake it. As I have every reason to believe that Malthus will not do it, it is probable that Torrens' offer may be accepted. I presented Torrens with one of the first copies of my book ; he was disappointed that I had not mentioned his name in it, and wrote to me to that effect, claiming some merit as the original discoverer of some of the principles which I endeavoured to establish. I had no design of neglecting his merits, and omitted to mention him because none of his doctrines appeared to me strikingly new and did not particularly come with[in the] [1] scope of the subject I was treating. There were so[me things] [1] in his book [about] [1] which I pointedly differed from him, but refrained from [noting] [1] them because I knew he was sensible they were wrong, and had adopted and was going soon to publish more correct views to the public. In the correspondence which ensued between him and me, I endeavoured to shew, and according to Mill's opinion I did shew, that on all those

---

[1] MS. torn ; the words in brackets suggest the probable reading.

points which I had as I thought for the first time brought forward, his published opinions were in fact in opposition to mine, and on those which he said we agreed upon and for which he claimed the merit of originality, they were all to be found in Adam Smith or Malthus, and therefore neither of us could be called discoverers [1]. Our altercation was carried on without the least acrimony, and ended by a complete restoration of cordiality, though accompanied with rather more reserve than before. He has dined with me twice since, and the last time he met Mr. Malthus for the first time and stoutly defended my doctrines, to which he is quite a convert, against Mr. Malthus' opposition to them. You will oblige me not to mention his application to the Editor of the Review unless you hear it from some other quarter [2].

I only staid one day in town on my journey from Paris to Gatcomb, so that I am ignorant of the proceedings of the savings Bank Institution. Your plan [3] is a good one if it do not too much encroach on the fund for expenses. I fear that our reduced treasure can bear no further diminution.

Our crops are abundant, but we are in bad spirits at the appearance of the weather. We hardly pass a day without heavy rain, and the atmosphere is so cold that we are never without a fire. An abundant harvest is at the present moment of the first importance,—it is at all times a great ingredient towards the happiness of the mass of the people, however it may on some occasions affect the interest of a particular class of individuals. Do you not

---

[1] For the economic doctrines of Torrens, see Mr. Cannan's 'Production and Distribution, 1776-1848' (1893).

[2] The notice in the Edinburgh Review was written by McCulloch. See Letters of Ricardo to McCulloch (Amer. Ec. Assocn., 1895), p. 9. Torrens reviewed Ricardo's 'Principles,' or at least the doctrine of Value contained therein, in the Edinburgh Magazine, Oct., 1818. See Letters of Ricardo to McCulloch, p. 15. As to the general attitude of Torrens, see Ricardo to Malthus, p. 112.

[3] We have not traced this in the Trower MSS.

think the funds enormously high with a revenue so deficient? Mrs. Ricardo joins with me in kind regards to Mrs. Trower.

Yrs truly
DAVID RICARDO.

NOTE.—A full account of Robert Owen's proceedings in 1817 is given in the 'Life of Robert Owen' by himself, publ. Effingham Wilson, 1857–8. See vol. i. pp. 154 seq., vol. ii. (called vol. i. A) pp. 53 seq. He proposed to arrange the Unemployed Working-classes into Agricultural and Manufacturing Villages 'of Unity and Mutual Co-operation' limited to a Population of from 500 to 1500 persons. 'This was the announcement of that new state of existence upon earth, which, when understood and applied rationally to practice, will cordially unite all as one good and enlightened family, will enable all rapidly to progress in knowledge and wisdom, and to enjoy without interruption the highest earthly happiness to which man can attain.

'The proceedings connected with these first public meetings which I held in the City of London Tavern, were minutely and accurately narrated in all the London morning and evening newspapers, published for general news at that period. And in this work the *Times* took the leading interest. And until the meeting at which I emphatically and solemnly at the risk of all that men hold dear, even to life itself, denounced in the strongest terms all the religions as they were taught to the world the *Times* was the warmest in my praise and in praise of the measures which I recommended,—often giving columns in the same paper to the development of the system as I gave it to the public,—as may be seen by referring to its pages from the 30th of July to the 10th of September 1817' (i. 154–5). The denunciation of all the religions took place at the meeting held on the 21st August (ii. 108 seq.).

XVII[1].

MY DEAR TROWER GATCOMB PARK 10 *Decr.* 1817.

You make your excuses with so good a grace, that I could not be angry with you if I would, but what perhaps

---

[1] Addressed on last page, 'Hutches Trower, Esqr., Unsted Wood, Godalming, Surry.'

more certainly determines me to shew charity to you, is the necessity I am under of frequently throwing myself on the charitable judgment of others—I shew mercy that I may receive it.

We have here, equally with every other part of the country, mourned over the untimely fate of our late princess[1], and are equally sensible of the great national loss we have sustained. All the Princes of the Royal Blood probably now expect to wield the sceptre in their turn, but the probability is that in this expectation they will be disappointed. It is a singular circumstance that with so many children our old King should not have one grand-child. A writer in the Morning Chronicle, whose letter I had not time to read, ascribes this to the Royal Marriage Act, and I think the remark well founded. Marriage would be a different thing to all of us if our partners were selected for us, and were necessarily strangers to our sympathies. I know that there are some good state reasons to be advanced in its defence, yet I cannot help thinking that it would be wise not to prevent the younger branches of the family from marrying subjects, either with a view to their own happiness and respectability, or to the interests of the country. Our Princes have certainly not refrained from marriage from a consideration of Malthus' prudential check, and from a fear of producing a redundant Royal population. If they had they would now be actuated by different motives and we might expect that the great demand for Royal infants would be followed by so ample a supply as to occasion a glut.

I have read the report of the Committee of the House of Commons on the Poor Laws with much satisfaction[2].

---

[1] Princess Charlotte Augusta, daughter of the Prince of Wales, and wife of Prince Leopold George Frederick of Coburg, died at Claremont on Nov. 6, 1817, and was buried in Windsor Chapel.

[2] See Letters to Malthus, p. 126, n.

I am glad to see sound principles promulgated from that quarter, though I should have been still more pleased if they had insisted more strongly on an *efficient* remedy. On this part of the subject they shew too much hesitation—recommend measures, and then qualify or abandon them. The whole country is feeling the inconvenience of the present system, and will, I hope, be brought to understand the origin of the evil. All the principal Reviews write well on the subject. In the last number of the British there is a very good review of the Commons' report, which is worth your reading. In the same number there is also a review of my book[1], in which in every page I am charged with ignorance and absurdity ; yet it is not done in an ungent[le]manly way, and I have the pleasure to have my friend Malthus associated with me in the censure of having made the subject of rent, which was well explained by Adam Smith, and is perfectly clear, obscure and unintelligible. The writer does not in fact see the important part of the subject ; he has read but not studied it. He has kindly left unattacked those points which were most assailable, and has fastened on those which are incontrovertible[2]. My style and arrangement are fortunately for me not mentioned. A writer in a Scotch paper called the Scotsman has written a short Essay in my vindication, and has I think done it ably, for he has expressed my opinions in much clearer language than I could do it myself[3]. To compensate me also for the censure of the reviewer, I have been made acquainted with Lord Grenville's opinion of my book, which is favourable beyond my expectations. When

---

[1] See Letters to Malthus, pp. 145-7.

[2] Compare Letters to Malthus, p. 145. The assailable points included his doctrine of the effects of Machinery, afterwards altered, and his view of the effects which a tax would have on the volume of the currency. See Letter XXXIV. and Appendix B. See also Letter XVI.

[3] The writer was doubtless J. R. McCulloch ; see Letters of Ricardo to McCulloch, p. 10.

I go to London I am, at his Lordship's desire, to be introduced to him. For Lord Grenville's judgement on matters of Political Economy I have always had the highest re[spect].

We have established a Savings Bank in this neighbourhood in the formation of which I have been very active. I was the only one practically acquainted with such Institutions and therefore my services have been much more highly appreciated than they deserved. We give a half penny per month for every 13s. In six weeks we have received about £1100, which may be said to be tolerably successful, but we understand that a strong prejudice exists among the manufacturing classes against us. They think that we have some sinister object—that we wish to keep wages down. Time and good temper will overcome this feeling and convince the prejudiced how that the rich have no other personal object in view excepting the interest which every man must feel in good government,—and in the general prosperity. The success of these Banks would be great if the enormous abuses of the Poor Laws were corrected.

Several other banks have been opened since ours within 15 miles of us, but every where the same prejudice operates against them.

Mill's book waits only for the index to be published[1]. He has from the remarks I have heard him make given me a great desire to read and study it.

Malthus has a volume ready which I am also anxious to see, because he expressed in it his views on the subjects on which I have lately written, and which I know differ materially from mine[2].

I shall be in London in January, and shall not return

---

[1] 'History of British India.' 3 vols. 4to. London, 1817-18. Ricardo was then reading an early copy of the work; see Letters of Ricardo to Malthus, pp. 146, 147.

[2] Doubtless 'The Principles of Political Economy, considered with a View to their Practical Application'—not actually published until 1820.

again here. I hope soon to meet you. To secure a meeting I ought to kill an East India director, a contested election will follow, and then you will infallibly be brought to town. I am annoyed by the prospect of being Sheriff of our county this next year. Of the three named, Col¹. Berkeley, son of the late Earl, is first and I second. The Col¹. it is said is about to try again for the peerage and therefore it is probable that I may be chosen[1]. Mrs. Ricardo and my daughter join with me in kind regards to Mrs. Trower, to whom and to you I wish all manner of good.

     Very truly yours
        DAVID RICARDO.

XVIII[2].

MY DEAR TROWER,   LONDON, 26 *Jany* 1818.

 Your last kind letter reached London before I arrived there, and after performing a journey to Gatcomb, was again brought to town in my pocket on the 15th inst. I should have answered it before but I have been incessantly employed in business that required my immediate attention. I heartily wish with you that we had chanced to fix our residences near to each other, that we might in the calm of the country, have pursued those discussions which on many occasions engaged our attention even in the tumultuous scenes where we were accustomed to meet, but where we had neither leisure, nor favourable opportunities, to make them so serviceable to us as we should have done amidst groves, and fields, undisturbed by the stimulating interests which formerly engrossed us. I remember well the pleasure I felt, when I first discovered that

---

[1] The dignity came in due course; see p. 49, below.
[2] Addressed, 'Unsted Wood, Godalming,' on back of last sheet, but without postmarks. Probably sent by hand. The paper is gilt-edged, as is not infrequent in this correspondence.

you as well as myself was [*sic*] a great admirer of the work of Adam Smith, and of the early articles on Political Economy which had appeared in the Edinburgh Review. Meeting as we did every day, these afforded us often an agreeable subject for half an hour's chat, when business did not engage us. Everything that has since occurred has stimulated me to give a great deal of attention to such subjects: first, the Bullion Controversy, and then my intimacy with Mill and Malthus, which was the consequence of the part I took in that question. My discussions with Malthus have been innumerable, and in my eagerness to convince him he was wrong, on some points on which we differed, I was led into a deeper consideration of many parts of the subject than I had before given them, and though I have failed to convince him, and may not have satisfied others, I have convinced myself, and think that I have a very consistent theory in my own mind. This theory I have attempted to commit to paper that I might communicate it to others, but owing to my little knowledge of the art of composition I have not succeeded to my wish, and I now quite despair of ever knowing how to wield that admirable instrument for conveying information.

The new publication of Malthus, which I mentioned to you, is not yet in the press [1]. It has no connection with any former work of his. Among other things it is to contain some examination of my opinions, to which I wish them to be submitted. He has a great aversion to controversy; I hope this aversion may not induce him to withhold it. The Review of his Essay in the Quarterly is [2] I think well done, and I am glad to see that so popular a Review is at length employed in advocating the cause of truth [3]. The reveries of Southey on questions of Political

[1] See above, p. 44, note 2.
[2] 'Is' is repeated in the original by oversight.
[3] See 'Malthus and His Work,' p. 364. Quarterly Review, July, 1817, pp. 369 seq

Economy will I hope no longer be admitted in any respectable journal. He quite mistakes his talent when he writes on such subjects, and is really no more deserving of attention than Mr. Owen or any other visionary [1]. The writer of the article in the Quarterly I suppose you know is Mr. Sumner, a clergyman, the author of a clever book on the Records of the Creation, in which Malthus' system is not only defended for its truth, but for its affording proofs of the benevolence and goodness of the Creator. Mr. Sumner's work was reviewed in the Quarterly and report says that Mr. Weyland was the reviewer [2]. He has of course carried his own erroneous principles into the Review, and does not do the author justice.—I am sorry to hear that Mr. Sumner does not intend writing any more on political economy—his whole attention in future is to be devoted to the study of theology. Whether in this latter pursuit he will have an equal chance of benefiting mankind, as in the former, I have great doubts, or rather I have no doubt at all; and I very much regret that the science will no longer be assisted by his distinguished talents.

I would gladly compound for such a change in the Poor Laws as should restore them to what appears to have been the original intention in framing them; namely, the relieving only the aged and infirm, and under some circumstances, children. Any change would be an improvement which had not a tendency to increase the evil which it proposes to remedy. The present plan creates

---

[1] Robert Southey, the poet, contributed regularly to the first four volumes (1802-1805) of the Annual Review, and was connected with the Quarterly Review from its establishment in 1808 until 1838. His contributions to the latter journal numbered nearly one hundred in all, upon the widest range of subjects. A complete list is appended to Rev. C. C. Southey's 'Life and Correspondence of Robert Southey.' 6 vols. London, 1849-50.

[2] For Weyland's writings see above, Letter IX. Sumner was afterwards Archbishop of Canterbury.

objects of distress, and these must necessarily go on increasing in a geometrical ratio. No man in his sober senses would wish for any sudden alteration of the present plan. The great object should be to teach the labouring classes that they must themselves provide for those casualties to which they are exposed from occasional variations in the demand for particular manufactured goods, and which should not be the subject of legislation. A man's wages should, and would on a really good system, be sufficient not only to maintain himself and family when he is in full work, but also to enable him to lay up a provision in a Savings Bank for those extraordinary calls which you mention.

To relieve the poor by any *extended* exercise of private charity would hardly be less objectionable than the evil of which we now complain. Your objection to this tax, or any of the taxes being paid by voluntary contribution is most sound—the selfish would pay nothing, and the whole burden would fall on the generous and humane! Great evils however result from the idea which the Poor Laws inculcate that the poor have a *right* to relief. In the British Review, which I send you, I think you will find a good article on this subject.

I have gone through my friend Mill's book, 'The History of India.' It is not a mere dry detail of facts, but contains ample discussions on the most important points, which refer not only to the Government of India, but to the Government of every other country. His observations on Legislation, on Law and on the rules of Evidence, are very interesting, and he shews most triumphantly, I think, that the administration of Justice, on which so much of the happiness of every people depends, is still very deficient in these countries which are considered the most civilized in Europe. I do not see what plausible objections can be made to him. Hastings' Trial,

Mr. Fox's and Mr. Pitt's India bills, give him very good opportunities for entering into these discussions. He endeavours to refute the prevailing opinion that the Hindus are now, or ever have been, a highly-civilized people, and enters very fully into an examination of the state of their religious opinions, their customs, their laws, their literature, and their knowledge of the arts and sciences, with a view to prove that they have never made more than the first steps in refinement and civilization. I am exceedingly pleased with the work,—it is replete with entertainment and instruction, and cannot fail to be acknowledged as a proof of great talents in the author. By special favour I had it before the maps and indexes were completed, and therefore several weeks before it was published. Mrs. Ricardo joins with me in kind regards to you and Mrs. Trower.

Very sincerely Yours

DAVID RICARDO.

XIX [1].

MY DEAR TROWER   LONDON, 22 *March*, 1818 [2].

I thank you for your congratulations on the occasion of the high honours which I have attained. The hour is fast approaching when I shall have to appear before the Judges, arrayed in the masquerade suit which I have been obliged to provide. The Assizes for our County commence on the 1st April. I hope I shall sustain my high office with becoming dignity—the difficulty is much increased by my being so much a stranger in the county, never having been present on any public occasion whatever. From this moment however I may date my public life ; as the ice once broken, I shall not fail to meet my neighbours two or three times a year at Gloucester.

---

[1] Addressed on last page, as before, 'Unsted Wood, Godalming.'

[2] Ricardo was chosen Sheriff of Gloucestershire in this year. See Ann. Reg. 1818 (*Chron.*) p. 207.

The expense of the office in our county does not exceed £450, so that on that score I shall be better off than you [1]. You may depend on having all the advantage which my experience can give you in the way of instruction previous to your election.

The perusal of the article in the British Review, has called forth much too favourable a criticism from you on my book. I am well aware of its great deficiencies which I much fear I shall not be able to remedy in a new edition, if it should be called for. Your suggestion of a copious chapter of clear and concise definitions would be of great use, but it requires a degree of precision and accuracy beyond what I could furnish. My scotch friend continues every now and then to allude to my work with the greatest respect [2], and in an interview which I lately had with Lord Grenville I received from him the most flattering testimony of his favourable opinion of my endeavours to throw additional light on the science of Political Economy. Praise from Lord Grenville on this subject is particularly gratifying to me, because he has given many proofs of his persevering attention to it, and on all great discussions, of the correctness of his opinions.

Birkbeck's account of his expedition to the back settlements of America is highly interesting [3] — I hope he will

---

[1] Trower became High Sheriff of Surrey in 1820.

[2] See above, p. 43.

[3] 'Notes on a Journey in America, from the Coast of Virginia to the Territory of Illinois.' London, 1818.

The author, Morris Birkbeck, accompanied by a friend, George Flower, came to America in 1817, in the hope of bettering his prospects. In his book, Birkbeck describes the long journey from the sea-board to Edward's County, Illinois, where both men settled, purchasing large tracts of land, and founding the town of Albion. Birkbeck was Secretary of State under Governor Edward Coles, and contributed 'more by his writings than perhaps any one else' to prevent the introduction of slavery into Illinois in 1824. He was drowned soon afterwards, while returning from a visit to Robert Owen at New Harmony, Indiana. See Davidson and Stuvé, 'History of Illinois' (Springfield, 1876), p. 349.

from time to time furnish us with an account of the progress of the little colony which he will soon have about him. His success will not fail to induce many from Europe to follow his example, and there is some reason to fear that the artificial state of things in England in consequence of our enormous debt will co-operate with the natural advantages of a new and fertile country to attract capital to a place where profits are so high that with moderate industry a certain provision may be made for a family [1]. I am told that many individuals with an aggregate capital of £100,000 are preparing to follow Mr. Birkbeck to the Illinois Country.

It is not expected that the dissolution of Parliament will take place before October. It is said that no attempt will be made to increase taxation, so that our nominal sinking fund of 15 millions will be really reduced to 3 millions. Mr. Vansittart had a ridiculous project, I hear, of creating a new circulating medium and legal tender, called stock notes, which were to be advanced without any limit, on stock, at the rate of £50 for every £100 stock. If such a plan had been carried into execution it was possible that our money might have been increased to 400 millions. I am told that he has now abandoned it, and indeed it is difficult to believe that he ever entertained so ridiculous a project, tho' my authority for the fact is no less than that of Mr. Tierney [2].

If I could, without much trouble, get into the New Parliament, I would. I should neither be Whig nor Tory [3], but should be anxiously desirous of promoting every measure which should give us a chance of good government. This I think [will] [4] never be obtained without a reform in Parliament. I do not go as far as Mr. Bentham.

[1] Cf. Letters of Ricardo to McCulloch, xv. seq.   [2] See below, p. 101.
[3] See Letters of Ricardo to Malthus, pp. 151, 152; also below, p. 62.
[4] MS. torn.

I regret that his book [1] is so full of invective against those
from whom he differs, yet I am convinced by his arguments.
There is no class in the community whose interests are so
clearly on the side of good government as the people; all
other classes may have private interests opposed to those
of the people. The great problem then is to obtain security
that the representatives shall be chosen by the unbiassed
good sense of the people. The suffrage must be extensive
to secure the voters against corrupt influence and the
voting must be by ballot for the same reason. There
must be an intimate union between representatives and
their constituents in order to destroy the dependence of
the former on [2] the executive government. The elections
should not be less than triennial. Mr. Burke has said that
the people may err but it can never be from design [3]. The
ability of representatives when their interests are opposed
to those of their constituents is a great evil because it can
only be employed in promoting objects which are mischievous to the latter. If the suffrage is not universal
there can be no danger of anarchy. A man with a very
small property can have no wish for confusion if he be
actuated by those motives which have always been found
to influence mankind. I have only partially read the
memoirs of the Bishop of Landaff and liked much what
I have read [4]. He was a reformer and saw pretty clearly

[1] 'Plan of Parliamentary Reform in the Form of a Catechism, with an
Introduction, showing the necessity of Radical, and the inadequacy of
Moderate Reform.' The work was written in 1809, but not published
until 1817.
[2] 'On' repeated in the original by oversight.
[3] 'Thoughts on the Cause of the Present Discontents,' fifth edition, 1775:
'The people have no interest in disorder. When they do wrong it is
their error, and not their crime. But with the governing part of the
State it is far otherwise. They certainly may act ill by design, as well as
by mistake.'
[4] Richard Watson, Bishop of Llandaff, born 1737, died 1816. 'Anecdotes
of the Life of Richard Watson, D.D., Bishop of Llandaff, written by himself at different intervals, and revised in 1814'—edited by his son—
appeared in 1817. See Edinburgh Review, June, 1818.

the evils of our present representation but I doubt whether he as clearly saw the remedy.

I am glad to hear that we shall soon see you in London. Mrs. Ricardo joins with me in kind remembrances to Mrs. Trower.

Believe me
Ever most truly yrs,
DAVID RICARDO.

XX [1].

MY DEAR TROWER　　　　　　　　LONDON 27 *June* 1818.

Your kind letter dated the 7th June ought not to have remained so long unanswered, but various things have encroached on my time, and I have also been a journey to Gatcomb, and Gloucester, for the purpose of returning the members for our County to Parliament. As there was no contest my task was easy, and we have, with our usual consistency, sent one member to vote with ministers, and another to vote with the opposition [2], both I believe disposed implicitly to follow their leaders.

My own endeavours to get a seat in the House have not been attended with success, but I believe that amongst all those who are disappointed, in a similar manner, there is not one more resigned than I am [3]. I could meet with nothing where I should not have had a contest, which I was exceedingly unwilling to encounter, particularly as I should have been thrown, alone, amongst persons with whom

---

[1] Addressed on back, 'Unsted Wood, Godalming, Surrey.'

[2] Lord R. E. H. Somerset and Sir B. W. Guise, Bart. (Ann. Reg. 1818 (*Chron.*), p. 210). Guise was 'favourable to reform in Parliament, and advocated the immediate abolition of slavery.' He represented the county from 1812 to his death in 1834 (Annual Biography and Obituary for 1834 (Longman, 1835), p. 419). Richard Sharp was elected at this Election for Portarlington, the seat that afterwards fell to Ricardo. See below, pp. 72, 107.

[3] See above, p. 51.

I was wholly unacquainted, and therefore ignorant how far I might depend on their statements. From all that I have seen I am more and more convinced that the system requires great amendment—that Parliament should really represent the good sense of the nation—that the expences of election should be reduced to the minimum—and that the choice should be made by ballot. Under such a mode of choosing representatives we should get rid of the disgusting spectacle of the lowest blackguards in every town assembling about the Hustings, and insulting in the grossest, and most cruel manner, those respectable candidates against whom their antipathies are excited. Why is such a man as Sir Murray Maxwell to be exposed to the disgraceful treatment which he has received[1]?—I am for Sir Samuel Romilly's system of Reform, as avowed to a gentleman whom he authorized to communicate it to Mr. Bentham, and to any other person.—His system is to extend the suffrage to Householders—to limit the duration of parliament to 3 years, and to vote by ballot. This is all the reform that I desire, and I cannot help thinking that if you had continued your walks with Mr. Mill and me, we should have got you to join in so moderate a scheme. Mill says you distinctly admitted that there should be an effectual check on the Government in the people, and as you are a fair and candid reasoner, he is persuaded that you could not fail to admit the conclusions also which would follow from that principle. Those conclusions are that the House of Commons as at present constituted does not afford that check—that it really represents the Aristocracy, or rather a narrow Oligarchy, and not the people.—You are I fear surrounded by Anti-reformers,—wealthy alarmists

---

[1] Captain Sir Murray Maxwell's misfortunes at Westminster are described by Miss Martineau, 'Hist. of the Peace,' Book I. ch. xiv. (Bohn, 1877, vol. i. pp. 250, 251). Romilly and Burdett were elected. The election lasted a full week.

who have in consequence of the French Revolution and the unhappy circumstances which attended it, associated the idea of insecurity of property with the exercise of popular privileges. They must necessarily have some influence on your opinions, but I pray you to counteract the effect by reading what the rational reformers have to urge in favour of their view of the question—read Madame de Stael's posthumous work on the French Revolution which contains an admirable defence of liberal institutions [1].

I cannot agree with you in thinking that Brougham's was a good speech [2] in answer to Burdett,—it was not in the least degree argumentative, nor did it shew what his own principles now are respecting reform. Brougham is a very clever man, but will never rank very high as a politician, for there is no steadiness in his opinions, and he appears to me [to] sacrifice too much to his immediate objects. Sometimes he wishes to conciliate the Whigs, and then the violent reformers receive no mercy at his hands,—at other times one would conclude that he went as far in the cause of reform as even Burdett himself. A man who wishes to obtain a lasting name should not be a vacillating statesman, too eager for immediate applause.

I am sorry that you could not consistently with your ideas of prudence seek to be returned for Guildford. You would be quite in your element in the House of Commons, and provided you started with the opinions which I deem right, there are few among my acquaintance whom I think would be more useful members, or whose talents would be

---

[1] 'Considérations sur les principaux événemens de la Révolution Française ; publiées en 1818 par M. le Duc de Broglie et M. le Baron de Stael,' in 'Œuvres Complètes de Mme. la Baronne de Stael' (Paris, 1820), vol. 12-14.

[2] Upon the resolutions for the Reform of Parliament, drafted by Bentham and introduced in the House of Commons by Sir Francis Burdett on June 2, 1818. See Hansard, Parliamentary History, xxviii. 1118; Bowring, 'Life of Bentham,' in 'Works,' vol. x. 491.

more likely to be made manifest by the discipline which the business of the House of Commons would afford.

We shall leave London in little more than a fortnight for Gatcomb. If Mrs. Trower and you should at any time during the next six months find it convenient to absent yourselves for a short time from home you will give both Mrs. Ricardo and me great pleasure if you will come into Gloucestershire and let me shew you the beauties of our country. We might take our walks and rides on the banks of the Severn instead of in Kensington Gardens and might too have Mill for our companion, for he has positively agreed to make me a visit this summer. Pray think of it, and if practicable come to us. Mrs. Ricardo joins with me in kind regards to Mrs. Trower.

Believe me ever
My dear Trower
very sincerely yrs
DAVID RICARDO.

XXI[1].

MY DEAR TROWER   GATCOMB PARK, 18th *Sept.*, 1818.

Our third assizes this year, as they may without much inaccuracy be called, commenced on the 31 Aug., and on that day I had again to go through all the ceremonies of meeting the Judges, attending them to the Court, and then to the Cathedral, all which had been so needlessly gone through on the former occasion[2]; but here my active services ended, for I had received the night before such an account of the alarming illness of one of my brothers, whom I believe you do not know, and of his wish to see me, that I was anxious to hurry to London as soon as my presence could be dispensed with. Nothing could be more humane and considerate than the Judges['] behaviour to

---

[1] Addressed on back 'Unsted Wood, Godalming.'
[2] See Letters to Malthus, p. 155.

me;—they no sooner knew how I was circumstanced than they insisted on my leaving Glocester [sic] immediately. I accepted their indulgence, and on my arrival in London found my brother in a less alarming state than I expected to find him. I passed a fortnight from home and am but just returned. I am happy to say that my brother's health improved daily while I was in London, and I left him with a fair prospect of complete recovery. It is to this interruption that you are to attribute my long silence after the receipt of your kind letter.

I am glad to hear that you are pleased with the review of my book in the Edinburgh Review. It gives me great satisfaction, and principally because the writer (Mr. M'Culloch) appears to have well understood me, and to have explained my doctrines with great clearness and perspicuity [1]. I am glad too to have had your observations on the review, for you have called my attention to the inaccuracy of the reviewer in a passage which had not before been noticed by me. In page 68 he has in the first quotation you make, used the word *price* instead of the word *value* [2]; substitute the latter word and the whole is consistent, though perhaps not quite satisfactory, for it supposes my definition of value to be correct, which may by many be disputed. In the next page he again speaks of real price as synonymous with real value, but his meaning is obvious [3]. The word *price* I think should be confined

---

[1] Edinburgh Review, No. LIX (June 1818), Art. II (On 'Ricardo's Principles of Political Economy and Taxation'). See Letters of Ricardo to McCulloch, pp. 9, 10.

[2] 'Should the quantities of labour necessary to bring every different species of commodities to market be increased in exactly the same relative proportions, their comparative exchangeable value would remain unaltered; while their real price would, however, be augmented.'

[3] 'The real price of commodities would, it is obvious, not be in the least affected by this increase of wages. The quantity of labour necessary to their production would not be increased; and it would, therefore, be equally easy to obtain them.'

wholly to the value of commodities estimated in *money*, and money only. If so confined, a commodity may rise in *real value* without rising in price. If more labour should be required than before to work the mines and to manufacture shoes, it is possible that shoes may continue unaltered in *price*, but both the shoes and gold (or money) will have *risen in value*. He is very able on the subject of rent, but if he answers the objections of any Review, it cannot be the Quarterly, for the work has not been noticed by it. In America I should think that there was no land for which a rent was not paid, but that is to be attributed to their particular institutions. The Government is proprietor of all uncultivated lands in the interior of the country, which it is ready to sell, and daily sells, at the moderate price at 2 dollars per acre. Rent then must amount in every part of America to the interest which 2 dollars would make, per acre, at the least; but this fact makes no difference in the principle, as you seem to be fully aware.

'The Fellow of the University of Oxford' is Mr. West, a barrister. His pamphlet [1] was ingenious, and he had a glimpse of the true doctrine of rent and profits. I am acquainted with him. He has I believe given up the study of Polit. Economy [2]. Mr. Mill has been staying a fortnight with me—he returned to London a day before

---

[1] 'An Essay on the Application of Capital to Land. With Observations showing the Impolicy of any great Restriction of the Importation of Corn.' By a Fellow of University College, Oxford. London, 1815.

The author, Edward West (born 1783), of the Inner Temple, became Recorder of Bombay, and, upon the establishment of the Supreme Court, Chief Justice of that presidency. He was knighted in 1822 and died at Poona in 1828. He published in 1826 a tract 'on the Price of Corn and the Wages of Labour,' which was in part a criticism of Ricardo. He was engaged on a more general treatise at the time of his death (Annual Biography and Obituary (1830), p. 109). Ricardo in the above passage wrote first 'Fellow of University College,' and then altered what he had written into the less exact phrase in the text.

[2] It was not so. See preceding note.

I went there. He is very much pleased with the review—he thinks it very well done.

Both he and I, I observe, have mistaken the extent of your admission respecting the House of Commons. You admit that there should be an effectual check on the Government in the people, but you think that as that House is at present constituted it practically and in effect affords such a check, because it feels the force of public opinion. We are of opinion with you that the force of public opinion is felt, and strongly felt in Parliament, but not in consequence of its good constitution, but in spite of the badness of it. The Parliament itself is controlled by public opinion as manifested through the means of the Press, and therefore it is the Press which is the real check on our Government. The Public opinion and (p. . .)[1] force is irresistible, and it is of this both the monarchy and the oligarchy stand in awe, and to it we are indebted for all the liberty we enjoy. *Instead* of having this *check* for the people *out* of Parliament, would it not be better to have it *constitutionally* exerted *within it*—would it not be more efficacious *there* as an instrument of good Government? It would in that case be powerful in correcting abuses on which the fear of insurrection does not now operate. As Parliament is at present constituted can we reasonably expect any important improvements in the *law*, while there is such a phalanx of interested men who have the power to oppose them? Why is not a general inclosure bill passed? because the lawyers['] interest is opposed to the general interest. Why are there so many obstacles to the transfer of landed property? Why is justice so tardy, and its expenses so great? And a thousand more whys,—all for the same reason. No, my friend, Parliament is no check *for* the people, but happily is yet checked *by* the people, whose voice and power cannot be wholly stifled

---

[1] Word destroyed by seal. 'Popular'?

while the press is tolerably free. You talk of your preference to a *mixed* Government, over that of a republican. I have *no objection* to the former provided it be administered for the happiness of the *many* and not for the benefit of the *few*. I know of no security under any form of Government for the happiness of the people, but that the people themselves, through the means of their representatives, should have a preponderating voice. I rejoice that you are not one of those who have an *antipathy* to election by ballot, for of all those who object to that mode of election I have never heard any solid reasons for their objection; they are all to be resolved to an antipathy, for which they can give no account.

Mill was exceedingly pleased with the view of some parts of our County. We performed a little tour to some estates which I have at 27 miles distance from home, and then we went to Hereford and surveyed the beautiful country about the cities of Hereford and Ross. I think you have been in those places.

Pray remember us all most kindly to Mrs. Trower and believe me very sincerely yrs

DAVID RICARDO.

I believe a Serjeant only can open the Court, and no serjeant accompanies the Judges in this Circuit.

XXII[1].

MY DEAR TROWER   GATCOMB PARK, 2nd *Nov.*, 1818.

I am not so guilty as you, in the affair of the Partridges, and pheasants. I eat them it is true, but their death, or that of some other animal, is necessary for my subsistence, and I may legitimately pursue them for that purpose. I employ a skilful man who brings them down

---

[1] Addressed on back, 'Unsted Wood, Godalming, Surry.'

with the least sum of pain, that can be inflicted in such a warfare. Are you no more guilty than this? If our judges were the birds themselves, I should be condemned to the guilotine [sic] simply—you would have to sustain the death of Damiens [1].

I think it is possible by what you say that you may be mistaking the gentleman who reviewed my book; it was not Dr. M'Culloch of London [2], but Mr. M'Culloch of Edinburgh, the editor of the Scotsman.

I am very much pleased at the approbation you express yourself, and which has been expressed by others, in your presence, of my humble efforts to improve the science of Political Economy. The reward which I have received for my labours has far exceeded my expectations.

I wish with you, that we could more nearly agree in our political opinions, this agreement we shall not probably be able to effect, but we may continue to esteem each other, and give each other credit for sincerity, whether we do or not. You speak with energy of the superior advantages of a mixed government, over that of a republic, as of a question not admitting of a doubt, and seem shocked that any hesitation should be expressed in agreeing to so clear a proposition, and you place it so far on the proper footing, that you prefer a mixed government, only, because, in your opinion, it is best calculated to promote the happiness and prosperity of the people. This you appear to agree is the only legitimate end of all government. Democracy, Aristocracy, Monarchy, or the three mixed, wherever they prevail *ought* only to be considered as means to that end. Yours is either a solid well-founded opinion, or it is not. If it is not, then, as you observe, there is an end of that

---

[1] Damiens, who tried to kill Louis XV, on January 5, 1757. was torn to pieces by horses, after the tortures to which Pope alludes in the line—
'Luke's iron crown and Damiens' bed of steel.'
[2] John McCulloch, M.D , physician, mineralogist, and geologist (b. 1773, d. 1835).

argument against a reform of parliament that it will make the popular branch of our constitution too strong. and so destroy the other branches; for if a republic be the best form of government, and will best promote the happiness of the people, we must not quarrel with reform for its tendency to give us a republican government. But let us suppose, or take for granted, which I do, that the contrary opinion is well founded, and that a mixed government such as ours, consisting of King, Lords, and Commons, is the best form of government, and let us examine the question of a reform in parliament on that supposition. You and I, and all *reasonable persons*, impressed with this opinion, having representatives to chuse, would select those only who acknowledged this demonstrable principle, and who would engage to maintain the monarchical and aristocratical branches. Having no *private interest* to serve, it would be folly or madness in us, if thinking that one form of government would be productive of advantage and happiness, another of disadvantage and misery, we should obstinately and deliberately reject the former, and prefer the latter. This is evidently improbable, if not impossible. If then the representatives of the people were fairly, and unbiassedly chosen, by the *reasonable part of the country*, you cannot shew that any motive could exist for chusing any but such as would uphold those branches of the constitution which are demonstrably essential to good government. If you say that the superiority of a mixed government, over a republic, cannot be demonstrated, but can only be inferred as a probable truth, I ask to whom would you refer the question for decision? not to the King, nor to the House of Peers, but to the *reasonable* part of mankind in the country, and who have no *sinister interest* to influence their decision. This then brings us again to the conclusion which I wish to establish, that there is no such security for good government as that of

Who should have the Franchise? 63

leaving the choice of representatives to the *reasonable part* of the community, for they have every motive to wish to be well governed, none to be ill governed. This being *demonstrated*, we must extend the elective franchise to all *reasonable men* who have no *particular interest* in opposition to the general interest, and the most you can require of the friends of reform is the right to challenge such electors as are *without the necessary qualifications*. Now this right I freely yield to you; shew the *sinister interest*, or the probability of a bad choice, and I will consent to deprive the individual to whom they attach of the right of electing members. But I will not allow you to challenge peremptorily and without shewing cause. Does not your argument run thus? The advantages of a mixed government are so evident that I am surprised any reasonable man can have a doubt on the subject—let me but fairly state the case, and all who are not biassed by prejudice, or interest, will admit my conclusion. Yet, though they admit it, I dare not trust them with the choice between a mixed government and a republic—these *reasonable people* are so besotted that they will give up a *greater good for a smaller*, and if once I allow the democratic part of our constitution to preponderate there will be immediately an end of the Monarchical and Aristocratical branches, although it is proved that they are essential to good government. It is not sufficient for your argument to prove, as you appear to think, that the popular part of the constitution would become irresistible if we had a reform; you are bound also to show that this irresistible power would be mischievously employed, and to do that you must shew an *adequate motive* for such an abuse. Men have the power, which is almost uncontroulable, of destroying themselves, but we confine them in straight [*sic*] waistcoats only when we discover that they think they have adequate motives for employing this power to their own destruction.

In answer to my question whether it would not be better that the operation of public opinion should be within the House of Commons, instead of without, you say that it would not be *instead*, but that the *two* powers acting constantly within, and without, would set at nought the other branches of the Constitution, and presently precipitate us into a democracy. To the last of these propositions I have already replied, and you must shew me where my argument is defective. To the first, I say that it is a fallacy to speak of two powers, one acting within the house, the other without; I know only of one power that we were speaking of. the power of public opinion. If it operated within the house, it would be inert without, as indeed it always is there, until the people actually resist. It is only by its operation on the fears of those *within* the house that public opinion produces any effect in our government. If the opinions of the representatives of the people within the House of Commons after a reform coincided with those [of] their constituents without, one power, namely, public opinion, would controul the government, as it ought to do in all governments whose end, and object, is the happiness of the people. If they did not coincide, those within would have the power of opposing public opinion no longer than till the followin election, when if the constituents were not convinced that they had been in error, representatives would be chosen more obedient to their views. It surely cannot be correct to say that because you take measures to ascertain the real opinion of the people in their own house of Parliament, that you double the effect of public opinion, and give it a strength which would be mischievously employed. According to your view of this question, the right of electing the House of Commons might be safely left with the house of Lords, or we might get rid of the House of Commons, and preserve the house of Lords only. The check from without, whilst we have a free press, would continue to exist, and would operate on the fears of the Lords, as it now operates on the house of Commons, and all the objects of good government would be obtained, for it would still be a mixed government of Monarchy, Aristocracy, and Democracy. The democratic part of it indeed would shew itself somewhat irregularly, as it now does, without, but that is the way in which you think its operation is salutary. If this is not your opinion shew me what the advantages are of the present House of Commons, for it seems to be agreed upon between us that it does not fairly represent the people, and that you seem to consider one of its great merits[1]. All the advantage that I can find out in it is that it is a more enlarged representation of the aristocracy than the House of Peers would be—that it admits the great landholders and wealthy merchants, and manufacturers to a share of power, and distinction,—that a few popular representatives are somehow or another admitted there whose votes go for nothing but whose opinions are expressed there through the press more effectually than they would be in any other manner, and thus that salutary fear which we both like, but which I would have more regularly and legitimately excited, is kept alive—these I think are all the advantages which flow from the present constitution of the House to the great body of the people.

After all that I have said about the Hon[ble] House, it is highly probable that I shall take my seat in it,—the business is not yet quite settled[2]. No one is more sensible of the capabilities and resources of the Country than I am, but I wish to have security for their continuance, and

[1] Ricardo's views on these subjects are fully stated in the 'Observations on Parliamentary Reform,' printed among his works (ed. McCulloch), pp. 551–556. McCulloch received the MS. from Ricardo a short time before Ricardo's death, and first published it in the Scotsman of 24th April, 1824.

[2] Letters of Ricardo to McCulloch, p. 24, note. Letters to Malthus, pp. 152, 154.

above all I wish that door to be opened by which those reforms which you acknowledge to be necessary might enter,—at present it is doubly and trebly barred.

Will you have patience to get to this line? I have severely put it to the test, but you must forgive me. My brother is getting better. Mrs. Ricardo unites with me in kind regards to Mrs. Trower. Believe me ever

My dear Trower

Very truly yrs

DAVID RICARDO.

Torrens I understand is to attack my doctrine of value in the next number of the Edinburgh Magazine, and in the number following M'Culloch is to defend it. It is a friendly contest. These gentlemen have lately met at Edinburgh [1].

XXIII [2].

MY DEAR TROWER

GATCOMB PARK
20th *Dec.* 1818.

I was sure that I was not mistaken in judging of your sentiments by my own. I was sure that you would not have a worse opinion of me because I differed in opinion with you on a subject on which we had neither of us any interest to come to a wrong decision, and yet I am glad that I stated this conviction in my last letter, because it has drawn from you an assurance of your regard and friendship, which has given me great satisfaction. I shall proceed now without fear to consider the different arguments contained in your last letter, and first I must observe that in an enquiry into measures which are likely to produce good government, we must not confine ourselves to the question whether parliamentary reform would or

---

[1] Letters to McCulloch, pp. 15, 16, note.

[2] A sheet and a half. Addressed on back of last half: 'Unsted Wood, Godalming, Surry.'

would not endanger the establishment of King, Lords, and Commons. We must look steadily to the end of all government, which we agree is the happiness of the people. As we both think that the establishment above-mentioned is best calculated to secure the object which we have in view, we should if we were legislators, acting under the proper influence, make it our endeavor to establish it; but still it must be considered only as means to an end, and those regulations are the best which give us the greatest security that the end will be obtained. It is surely unwise to make the means the end, and thereby limit our enquiry to whether we may chance to strengthen or weaken one of the branches of our constitution.

I want to get all the wisdom and virtue of the country to act in the Government. Whether that end can be attained by a parliamentary reform is a different question, and remains for discussion, but your argument is that even if it could be attained you would not make use of it. Why? because it would endanger the independence of the monarchical and aristocratical branches of the constitution. Is not this saying 'I think a certain form of government the best, and on this point I will not admit the wisdom and virtue of the country to decide.' Now I am a more warm admirer of our constitution than you are, for I am so persuaded of its excellence that I have no fear of putting it in the power of the wise and good to overturn it. Instead of so using this power, they would more firmly establish it. Without being aware of it you are guilty of a species of intolerance, and on the same principles, you might insist on any particular system of religious belief—any particular doctrines in political economy, or any other opinions that you may have justly or unjustly imbibed. You might say these opinions appear to me essential to the people's happiness and I will not admit even wisdom and virtue to decide upon them. I think that you will agree I am justified in these remarks when I call to your recollection the following passage in your letter, 'But even admitting the electors should become as qualified for the discharge of their important duty as could reasonably be expected, under any circumstances, still I contend that if you were to let loose in the House of Commons the full force of the popular part of our constitution it would be impossible for the other branches to preserve for a continuance, anything beyond a mere nominal authority . . . unless the influence of the other branches was silently suffered to operate to a certain extent in that House the whole form of the constitution would be changed . . . it would be merely a mixed government in form, but a Republic in substance.' You appear to me to have changed the subject in discussion—it is no longer an enquiry into the best means of making the people happy, but into the best means of preserving the monarchical and aristocratical branches of the constitution, for you admit that if the practice of the constitution conformed to its theory—if the people were really represented in their house of parliament and were free from the influence of the other branches, irregularly and corruptly applied, they would be the only real and efficient power in the state. Is not this admission at variance with another part of your letter, where you speak of this government being formed on a principle of the due balance of powers, the preservation of which you say is essential to its existence? If influence is necessary to the preservation of this balance—influence too not defined nor capable of being either defined or controlled,—which you yourself say 'should be measured and regulated to prevent its undue preponderance,' how can there be in the constitution itself a due balance of powers? No; depend upon it, there is no check in the constitution against this influence—it will be used at all times for the benefit of those who happen to be in possession of it, and will be under no other controul than that of their own views of advantage. The check is not in the constitution —it is as I said before in public opinion, expressed through the medium of the press—in the trial by jury—in the published speeches of a few popular members of parliament, who have no influence by their votes, but by their tongues, and in the right of convening public meetings, and thereby organizing opposition—these are the checks to which we owe all the happiness and liberty we enjoy. You may think that this is the most eligible mode for the people to control their government,—I should differ with you, but this is the real question to be discussed with those who are friends to a reform of parliament, and who wish to extend the elective franchise to such of the people as would make a good use of it. It is to this point I want to conduct our argument. I want those who oppose me to acknowledge candidly that the people are not represented, and that they do not think it expedient that they should be; instead of which I meet daily with people who avow themselves friendly to moderate reform, but when they explain their views it becomes manifest that they wish for no reform at all, for they say that it would be impossible for government to proceed to any good purpose, if the people had even a majority in the House of Commons whatever precautions you might take in bestowing the elective franchise. This is Malthus's argument, who has been staying with me for a few days, and has just left me. I could not, however, bring him to confess that he really wished for no reform at all.

It must I think be admitted without qualification that there is no such thing as a balance of the three powers in our government. If it could for a moment exist it would disappear immediately that either of two out of the three powers should combine their interests against the third. In our government the mutual interest of the monarchy and the aristocracy to combine cannot admit of a doubt, one possessing the privilege of bestowing every place of honour and emolument, and in a degree never possessed perhaps by any former government,—the other having an overwhelming influence in the legislature, which may be advantageously disposed of to the minister. No reform would be effectual to counteract this powerful combination but such a real representation of the people as should give them a majority in the house of commons.

In one part of your letter you were disposed to yield the substance of all that I am contending for, but you suddenly recollected that it might endanger the independence of the monarchy and aristocracy, and you withdrew your concession. You say that if my scheme of reform went further you would be more disposed to go along with me. You call upon me to 'limit the right of voting at Elections to such persons who by their education have the ability to decide correctly,' and then you would have fewer objections to reform. In other words, you would require security for a good choice of representatives, and this is precisely what I want. If I can not obtain it without limiting the elective franchise to the very narrowest bounds, I would so limit it; but I am persuaded that we should most securely get our object, and should be less exposed to hazards of a different kind, by extending the elective franchise,—not indeed universally to all the people, but to that part of them which cannot be supposed to have any interest in overturning the rights of property. Come back to this admission, and our difference will not be very difficult to settle, but do not mock us with the name of a representative government, denying us all the advantages which may be derived from that form.

The report that you have heard respecting my daughter's approaching marriage is true, but it is not a subject of congratulation to me.

Everybody joins in lamenting the untimely end of Sir

S. Romilly[1]. He was a very useful man, and would have laboured effectually in procuring for us an amelioration of the criminal law.

The second edition of my book is in the press[2]. I have made very few alterations in it. Murray has just received a copy of a French translation of the first edition, the only copy in London—with notes by M. Say[3]. I have looked over the notes—they may be considered as M. Say's defence of those opinions of his on which I have animadverted. It would not be becoming in me to decide which of us is nearest to the truth. I must leave impartial readers to do that. They are written in perfect good temper, and where his conscience will allow him to praise me, he does it in the most flattering manner. The French edition is in two volumes.

Malthus came over from Bath, and stayed with me at Gatcomb for a very few days. We have neither of us lost our interest in the discussion of questions which we have so often debated before. His work will not appear till the end of next year. Mrs. Ricardo joins with me in kind regards to Mrs. Trower.

Ever truly yours

DAVID RICARDO.

XXIV[4]

MY DEAR TROWER   LONDON 28 *Feb.* 1819

Your last kind letter ought not to have remained so long unanswered, but my natural indolence conspired with a multiplicity of occupations to induce me to defer writing

---

[1] On November 2, 1818, in his sixty-second year.

[2] See Letters of Ricardo to McCulloch, pp. 12-21 passim; the second edition of the 'Principles' appeared early in 1819.

[3] 'Des Principes de l'Économie Politique et de l'Impôt, traduit de l'anglais par M. F. S. Constancio, et avec des notes explicatives et critiques de M. J. B. Say,' 2 vols., Paris, 1819.

[4] Addressed on back of sheet to 'Unsted Wood, Godalming,' and franked by Ricardo himself.

to you. Besides, the information you gave me that you would be in London in March, made my negligence appear less unfavourable in my own eyes. Before March actually begins however I must assure you of the pleasure which I shall have in seeing you in London, and I hope you will, on the earliest day you can, announce your arrival to me by presenting yourself in Brook Street at our breakfast hour at half-past nine. At that time I am sure to be found, but at any other I may be engaged from home in some of the many objects which now draw my attention.

My efforts have been at last crowned with success, and I am now a seated member of the House of Commons[1]. My introduction there was nowise disagreeable as the ceremony of taking the oaths is not very formidable, and the kind expressions of welcome given to me by my friends set me quite at my ease. I fear that I shall never become a very useful member[2].

The inquiry into the state of our currency and exchanges is proceeding in both houses very satisfactorily. I have had many conversations with several of the Committees of both Houses—with Lord Grenville, Marquis of Lansdown, Lord King, Mr. Huskisson, Mr. F. Lewis, Mr. Grenfell, and others. All have a very perfect knowledge of the subject, and all agree that the progress of the public in comprehending the question has been very great. The Bank Directors themselves have improved, and they are far behind every other person. I confidently rely on measures

---

[1] Ricardo was elected as member for Portarlington, an Irish pocket borough, in Queen's County, on February 20, 1819. Cf. Letters of Ricardo to McCulloch, p. 24, and to Malthus, p. 154. Compare Bentham, 'Works,' vol. x, p. 450, where Bentham says he himself took some pains to get Ricardo a seat.

[2] For outlines of his speeches, see Letters to Malthus, Introduction x, and passim; also Mr. E. Cannan's two articles on 'Ricardo in Parliament' (Economic Journal, 1894, pp. 249 seq., and 409 seq).

being taken to place our currency in a satisfactory state. I am told that I shall be examined[1].

Believe me
My dear Trower
Very truly y^{rs}
DAVID RICARDO.

XXV[2].

MY DEAR TROWER   LONDON 28 *May* 1819

I take advantage of a little respite in the business of the House to acknowledge the receipt of your kind letter, and to inform you that I am every day rejoicing with increased satisfaction at the triumph of science, and truth, over prejudice, and error. You will perceive by the Newspapers that Parliament has at length decided that we should revert to a sound currency[3]. The feeble resistance, in point of argument, of the Bank Directors, was easily overcome. I had the courage to set myself foremost in the battle, and was amply rewarded by the support of the House, which enabled me to get to the end of my speech without any great degree of fear or trepidation. I hope that during the next fortnight we shall give the death-blow

---

[1] Ricardo was examined before the Committees on the Resumption of Specie Payments, 24th March, 1819, &c. See Ricardo's Letters to McCulloch, p. 26, note.

[2] Addressed on back as before. Franked by himself.

[3] Two days earlier (May 26), the House of Commons had agreed to a series of eight Resolutions respecting the Resumption of Cash Payments, and had ordered a bill to the same effect to be brought in. The Resolutions adopted Ricardo's 'Proposal for an Economical and Secure Currency,' and recommended that gold bullion, assayed and stamped, should be given in quantities of not less than 60 ounces for bank-notes, at the rate of £4 1s. per ounce, after February 1, 1820; of £3 19s. 6d. after October 1, 1820; of £3 17s. 10d. after May 1, 1821; in legal coin, after May 1, 1823. The repeal of laws prohibiting the melting and export of gold coin, and the repayment to the Bank of £10,000,000 of the advances made to the Government were also recommended. See Hansard, Parliamentary Debates, vol. xl. 802-804. Cf. Letters to McCulloch, p. 27.

to the theory of an abstract pound sterling. The alarm that prevailed in the City is incomprehensible; it must have been occasioned by the imprudent remonstrance of the Bank to Government setting forth the great danger which would attend the reduction of the currency[1]. I regret that the Committees have not adopted the measure of obliging the Bank to buy gold at £3 17s. 6d. whenever it is offered to them at that price—the reverting to specie payments appears to me unnecessary, and not likely to be attended with any advantage.

I sent you by the coach the Lords' Report, as I had two, one from the Lords as a witness who had given evidence before them, the other as a member of the House of Commons, but I have only one copy of the report from the Commons' Committee which I will lend you with pleasure, but which I must keep as a valuable document. Tell me whether I shall send it to you.

There were I think very serious objections against the Poor Law settlement bill[2].—It would have borne very heavy on the towns, particularly on some that are in the neighbourhood of the mines. Why is not a more efficient measure proposed? The fact I believe is that no party in the House dare take upon themselves to propose or support any plan which may make them unpopular. This is one of the ill effects of party; the public interest is neglected.

I agree with you that we ought not to add to our debt by loans, we should have the firmness to raise taxes for any deficiency that may now be wanted [*sic*]. Our sinking fund is gone, and I am not disposed to raise a new one, for

---

[1] This was a 'Representation, agreed upon 20th day of May, 1819, by the Directors of the Bank of England, and laid before the Chancellor of the Exchequer.' It was laid before the House of Lords by the Earl of Liverpool, on May 21, 1819. Hansard, 'Parliamentary Debates,' vol. xl. 600–604.

[2] Ibid., vol. xl. 284 et seq. (May 10, 1819).

the purpose of placing it again at the disposal of ministers. Do what you will, they will not respect it, and after a few years we should be as much in debt as ever. I am for a vigorous system of taxation, if it is for the purpose of paying off debt once for all, but I am sure that ministers will never respect any fund, which is to accumulate at compound interest. With the slightest pressure on the finances such a fund would be diverted from the employment to which it had been destined.

Mr. Elwin is in London—I saw him for a moment on tuesday—he is looking very well.

Mrs. Ricardo unites with me in kind regards to Mrs. Trower.

Believe me ever
My dear Trower
Very truly y^{rs}
DAVID RICARDO.

I have omitted saying that your name will be remembered when we prepare our list.—I have not sold any stock against the loan, for I have been thinking the price low ever since they were 74.

XXVI[1].

MY DEAR TROWER LONDON *June* 1—1819.

I write to you without delay to give you my opinion respecting an investment of money in Bank Stock at the present price. The fall has been great, but I think not so great as the facts with which we are now acquainted warrant and justify. I calculated on the Bank having a much greater surplus Capital than the reports of the Committees inform us they have. That Capital is stated to be 5 millions[2], I thought it more than double, and so

---

[1] Addressed on back as before. Franked by himself.
[2] On January 30, 1819, £5,202,320; see 'Second Report from the Secret

it would have been if the Directors had managed the concern intrusted to them with the ability and economy that they ought to have done.

Let us try if we cannot ascertain what under a good system of management should now be the profits of the Bank, and then let us make a due allowance for the management which the affairs of the Bank will receive under the present Directors—

Savings (see Reports of Committees)	£5,000,000
Bank notes in circulation after the necessary reduction—estimated at	23,000,000
Deposits, Public and Private,—estimated at	6,000,000
	34,000,000
Deduct Treasure to meet demands	4,000,000
	30,000,000
Suppose these 30 millions to be lent on an average at 4 per cent. and if peace continues that is not too low an estimate they will receive annually	1,200,000
Interest on capital lent to Government at 3 per cent.	440,604
For Management of the Debt	280,000
	1,920,604
Expences and Stamps . 465,304	
Dividend, 10 per cent. . 1,455,300	
	1,920,604
	,, ,, ,,

If the Bank should have a circulation of 23 millions and manage their affairs well they may continue to pay a dividend of 10 per cent. till 1833 when their charter will expire, and a deduction must be made in consequence of the price they must be obliged to pay for a renewal of

Committee of the House of Commons on the Expediency of the Bank of England resuming Cash Payments,' Appendix I.

their privileges—if they are renewed—and if they are not they may probably divide 130—or 140 for every £100 Stock. —But will they be able to keep 23,000,000 in circulation— certainly not if specie payments are to be restored—that circumstance may probably sink the amount to 15 millions in which case they could not pay more than 8 per cent. dividend.

After examining these statements you will be able to judge whether it would be expedient to [buy]¹ Bank Stock.—I have thought it right to sell s[ome of]¹ mine, not much indeed (£2500) being firmly persuaded that it is much too high, and that after a little sober examination the price will fall.

Your brother called on me this morning when I communicated to him my sentiments on this subject.

In great haste I am

My dear Trower

Yrs truly

DAVID RICARDO.

XXVII ².

MY DEAR TROWER   LONDON *July* 8—1819

You have calculated right—I shall in a few days leave London for Gatcomb, no worse in health for irregular meals, and late hours, during my first Parliamentary campaign. Though not necessary to my health I shall see the green fields, and hills of Gloucestershire, again, with great satisfaction. These objects are always pleasing to me, but will be more so now on account of the contrast which a little leisure will afford me to the busy and bustling life which I have lately been passing. The daily attendance in the House of Commons, and the time necessary

¹ MS. torn.   ² No cover or address.

to look over the Reports and papers which are so profusely delivered,—to say nothing of Committees which sit in the morning, leave a member no leisure to read even the light publications of the day, so that I am not acquainted with the Legend of Montrose yet[1], and have not read more than two or three articles in the last Quarterly and Edinburgh Reviews.

The triumph of science and truth in the great councils of the Nation, this Session, gives me great satisfaction, which is not a little increased by observing the present state of the price of bullion and the foreign exchanges. Gold is I believe at £3 18s. per oz., silver at the mint price, and the exchanges very nearly at par. The best friends to the measures lately adopted could not have anticipated less pressure than what has been hitherto experienced, and I think it but reasonable to hope that the permanent price of bullion will settle at the present rate, without adding much to the slight difficulties which we have already suffered. Our opponents, whose prophecies are all proved to be unfounded, now say that we have had great good luck—that the natural course of events has been favorable to us—they will admit any thing but the truth of our principles. Even Lord Lauderdale, whose theory respecting Mint regulations requires that silver should never be under 5s. 6d., that price which he calls the mint price, maintains that the present market price of silver is an unnatural and disturbed price, which cannot have a long duration[2]. I have heard much of Mr. Turner's pamphlet[3], but I have

---

[1] Cf. Letters to McCulloch, p. 32.

[2] Lauderdale had published in this year a second edition of his 'Public Wealth' (1st ed. 1804).

[3] Letter to Sir Robert Peel, by Samuel Turner, Esq., 1819. He maintained that there was no connection between the price of bullion and the value of bank notes, and opposed Resumption as ruinous to trade and agriculture. See also Turner's 'Considerations on the Agriculture, Commerce, and Manufactures of the British Empire,' 1822, p. 65; cf. pp. 32-9, &c., where he applied mathematics to economics.

not seen it—I did not buy it because I have already such a number of publications by me which maintain the same doctrine which he maintains that I did not think it expedient to make the trifling sacrifice which its purchase would cost, to add to the mass. I saw extracts from it in the New Times, which paper has been as loud in his praise as it has been in condemning me.

I am not a member of a Committee to *further* Mr. Owen's plans—the Committee was appointed for the purpose of examining, and not of approving those plans. I attended the meeting and had very successfully resisted all entreaties to let my name be on the Committee till attacked by the Duke of Kent and Mr. John Smith. It was in vain that I protested I differed from all the leading principles advanced by Mr. Owen,—that, I was told, was no objection, for I was not bound to approve, only to examine. With very great reluctance I at last consented, and have attended the first meeting, at which I gave my reasons at some length for departing from all Mr. Owen's conclusions. The scheme was chiefly examined with a view to a pauper establishment or a well regulated workhouse, but even to that limited plan there are insuperable objections. Owen is himself a benevolent enthusiast, willing to make great sacrifices for a favorite object. The Duke of Kent, his great supporter, is also entitled to the praise of benevolent intentions, but he appears to me to be quite ignorant of all the principles which ought to regulate establishments for the poor—he has heard of Malthus['] doctrine, and has an antipathy to it, without knowing the reasons on which it is founded or how his difficulty may be obviated. He, Mr. Preston, and Mr. Owen, appear to think nothing necessary to production, and the happiness of a crouded [*sic*] population, but land. We have land; it may be made more productive, and therefore, we cannot have an excess of population.—Can any reasonable person believe, with

Owen, that a society, such as he projects, will flourish and produce more than has ever yet been produced by an equal number of men, if they are to be stimulated to exertion by a regard to the community, instead of by a regard to their private interest? Is not the experience of ages against him? He can bring nothing to oppose to this experience but one or two ill authenticated cases of societies which prospered on a principle of a community of goods, but where the people were under the powerful influence of religious fanaticism. I was in hopes that Sir Wm. de Crespigny would have given me an opportunity to state my opinions shortly on this subject in the House of Commons, but he thought fit to withdraw his motion for a Committee, and therefore I was obliged to be silent [1].

Mrs. Ricardo unites with me in kind regards to Mrs. Trower and yourself. Believe me ever

My dear Trower

very truly yours

DAVID RICARDO.

Torrens tells me he is proceeding with his work on Political Economy. Malthus has been staying a few days with me. He calculates on publishing his book by the end of the year. Mill appears to be well satisfied with his new office at the East India House [2].—Mr. Bentham's mind and pen are employed at the present moment in elucidating the principles of Government and the safety of extending the representation.

[1] The opportunity was actually presented some months later, on December 16, 1819, when Ricardo addressed the House on Sir William de Crespigny's motion for the appointment of a select committee 'to inquire into the plan of Mr. Owen for ameliorating the condition of the lower classes.' See Hansard, Parliamentary Debates, vol. xli. 1206-1209; Letters to McCulloch, p. 47; Mr. Cannan on 'Ricardo in Parliament,' Economic Journal, 1894, pp. 415-7.

[2] Mill was appointed Assistant to the Examiner of India Correspondence, 12th May, 1819. See Bain's 'Life of Jas. Mill,' p. 185.

NOTE.—Mr. Owen's proceedings in 1819 have been already mentioned. (See above, p. 79.) The object of the Committee to which Ricardo so unwillingly belonged was to 'investigate and report on Mr. Owen's plan.' They hoped to get large enough subscriptions to enable them to found something like a New Lanark in England. 'It is now proposed to form a new establishment in which agricultural and manufacturing employment shall both be used, but of which agriculture shall be the basis. Mr. Owen's increased experience and the advantage of beginning *de novo* will enable him to make arrangements much superior to those which exist at New Lanark; he expresses the most confident opinion that the capital employed will be rapidly repaid with interest, that the labourers may be placed in a state of comfort hitherto unknown to that class; he offers to take upon himself the superintendence, at the same time that he entirely precludes himself from deriving any profit, and he is desirous to communicate in the most open and unreserved manner the whole details of his plans.' ('Life of Owen,' vol. ii. pp. 213-4, Address of the Committee to the Public, Aug. 23rd, 1819.) The Committee considered the plans practicable; but (in December, 1819) in view of the smallness of the subscriptions they were obliged to give up their task. £100,000 had been needed, and only £8,000 had been collected, in spite of the efforts of the Duke of Kent, their chairman (ibid. 249, cf. 242).

XXVIII [1].

MY DEAR TROWER   GATCOMB PARK 25 *Sep.* 1819

I was well pleased to see your well known handwriting after the very long interval which had elapsed since I received your last letter. I was on the point of writing to you, to shew you that I was not disposed to relinquish my intercourse with you, imperfect as it is, when your letter arrived, and my murmuring ceased.

By rising early in the morning I have two hours to myself for any object I may have in view, without interruption, even when visitors are in my house; of course

[1] Cover wanting.

when I am alone or when my visitors are those who are nearly related to me there is much more time in the course of the day that I can call my own. It is easier to find time, than to use it profitably. I have been very much drawn away from all serious occupation since I have been in the country by the desire I have felt to enjoy the fineness of the weather. I cannot often refuse the solicitations of my two little girls to accompany them in their morning rides and we are often to be met with in full canter on our respective ponies.

For the last fortnight I have confined myself a good deal to my desk, endeavouring to put my thoughts on paper on the subject of the Sinking Fund. I was requested to do so by Mill, who had been applied to by Mr. Napier to forward such a request to me. Mr. Napier is the Editor of the Supplement to the Encyclopedia Britannica, and he wished for an article on the Sinking fund, from me, to appear in the next half volume of his work. I, at first, refused, but on being strongly urged to do it by Mill, I consented to make the attempt. I have made it, but I have not succeeded, and it is now a very doubtful matter whether I shall persevere in my task [1]. The truth is that Dr. Hamilton's book on the Sinking Fund [2] is so good that very little of original observations can be made on the subject. It would be unjust not to refer to him on all occasions, and if you do so it may be asked, whether you have done any thing yourself? The only point of difference between Dr. H. and me is this,—he would I believe support the Sinking Fund, I would get rid of it entirely, or leave

---

[1] The article was completed and published in the 'Supplement to Encyclopaedia Britannica,' vol. iv; it is reprinted in 'Works' (ed. McCulloch) pp. 515-548. See Letters to McCulloch, p. 46; Letters to Malthus, pp. 157-158, 165.

[2] 'An Inquiry concerning the Rise and Progress, the Redemption and Present State, and the Management of the National Debt of Great Britain and Ireland.' Edinburgh, 1813.

it at that small amount as to give security that if the revenue suffered any unexpected defalcation there was this surplus to apply to. I am equally impressed with Dr. Hamilton with the importance of diminishing our enormous debt, the question with me is, will the Sinking Fund effect it? I am persuaded that it never will, for it will never be safe from the gripe of ministers. Have you virtue enough to pay a great part of your debt by the sacrifice of a portion of your property? This is the question to be put to the country—if they answer in the negative, then I say the next best thing is to submit to the burden of your debt without aggra[va]ting it by new imposts which will certainly be misapplied. But I must remember that I am not now writing my essay, and that I must not forestal the only point on which I think I am entitled to attention.

I have pretty nearly discarded the subject of bullion from my mind. Every thing regarding its price and the foreign exchanges is going on so much to my satisfaction that I have nothing to wish for. I repose in full confidence on the wise checks which have been put on the Bank Directors[1]—if they had been unrestrained they would again have mistaken the object which they ought to have in view; instead of taking measures to equalise the value of paper and gold they would have been thinking of the public good, and under a mistaken idea of promoting that, they would have administered an increased dose of paper.

On the subject of taxation[2] a wide field is open for those, who will patiently think, to give instruction to the Public; but the first step must be to make the first principles of Political Economy known, and that remains yet to be done. Without correct notions of rent, no man can be made to understand that a land tax does not ultimately

---

[1] See above, p. 73, note.
[2] Cf. *Letters to Malthus*, p. 164 (Nov. 1819), where for Turner should probably be read Trower: Trower had regretted that the political economists gave so little attention to taxation.

fall on the landlord, and it would be in vain to talk to him, till he did admit the new doctrine on the subject of rent. We are advancing, and the discussion which Malthus' new work will provoke as well as the other productions which we lately have had, and which we shall have, will tend to the diffusion of right principles. I am very much mistaken indeed if the delay in the publication of Malthus['] book will not have had the effect of very much improving it. I think I perceive in him a very sensible approach, under different words, to opinions which at first appeared to him most preposterous and extravagant.

This is as it should be. Even Sismondi's errors will be of use to the diffusion of correct opinions [1]. Why do not you give your assistance? It is a path in which much may be done, and in which the stimulus of public opinion and public approbation for success, is not wanting. The truth is you are an idle fellow, and are glad to avail yourself of any excuse, such as a want of time and an abundance of other occupations, rather than undergo the toil of writing.

One word on the Manchester proceedings [2]. I am glad to find that the opinion is general amongst all those whom I meet or converse with that the interference of the Magistrates at the late meeting was unwise and inexpedient. I hope it will appear too that it was illegal, for I hope that no law can be produced to justify the violent interference of magistrates to dissolve a meeting of the people, the avowed object of which was to petition legally for a redress of real or imagined grievances. If the right to petition is only to be exercised at the discretion of magistrates, or of any other body in the state, then it is a farce to call us a free people. These large assemblages

---

[1] 'Nouveaux Principes d' Économie Politique, ou de la richesse dans ses rapports avec la population.' 2 vols., Paris, 1819.

[2] 'Peterloo Massacre,' August 16, 1819. Cf. Wallas, 'Life of Francis Place,' (London, 1898), pp. 140-141. Miss Martineau, 'History of the Peace,' *sub dato*.

of the people may be regretted—they may in their consequences be productive of mischief, but if the security of our freedom depend on our right to assemble and state our wrongs, which in the absence of real representation I believe it does, then we must patiently suffer the lesser evil to avoid the greater.

Accept my sincere wishes that Mrs. Trower may pass through her time of anxiety with safety. My friend [1] Malthus would not have thought your case one which required his skill, had he been a physician, and possessed of a remedy to prevent the too great increase of population. You would be only legally and beneficially employed in furnishing citizens to the state, whose exertions might benefit, but whose reasonable wants could not injure the rest of the community. Mrs. Ricardo and my family are well; they unite with me in kind regards to Mrs. Trower.

I am ever my dear Trower
Truly yours
DAVID RICARDO.

XXIX [2].

[To Francis Place.]

Gatcomb Park, Minchinhampton,
1 November 1819.

Dear Sir

My object, as well as yours, is the discovery of truth, and therefore there is no occasion for apology on either side, for freely commenting on each other's opinions.

You say, that you do make a distinction between a Sink^g Fund provided by taxes, and a Sinking Fund

---

[1] 'Friend' repeated by oversight, in the original.

[2] Addressed on back: 'Mr. Place, Charing Cross, London.' Franked by Ricardo himself. These letters (XXIX and XXX) are in the 'Place' Collection in the British Museum, Add. MSS., 27836, ff. 113-118, and were first printed, at the suggestion of Mr. Graham Wallas, in the Economic Journal, June, 1893. For Ricardo's relations to Place see Wallas' 'Life of Place '(1898), and Ricardo's Letters to Malthus, pp. ix, 43, 96, 207, 209.

borrowed, but that in both cases there is nothing but delusion. 'To a S. F. borrowed,' you say, 'that there has been no other kind since 1793.' Now I cannot agree to this; I wish to ask whether during a portion of the time from 1793 to the present day, there was not, in consequence of that which you deem an unfounded and delusive name, less debt contracted than there would have been if no such name had existed. Twenty millions, for example, were required for the extraordinary expences of 1796. Besides a million a year for interest, 200,000 pr ann^m were also provided, by taxes, for what was improperly called Sinking Fund. Suppose this to go on for several years, say ten years, is it not true that we shall, at the end of those years, be less in debt, than if we had continued our expenditure of twenty millions, and had provided only one million per ann^m for interest? It is demonstrable that the difference of our debt would be precisely equal to the sum which £200,000 pr ann^m, for ten years, another 200,000 for nine years, another for eight years, and so on, would amount to, at compound interest, in ten years, and therefore in comparing these two modes of providing for expenditure together, it conveys no erroneous idea, to say, that we shall owe less in one case than the other, by all the amount of the sinking fund and its accumulations. Strictly speaking there is no fund, for there can be no fund, and no accumulation, while we are in debt. All that is received is applied to the payment of debt, or to prevent the contracting of it, but still it is correct to say that the difference between A and B is equal to all the accumulations which a fund of any named amount would yield in a given time. Now suppose the S. F. to be borrowed every year, then indeed, you may justly say that the whole is a delusion, for it may be demonstrated that with a given expenditure you will be just as much in debt at the end of ten, or any other number of years, without, as with a sinking fund. Is there not a very marked difference between the effects of one or other of these sinking funds, yet your language would lead us to suppose there was none, for you say, 'that neither in the one case nor in the other is there any thing but delusion.' Suppose Mr. Pitt's plan to have always been fairly acted upon, and I should ask any of its supporters what benefit we had derived from it in diminishing or in preventing the accumulation of debt, would he not be correct if he showed me the amount of stock standing in the names of the commissioners, and told me that but for the operation of the Sinking Fund, the nation would really have owed that amount in addition to the unredeemed debt. How, then, can you call the whole a delusion? I say that the delusion is in ministers not having performed what they promised—they did not provide what they have always called a sinking fund from the taxes, but have *for the last few years* not only borrowed the sinking fund on the loans which they have created, but have not even provided the interest for them, and therefore it has become necessary to take the interest from the sinking fund. I hope now I have made myself understood; I concede to you that there is no real fund, nor can there be, while we are in debt, but that no delusion will arise from considering the Sinking fund as a real fund, if we wish merely to make a comparison between the actual state of our debt, with a certain provision to check its accumulation, and its state if no such provision were made.

You deny that Mr. Vansittart took anything from the S. F. when he made his arrangements in 1813, you say 'there was nothing to take.' We will suppose a country to owe twenty mill^{ns} pr ann^m, and to consent to pay twenty-five millions pr ann^m. It pays the five millions with the intention of arriving at a term when it shall not be called upon to pay anything, or, in other words, it prefers paying twenty-five millions pr ann^m for a limited number of years, to paying twenty millions pr ann^m for ever. With the five millions pr ann^m payments of capital are to be made, but without affording any relief to the country, which is always to pay twenty-five millions, till the whole debt is paid. The first year twenty millions are paid to the public, and five millions to the Commissioners; the second year 19,750,000 to the public, and 5,250,000 to the Commissioners; and so from year to year the payments to the public diminish, while those to the Commiss^{rs} increase. Suppose that at the end of a certain number of years, seven millions only are annually paid to the public, eighteen millions to the Commissioners; and suppose at this time the minister requires a loan of twenty millions. If he provides one million from the taxes, for the interest of this loan, he will pay annually for interest and sinking fund on debt twenty-six instead of twenty-five millions, and though the debt will increase, the sinking fund will not diminish, but suppose he does not so provide the million for interest, he will only pay twenty-five millions pr ann^m: instead, however, of paying as before seven millions for interest, and eighteen millions to the commissioners, he must now pay eight millions for interest, and seventeen millions to the commissioners; and if foreseeing that he shall want loans of an equal amount for several years to come he should obtain an act of Parliament allowing him to reduce the payment to the commissioners to eleven millions, and increase that to the public, by the creation of new debt, to fourteen millions, will he not have made a substantial inroad on the plan for the payment of debt? This is what Mr. Vansittart has done, and yet you say, 'Nothing was in fact taken, nothing could be taken, because there was nothing to take.'

If you say so because, strictly speaking, there is no fund,

I will not dispute the matter, for it is in fact a dispute about words. But you observe that it is not a dispute about words, what then do we differ about? If we have not the means of paying off our debt so quickly as we otherwise should do, or, if we cannot check its increase so effectually in consequence of the new arrangement proposed by Mr. Vansittart, then I say he has taken something, and not nothing. Call it S. F., or call it what you please, he has diminished the necessity for laying on new taxes, but he has done so, by accelerating the increase of debt.

'A S. F. from taxes can only exist when the taxes produce more money than the current expenses of the Government consume, and this has never been the case in any one instance since 1793, so there has been no sinking fund from taxes.' This is in other words saying, 'I call nothing a sinking fund which does not actually diminish debt.' My idea of a sinking fund is not so strict as yours,—it is a fund which holds out a fair prospect of one day being effective to the diminution and the annihilation of debt. If we had a surplus of permanent revenue above permanent expenditure of twenty millions, and for one year only expended more than our permanent income, you would say that we had no sinking fund that particular year — I should on the contrary contend that inasmuch as we had twenty m. pr ann^m *for ever* to set against one single year[']s expenditure of twenty-one m. we had a very substantial and a very efficient fund. 'If we had lent out a sum at compound interest, notwithstanding our continual borrowing, we should have a real sinking fund, and might in time pay off our debts, but this we have never done and never can do.' That we have not lately done it I agree, but why the thing is impossible, except from the bad faith of ministers or parliament I can not see.

What reason do you give why we can not do it? 'because we can not create stock with the produce of the taxes,' but the commissioners can appropriate the interest on stock already created with the produce of the taxes, and this will be attended with precisely the same effects as if they had lent the money at compound interest. If you admit which you unequivocally do that if we lent out a sum at compound interest notwithstanding our continual borrowing, we should have a real sinking fund and might in time pay off our debts, you must admit that an equal fund given to the commissioners to purchase stock in the market with the power of appropriating the dividends on the stock purchased to the making of new purchases, would be equally efficacious. You must withdraw your first admission or you must be prepared to yield the second—it is impossible consistently to maintain one of these propositions and to refuse one's assent to the other.

I am Dear Sir
Truly Yours,
DAVID RICARDO.

Be so good as to show this letter to Mr. Mill that he may judge between us.

XXX [1].

GATCOMB PARK,
DEAR SIR 3 Novemb^r 1819.

I have looked carefully at the passage which you quote from Dr. Hamilton, but do not see that the Dr shows that there cannot be a sinking fund from taxes.

The case he supposes of borrowing money at simple interest and lending it at compound interest, I do not clearly understand. If the nation borrows a loan of a

---

[1] Franked by himself. Addressed on back: 'F. Place Esq., Charing Cross, London.'

million, for which it taxes itself £50,000 pr ann^m to pay the interest, and then employs the million at compound interest in the discharge of debt, it will the first year discharge the debt of the million, and will from that time employ £50,000 pr ann. at compound interest in the discharge of old debt. In fact it taxes itself £50,000 pr ann. for a Sinking Fund. When a nation or an individual borrows money at simple interest, and lends it at compound interest, it has the interest to pay every year, but never receives any thing in return while it continues the original loan, or, which is the same thing, the annual interest of it, at compound interest. So far from this case proving your proposition it appears to me to establish mine. A nation taxes itself 50,000 pr ann. without increasing its expenditure. If the revenue and expenditure were before equal this surplus of £50,000 pr ann. being devoted to the payment of debt, will produce the same effects, as if it were lent to A or B at compound interest, and when arrived at a certain sum were employed for the payment of debt. Do you mean to say (I am sure Dr. Hamilton does not) that if our income exceeds our expenditure £50,000 pr ann^m, and is devoted to the payment of debt, that it will not diminish our debt at a compound rate of interest? Shall we not be less in debt by £50,000 the first year, £52,500 the second, £55,125 the third, and so on. Call this a S. F. or what you please, for I will not dispute about a name, will not this be the result? If you say it will what is our difference? On this subject I agree entirely with Dr. Hamilton — pray look at Page 53 and following pages of the last edition of his book.

I am
Sincerely Y^{rs}
DAVID RICARDO.

I am very much obliged to you for sending me the

account of the proceedings at the Westminster election. I have read it with a great deal of interest.

XXXI [1].

My dear Trower   Gatcomb Park—12 *Nov*—1819.

Think not, I pray you, that I meant to make a charge of idleness against you—I knew full well that if you were not employed in sedentary occupations, that you were nevertheless usefully employed [2]. Nothing can be more useful to the public than that enlightened men, with no motives for the misapplication of the powers entrusted to them, should take upon themselves the duties of magistrates. I am convinced that you are performing very essential services to the community about you by settling the disputes,—preserving the peace, and affording securities for the protection of property within the circle of your influence. Nor do I undervalue your farming pursuits; I am well satisfied that great benefits arise from men of education and liberal views engaging in such speculations. They contribute much to introduce improvements in agriculture, and to break down those obstinate prejudices against innovation, which are perhaps more conspicuous in farming concerns than in any other. My regret was perhaps selfish. Wishing ardently [3] for the diffusion of correct principles in Political Economy, I wanted the assistance of one to effect that object who appeared to me to have imbibed correct opinions himself, and to be qualified to aid in the further improvement of the science.

[1] Cover wanting. On back (in another hand) 'Mr. H. Trower from Ricardo.'
[2] The quantity of MSS. left by Trower, and now in the possession of Mr. Walter Trower, would be a sufficient proof that he was never idle.
[3] Written 'ardendtly.'

The subject you mention is very important to be well analysed, and explained—namely, the best means of raising the funds which may be necessary for future expenditure; it is highly interesting, and merits the most patient investigation. The difficulty which encompasses it is almost sufficient to deter one from entering upon it. For my own satisfaction however, and not with any hope to throw much light on so very intricate a question, I would employ my time upon it, if I had any time at my command, which at present I have not: on some future day I will bend my whole mind to the consideration of this subject.

I am sorry to find that Malthus, whose work I believe is now actually in the press, has left off, without treating on the subject of taxation. Political Economy, when the simple principles of it are once understood, is only useful, as it directs Governments to right measures in taxation. We very soon arrive at the knowledge that Agriculture, Commerc[e], and Manufactures flourish best when left without interference on the part of Government, but the necessity which the state has for money to defray the expences of its functions, imposes on it the obligation to raise taxes, and thus interference becomes absolutely necessary. It is here then that the most perfect knowledge of the science is required, and I cannot but regret that Malthus has not given us his thoughts on this part of the subject. I hope he will immediately after publishing his volume seriously set about it.

I am pleased to find that you are friendly to the preservation of the right to the people to meet, and to state their real or supposed grievances. This right may occasionally be attended with grave inconveniences, but I do not think that you can provide against these, in the way you mention, without making the privilege itself a mere nullity. A Government is free in proportion to the facility with which the people can overthrow it. What security for freedom should we have if no meeting, larger than a parish meeting, was legal. Such meetings might indeed talk of their grievances, but their talking would be no motive to their rulers to alter their measures, but might indeed be an inducement with them to get rid of such meetings altogether. The fear of insurrection, and of the people combining to make a general effort are the great checks on all governments—these we might have thro the means of a reformed House of Commons—now we have them by the privilege which the people have of meeting—I can not consent to weaken the latter check without having some security for the obtaining of the former, and even if we did obtain it, I am doubtful how far it might be safely accepted as a substitute for the privilege which we now enjoy.

I agree with you in thinking that the ministers have shewn very little wisdom, and as little liberality, in their dismissal of Lord Fitzwilliam [1]; as for the conduct of the opposition, in taking advantage of the present circumstances, or any other which may occur, to oust ministers from their places, it is quite in the regular course of ministerial and opposition tactics,—they appear to me to have no more chance of succeeding now than on many former occasions.

Before I go any further, let me congratulate you and Mrs. Trower, which I most sincerely do, on the birth of your daughter. I am glad to hear that mother and infant are doing well.

I have not read Peter's letters to his Kinsfolk, they are in our book society but have not yet reached me [2].

[1] For signing the requisition to the High Sheriff of York to convene a meeting of protest against the Manchester Massacre, Earl Fitzwilliam was dismissed from the lord-lieutenancy of the West Riding. Martineau, Hist of Peace, I. xvii. (Bohn) p. 310.

[2] 'Peter's Letters to his Kinsfolk.' 3 vols. Edinburgh, 1819. A series

I was sworn in as sheriff at my own house, by, I believe, the Clerk of circuit, or Arraigns, in London, and in the month of Feby or march — perhaps April. I was not called upon to do any act in discharge of the duties of the office, till I went to meet the Judges at the Assizes.

I hear with great concern that an application will be made to Parliament to defer the payment of bullion for paper, at the rate of £4 1s. pr oz., in gold, from feb^ry next the time fixed by law, to a later period. I am told that ministers have not discharged any part of the Gov^t debt to the Bank, and are disposed to accede to the wishes of the Directors and of their friends to the undefined issues of paper, on condition of more time being granted to them for the payment of the money. Surely Lord Liverpool will disgrace himself by listening to any such compromise —nor can it be possible that after the solemn and grave consideration this subject has undergone Parliam^t will consent to further procrastination. What will you say of the House of Commons if it consents?

Have you heard anything of an intention to propose an income tax of 5 p.c^t.? I do not see the necessity for it. If the revenue is very deficient, it can hardly be so much so, as to leave us without any surplus at all for a sinking fund. If we are to be taxed only for the purpose of creating a sinking fund, I for one dissent from it. Besides, is it fair to infer that because the revenue is from peculiar causes deficient this year, it should therefore be deficient also for years to come. Ministers told us last session that they were then arranging a system which was to be the permanent system of the country and that they did not see any probability of their requiring any further assistance excepting only a loan for five millions.—Why do they not raise the interest on exchequer bills? What

of sketches of Scottish society, published anonymously, but written by John Gibson Lockhart, assisted by Professor Wilson.

reason have they to persevere in their endeavors to borrow money at 3 p.c. when the market rate is 5 p.c^t.? Before you come to this place you will be heartily tired with this letter—I hasten now to relieve you. With the united wishes of Mrs. Ricardo and myself for your and Mrs. Trower's happiness

I am ever yours

DAVID RICARDO.

XXXII[1].

[To R. HEATHFIELD.]

UPPER BROOK STREET,
19th *December*, 1819.

SIR,

I ought, long before this time, to have thanked you for the present of your excellent pamphlet[2], on the means of paying off the national debt, and to have expressed to you the pleasure which I derived from its perusal; but I have been so much engaged of late, that, till now, I have not had leisure to make the few remarks which I was desirous of submitting to you on some parts of your clear and perspicuous statement.

I entirely concur with you in your general view of the desirableness of extinguishing our debt, and declared my opinion to that effect in a publication of mine given to the public about two or three years ago[3]. During the autumn which is just passed I have been employed in giving my thoughts rather more in detail, on the same subject, in an article written for the Encyclopaedia Brittannica Supple-

---

[1] See note below, p. 98.

[2] 'Elements of a Plan for the Liquidation of the Public Debt of the United Kingdom; being the draught of a Declaration, submitted to the attention of the landed, funded, and every other description of Proprietor of the United Kingdom. With an Introductory Address.' London, 1819.

[3] 'Principles of Political Economy and Taxation,' 1817, ch. xv. 'Taxes on other commodities than raw produce,' p. 338; 'Works' (ed. McCulloch), p. 149.

ment, and which was to have been published last month[1]. Mr. Napier, the editor of this work, had my article in October last, but has deferred the publication of it till the next period of publication, because he found that he could not reach the Letter to which it was to be appended, without making the volume just published too bulky. As our opinions coincide remarkably on this question, I thought it right to make you acquainted with these facts, that you might not suppose that I had, without acknowledgment, borrowed your arguments. The chief difference between your opinions and mine are the following: You would pay the stockholder at 100, I think he will receive a full measure of justice, if he is paid at the present market price, or about 70, for his three per cents. As we are now proceeding in the payment, or rather, non-payment of debt, he can never reasonably expect to receive 100, but may more justly expect to be eventually a loser of the whole of his capital. Your reasoning on this point, p. 25, is not satisfactory, for you there assume that the stockholder would reinvest his capital at an interest of three per cent.; such a fall in the rate of interest being, in your judgment, the natural effect of the payment of the debt: but why interest should fall from five to three per cent. without any increase of capital, or diminution of population, I cannot conjecture, and I do not perceive that you have said anything in favour of such a conclusion.

We differ, too, on the effect which the reduction of the debt would have on the agriculture of the country. It would not, in my opinion, enable us to compete with foreign

---

[1] The article on the Funding System ('Encycl. Brit.,' Supplement to 4th, 5th, and 6th edd., vol. iv. 1824, pp. 410-26) is faithfully reproduced by McCulloch in his edition of Ricardo's Works, pp. 515-548. McCulloch has not even corrected a bad printer's mistake in the opening quotation from Professor Hamilton, making him say that the reduction of the legal rate of interest in 1714 was 'unfavourable' to the commercial state of the country, instead of (as Hamilton wrote) 'conformable' thereunto.

growers of corn, in a degree the least more favourably than we now can do, and, consequently, I think that if a corn law be now necessary to favour our landed interest, it will be as necessary when the national debt is paid. You say (p. 10) 'that under the supposed relief from impost, the people would be cheaply fed, and that great and powerful impulse to the agriculture of the United Kingdom would be experienced.' You think. too, (page 11) 'that the remission of duties and taxes would greatly augment the demand for manufactures:'—I cannot help thinking that we should not experience any such advantages.

I am sure you will forgive me for the remarks which I have taken the liberty of making on your ingenious pamphlet. If you are desirous of knowing the reasons on which these remarks are founded, I shall be glad to state them to you on any morning that you will favour me with a visit. I will make a point of being at home, any hour that may be most convenient to you.

I am, Sir,

Your obedient Servant,

DAVID RICARDO.

RICHARD HEATHFIELD, Esq.

NOTE (1).—The above letter is reprinted from a pamphlet entitled: 'Speech on The State of the Nation, delivered in the House of Commons on the Third Reading of the Reform Bill, on Tuesday, March 20, 1832, by General [C. K.] Palmer. To which are prefixed a letter from the late Mr. Ricardo to Mr. Richard Heathfield on the Liquidation of the Public Debt, and some observations thereon.' London (Longman, &c.) 1832.

The Speech is edited by Heathfield, who prefixes a general introduction, dated from 8, Regent St., London, 12th April, 1832. Ricardo's letter is given on pages 4 to 6. Palmer in his speech had referred in complimentary terms to Heathfield's pamphlet of 1819, in favour of direct taxation instead of taxation of commodities for the liquidation of the Debt.

According to J. R. McCulloch, the credit of first devising the plan of paying off the national debt by an assessment upon the wealth of the country belonged neither to Ricardo nor to Heathfield, but to Archibald Hutcheson, who in 1716 had proposed the scheme in the House of Commons, and had developed it in his 'Collection of treatises relating to the Public Debts and Funds' (London, 1721). Hutcheson's plan was referred to by David Hume, thirty years later, in his 'Essay on Public Credit,' and is said to have attracted some notice at that time. See McCulloch, 'Literature of Political Economy,' pp. 319, 337. See also Cobbett's Letter to Lord Liverpool on Heathfield's Plan for paying off the Nat. Debt, Pol. Register, 22nd April, 1820, p. 369, seq., and Cobbett's severe comments on 'Mr. Ricardo's plan of dividing the lands,' Weekly Reg., Oct. 27th, 1821, pp. 974-6; see also Edinr. Review, July, 1821, pp. 483-4, 'on the plan originally suggested by Mr. Hutcheson, and since recommended by Mr. Ricardo, for paying off the public debt by an assessment on capital.' This review was McCulloch's (see the lists quoted, p. 190).

It is curious that in the controversy raised, by J. Horsley Palmer in 1837 on the causes and consequences of the Pressure on the Money Market, Mr. Samson Ricardo took part, writing two pamphlets. But his allusions to his distinguished ancestor do not add to our knowledge of the latter.

NOTE (2).—Hume wrote in 1752 : 'There was, indeed, a scheme for the payment of our debts, which was proposed by an excellent citizen, Mr. Hutchinson [*sic*], above thirty years ago, and which was much approved of by some men of sense, but never was likely to take effect. He asserted, that there was a fallacy in imagining that the public owed this debt, for that really every individual owed a proportional share of it, and paid, in his taxes, a proportional share of the interest, besides the expences of levying these taxes. Had we not better then, says he, make a proportional distribution of the debt among us, and each of us contribute a sum suitable to his property, and by that means discharge at once all our funds and public mortgages? He seems not to have considered, that the laborious poor pay a considerable part of the taxes by their annual consumptions, though they could not advance, at once, a proportional part of the sum required. Not to mention, that property in money and stock in trade might easily be concealed or disguised; and that visible property in lands and houses would really at last answer for the whole: An inequality and oppression, which never would be submitted to. But though this project is never likely to take place 'tis not altogether improbable, that when the nation become heartily sick of their debts, and are cruelly oppressed by them, some daring projector may arise with visionary schemes for their discharge. And as public credit will begin, by that time, to be a little frail, the least touch will destroy it, as happened in France, and in this manner it will *die of the doctor*' (Essays published 1752, p. 406 of 4to. ed. 1768, vol. i. Essay ix, 'Of Public Credit').

J. S. Mill (Pol. Ec. Bk. V. ch. vii. § 2, 1st ed. 1848, vol. ii. p. 433) adds the argument, 'If those who have no accumulations, but only incomes, were required to make up by a single payment the equivalent of the annual charge laid on them by the taxes maintained to pay the interest of the debt, they could only do so by incurring a private debt equal to their share of the public debt' and at higher interest.

Hume's 'Public Credit' was reprinted in a Reform pamphlet in 1817: 'Insecurity of the British Funds. Essay on Public Credit by David Hume (Reprinted from the Edition of 1752), with observations on the sound and prophetic nature of its principles, shewing from indisputable facts, that a perseverance in the Pitt and Paper System must eventually produce a National Bankruptcy, and pointing out the only mode of averting so fatal a calamity, with remarks on the necessity of parliamentary reform, an analysis of Mr. Bentham's Plan, &c. Addressed to the British People by Imlac.' London &c., 1817. When Hutcheson made his proposal soon after the Peace of Utrecht, the Debt was about 50 millions. In 1752 when Hume wrote his Essay it was about 75, and in 1819 about 900 millions. It is now about 620.

XXXIII[1].

MY DEAR TROWER   LONDON, 28 *Decr*—1819.

At length we have obtained a little breathing time, and I am enabled to sit down and have a chat with you. All the important business in the house has been dispatched, and we are now to look forward to a long holiday: indeed

[1] Cover wanting.

I think we deserve one for our labours have been incessant during the last month, and it is matter of surprise to me how ministers undergo the fatigue of midnight watchings. added to their other duties. Mr. Tierney[1] is evidently much the worse for it, although his attention to the business, even of the House, is by no means unremitting; he declares himself that he can no longer undergo the harassing duty of a close attendance at the debates of the House of Commons. You, I have no doubt, approve of all the measures[2] which have been adopted to suppress the public discontent—I consider them as serious infringements on our liberties, and deprecate them because I expect that they will not allay the causes of discontent, but increase them. The people complain that they have not a due share in the formation of their government, and they are deprived of a portion of that which they really had. To me it appears that the radical reformers are very unfairly treated—they are all lumped together—without proof or even examination they are declared to be revolutionists in disguise, and on this assumption they are condemned without being permitted to say one word in their defence. That there was cause for apprehension from the large meetings of the people, and from the publication of atrocious libels, no one can deny, but the efficiency of the laws already in force was never fairly tried, and ministers were not justified in

[1] George Tierney (born 1756, died 1830), the well-known Whig leader. He fought a duel with Pitt in 1798. He held office both in the Addington ministry of 1802, and in the Grenville ministry of 1806 ('All the Talents').
[2] The 'Six Acts,' viz.: (1) An Act to prevent delay in the administration of justice in cases of misdemeanour; 2) An Act to prevent the training of persons in the use of arms and the practice of military evolutions; 3) An Act for the prevention and punishment of blasphemous and seditious libels; (4) An Act to authorize justices of the peace, in certain disturbed counties, to seize and detain arms; (5) An Act to subject certain publications to the duties of stamps upon newspapers, and to make other regulations for restraining the abuses arising from the publication of blasphemous and seditious libels; (6) An Act for preventing the assembling of seditious assemblies.

adopting new measures of rigour until the old measures had failed of remedying the evil complained of.

Our finance does not seem so very bad as had been represented—the deficiency this year must be serious, but not so great as to absorb the whole of the Sinking Fund, and unless the whole is absorbed I do not see either the policy or necessity of imposing new taxes. I suppose we shall now go on without any important measure in finance till a new war breaks out, and then it appears to me impossible, if faith is to be kept with the public creditor, to raise the annual supplies for the expences of such war, but by taxes equal to such expenditure.

There must I think be an end of loans; we cannot go on adding to a debt of 800 millions [1]. A great deal more has been said than I intended there should be of an incidental observation of mine respecting the payment of the debt and as it usually happens I am attacked by the most opposite parties [2]. By some stockholders I am accused of not doing justice to them, by suggesting that they are not fairly entitled, in ready money, to £100, for £100— 3 p. cts., but to the market price of £100 stock, or £70. By another party—the landholders—I am accused of wishing to give the lands of the country to the stockholders, and it is more than hinted that I have an interested view in making the proposal. I may be ignorant or prejudiced, but I am not conscious of being influenced by any motives of interest, and it would really be very difficult for me to determine how my particular interest would be affected by the adoption of the measure.

---

[1] Of funded debt; with the unfunded and annuities it reached 900.

[2] Four days earlier (December 24, 1819), in a speech in the House upon a representation of London merchants respecting commercial distress, Ricardo had urged his characteristic recommendation that the whole capital of the country be assessed for the discharge of the national debt. See Hansard, Parliamentary Debates, vol. xli. 1576; cf. also Letters to McCulloch, p. 50; to Malthus, p. xv. See also above, pp. 96 seq.

The most serious obstacle which I see against the adoption of the plan is the state of the representation of the House of Commons, which is such as to afford us no security that if we got rid of the present debt, we should not be plunged into another.

The debates have been very interesting—those of the last week[1] afforded an opportunity for the display of great eloquence and great talent, both on the part of Sir J. Mackintosh and Mr. Canning. This display was admirable, and I am told by those who have long had seats in parliament, has not of late years been surpassed. Plunkett and Brougham also have shewn very great abilities.

I hope Mrs. Trower and your children are well, and are enjoying without alloy the festivities of this season, usually devoted to mirth and cheerfulness. Pray give Mrs. Ricardo's and my kind regards to them.

I suppose you will be selected for the Sheriff for the ensuing year, in your County. I hope you will find the office an agreeable one, and that it will not be attended with any unusual portion of responsibility from the unsettled state of the times. Adieu my dear Trower.

Believe me ever Most truly yrs

DAVID RICARDO.

XXXIV [2]

MY DEAR TROWER   LONDON 28 Jan'y. 1820.

I very much regretted not seeing you at dinner on the day I met you in the Strand, we had a very agreeable day, and some discussions in which you would have liked to participate.

I am glad to hear that you are again looking at the subject of Political Economy, and that you still see no reason to

---

[1] On the third reading of the 'Newspaper Stamp Duties Bill'; see Hansard, Parliamentary Debates, vol. xli. 1459 et seq.

[2] Cover wanting.

doubt the truth of the principles which I have endeavored to establish. I have looked to the passages in my book to which you refer [1]. I quite agree with you that in most cases of taxes on income, or on profits, no effect would be produced on prices, and the burthen, which in every case would be equal, would fall on the producer, or the man enjoying the income. But I have supposed a case of our having the mines which supplied our standard, in this country, and that the profits of the miner were not taxed, then commodities would rise in price to the amount of the tax, or the miner[']s business would be more profitable than any other, and consequently would draw capital to that concern [2]. If then all commodities rose in price [to] what would they rise? not in proportion to their value, but in proportion to the capitals employed in their production, and therefore as commodities selling for £4,000 may be the result of the employment of the same amount of capital as commodities which sell for £10,000, these commodities would not rise in proportion to their prices, but if one rose £200 — the other would also rise £200. Now in this situation of things suppose money to rise in value and the goods which sell for £10,200 to fall to £10,000 the other goods which sell for £4,200 will fall to £4,000, but if money should continue to rise in value and consequently the goods which sold for £10,000 should fall to £5,000, then those which sold for £4,000 would fall to £2,000. Up to [a] certain point then they fall in proportion to the capitals employed in their production, but subsequently in proportion to the value of the goods themselves [3]. This is the opinion which I wish to express, whether

---

[1] 'Principles of Political Economy and Taxation,' in Works, chap. xv. ('Taxes and Profits'), esp. p. 127. Cf. Appendix B. I.

[2] Gold and silver would be relatively cheaper than other commodities, or, if they were not, competition of capitalists would soon make them so, till the flow was followed by the ebb and they became dearer again.

[3] The position seems to be as follows: The first effect of the tax will

Effects on Price of a Tax on Profits

it be a correct one is another question. On the hasty consideration which I can now give it I see no reason to doubt it.

A tax imposed on goods, exactly equal to the tax on profits which each man would have to pay, will have precisely the same effects.

I never contemplate as a good practical measure, a tax on profits, without also taxing all other sources of income. Profits can never be known without a minute scrutiny into the affairs of those concerned in trade, other sources of income are well known and may be easily come at. The landlord cannot well conceal the amount of his rent, nor the stockholder the amount of his dividend, and therefore it might become a question whether you should not tax the profits of trade indirectly, by taxing wages, or necessaries; and other incomes directly, as rent, dividends, annuities, &c., &c.

As a political economist I say that there is no tax which has not a tendency to diminish production, in the same way as a deterioration of soil or the loss of a good machine, but I mean nothing more than that it is an obstacle opposed to production. You say it is such obstacles as these which stimulate to exertion, and experience proves they are always overcome. I have no doubt that there is a degree of difficulty in production which acts in the way you mention; if too strong however it will oppose a physical difficulty

be uniform as regards profits, and therefore *not* uniform for prices, the high-priced articles and the low-priced (under competition) yielding a like rate of profits to the same amount of capital, but being various in number, and therefore not increased or diminished in price by the same figure per article; the eventual effect will be a uniform raising or lowering of the prices per article, through a change in the value of money generally. The first effect proceeds from the total to the items, the second from the items to the total. The process in any case is a slow one. See the chapter (xiii) of Pol. Econ. and Tax. (Works, pp. 113 seq.) on 'Taxes on Gold.' Compare Marx, 'Kapital,' vol. iii. (1894), ch. x. pp. 151 seq. (reproduced in 'Karl Marx and the Close of his System' by Böhm Bawerk, translated by Macdonald (Fisher Unwin, 1898, pp. 46-59). Marx was more Ricardian than Ricardo; but Ricardo had certainly left him models of over-subtlety.

which can not be overcome. I think the difficulties in our case are not precisely in the proper degree to ensure the greatest production. Still it is correct to record the obstacle and acknowledge it to be one. You compare the expences of the rich proprietors and the expenditure by Government of money received in taxes. With respect to future production it is indifferent whether this portion of the general revenue be expended by one or the other, excepting in this that in the expenditure of government a tax will be required for the future increased production, as well as for that which is usually produced and this may prevent the production of the increased quantity altogether. A tithe on land which cannot afford a rent will prevent that land from being cultivated until the price of corn rises. If there were no tithe the same land might be cultivated for the proprietor[']s benefit. If all I am to get is to be expended by the state I will not produce, if it is to be expended by me, I will. After it is produced it is not of much importance whether the state or I expend it, to the public at large, but it is of immense importance in determining me to be active or idle. Taxes for the benefit of trade itself, such as for Docks, canals, Roads, &c., &c., are on a different footing from all other taxes, and produce very different effects, they may and generally do promote production instead of discouraging it.—I am glad you have not persuaded yourself that taxes are very delightful things. I am very sorry to be obliged to agree with you that there are a very few who are perfect masters of the science of Polit. Econ.

I have been much entertained by reading Ivanhoe though not in an equal degree as by reading some of the other novels written by the same author.

Mrs. Ricardo joins with me in kind remembrances to Mrs. Trower.

Ever Y^{rs}
D. RICARDO.

XXXV [1].

MY DEAR TROWER LONDON 13 Mch 1820

Mr. Mill is so constantly occupied at the India House that I seldom see him, except on sundays, and therefore I delayed answering your letter till after I had met him yesterday. He, as well as I, are [sic] much obliged by your invitation, and we have agreed to accept it, if it will suit you to receive us on saturday the 1st, or the following saturday, the 8th of april. Mr. Mill is obliged to stipulate for Saturday, as that is the only day on which he can leave the India House. Our visit will necessarily be a short one, but if the weather should be as fine as it now is, we shall have an opportunity of seeing the beauty of the country immediately about you.

My late constituents at Portarlington appear to be a very good tempered set of gentlemen, and will I am assured elect me without hesitation to the next Parliament [2]. The report of my being a candidate for the county of Gloucester never had the least foundation, and was put forth I imagine with no other view than to provoke a contest. I do not soar so high, and am the most unfit of all men to engage in an undertaking so difficult and so expensive as that of contesting a county with an old and powerful family.

The plot in Cato Street [3] must no doubt be favorable to ministers in the general election, and yet at Brookes' they confidently anticipate rather an accession than a diminution to the ranks of opposition. On this point I am

---

[1] Addressed on back, but without postmarks or frank.

[2] McCulloch states that Ricardo never saw the borough of which he was the representative, and therefore 'could speak and vote as he thought proper, without being influenced in any degree by the opinions of his constituents. He was in every sense a truly independent member.' See McCulloch's 'Treatises on Political Policy' (second edit., 1859), pp. 555, 556, note. Compare Letters to Malthus, p. 154, and above, Letter XXIV.

[3] The plot of Thistlewood and others to murder the Ministers at a Cabinet dinner on Feb. 23. They were betrayed by a spy, and dispersed on that day, at their last head-quarters in Cato Street, Edgeware Road.

very little anxious, as whether the ministers have a majority of 200, 100, or 50, will not, I think, in any degree affect the important questions about which the country should be most particularly solicitous.—I should be glad to have some enlightened commercial men added to the small number usually in the House, and therefore I regret that Sharp [1] has been defeated at Maidstone—I hope however that Haldimand [2] will succeed at Ipswich. He is brother to Mrs. Marcet [3] and appears to be a clever man. He is rich and has much influence amongst his brother merchants. Sir Wm. Curtis's [4] commercial knowledge will not add much to the general stock.

My thoughts have not been engaged upon any particular branch of Political Economy exclusively, but have wandered over the whole field. At one time I have to defend and explain one principle against an adversary, at another time another, and I have the satisfaction of observing that the opinions which I deem the correct ones are daily gaining ground. Col. Torrens is becoming one of the most efficient advocates for the right principles, as may be seen both in his review of Owen in the Edinburgh [5], and in the last

---

[1] Richard Sharp, best known as 'Conversation' Sharp, had been Ricardo's predecessor as member for Portarlington.

[2] William Haldimand, a director of the Bank of England, and a strong advocate of the resumption of specie payments. In 1828 he removed permanently to his summer villa, Denantou, near Lausanne, and upon his death in 1862, left the bulk of his estate to the blind asylum at Lausanne.

[3] The well-known author of 'Conversations on Political Economy.' (London, 1816, and other educational writings. See Letters to Malthus, p. 132, and Palgrave's Dict. of Pol. Ec., art. 'Marcet.'

[4] Sir William Curtis, Bart. (1752—1829), the head of the Tory party in the City of London. He was several times Lord Mayor, and in 1819 was elected M.P. for Bletchingley, Surrey. He was first a biscuit maker, then concerned in the Greenland Fisheries, and finally a banker. In 1822 he donned the kilt with the king in Scotland.

[5] Edinburgh Review, No. LXIV (October, 1819), Art. xi: 'On Mr. Owen's Plans for Relieving the National Distress'; nominally a review of Robert Owen's 'New View of Society,' and three of his minor tracts. Cf. Letters to Malthus, p. 170; Letters to McCulloch, p. 52.

edition of his work on the impolicy of restraints on the importation of corn[1]. Lord King too, with whom I have lately conversed, is also marshalled on our side. M'Culloch has I am told an article in the Edinburgh just printed, in favor of free trade, and I dare say it is a good one[2]. That we are improving is manifest from this that a petition is preparing in the city to Parliament in favor of free trade, in which the merchants (the petitioners) with great ability urge the advantages which would result from unrestrained commerce. It is very respectably signed and will be presented to the H. of Commons by Mr. Baring[3]. That the merchants should condemn and expose the mercantile system is no unimportant evidence of the progress of liberal opinions.

I am glad that you are not to be plagued with a contested election in Surry. As Sheriff it would have involved you in a degree of anxiety and responsibility from which you must be glad to escape.

Mrs. Ricardo unites with me in kind wishes to Mrs. Trower.

Believe me Ever

Truly yrs

DAVID RICARDO.

[1] 'An Essay on the External Corn Trade,' &c.; 1st ed., London, 1815; 2nd ed., 1820.

[2] Edinburgh Review, No. LXV (January, 1820), Art. ix, on 'Taxation and the Corn Laws.'

[3] The petition was drawn up by Thomas Tooke, and signed by leading merchants of London. It was introduced in the House on March 8, 1820, by Alexander Baring, and after a debate, in which Ricardo participated, ordered to lie upon the table. Hansard, Parliamentary Debates, vol. i, N. S., 165-197. The text of the petition is reprinted in McCulloch, 'Literature of Political Economy,' pp. 57, 58. In 1857, the year before his death, Mr. Tooke prepared, for the sixth volume of the 'History of Prices,' a statement of the circumstances under which the petition was prepared; see Tooke and Newmarch, 'A History of Prices and of the State of Circulation from 1792 to 1856,' vol. vi, Appendix I (pp. 331-344. This interesting account, together with a portrait of Mr. Tooke and a facsimile of his hand-writing, is reproduced in vol. iv of the 'Proceedings of the Political Economy Club' (London, 1882).

XXXVI [1].

[TO SIR JOHN SINCLAIR.]

SIR,   11th *May* 1820.

I agree with you on the benefits resulting from a paper instead of a coin circulation, *and I never wish to see any other established in this country*; but we differ on the means of regulating its value and amount. That I think is to be done best, by making it exchangeable for bullion, at a fixed rate. I do not deny that the public has suffered much pressure from the limitation of circulation, but Parliament is not responsible for more than about 5 or 6 *per cent.* of that pressure, the limitation having taken place, and the currency having risen in value, to within 5 or 6 *per cent.* of the mint value, before the Bank Committee was appointed. An increase of currency now, would undoubtedly lower its value, raise all prices, and very much lighten taxation; but no measure could, I think, be more impolitic. It would be unjust to all creditors, and proportionally advantageous to debtors. If the payment of the interest of the national debt is a greater burden than we can bear, which I think it is not, and cannot well be, the fair way would be, to compound with the public creditor, and not make him only a pretended payment.

Respecting the paying off the national debt, we do not materially differ. I would pay it off entirely, and never allow any new debt, on any pretence whatever, to be contracted. You would only pay off a part, and would not object to contract a fresh debt, on any pressing emergence [*sic*]. You would not exempt foreigners from the necessary contribution. I would. You calculate that we consume as much corn, and other things, when prices rise from a scarcity, as when they are cheap from abundance. This I think impossible. If there were an equal consumption, there could be no

---

[1] 'Sinclair's Correspondence,' pp. 372, 373.

scarcity, and consequently no rise of price. You would give the home grower of corn the monopoly of the home market, while the operation of paying the debt is going on. I would, when it was completed, take off all restrictions on importation. I would leave the law as it is during the paying off, and would gradually take off all restrictions afterwards. To induce capital, by a monopoly, to go into agriculture, and then remove it afterwards, would be attended with ruin to the agriculturists. The restrictions, I think, should not be increased, with a view, finally, to get rid of them.

I fear that no plan for paying off the debt will receive any countenance from Parliament. Men do not like to make an immediate sacrifice for a future good; and they please themselves with imaginary riches, from which they really derive no advantage. Are not those imaginary riches, from the possession of which we only derive a revenue, which we are immediately obliged to pay to the tax-gatherer? I remain, Sir, your faithful servant,

DAVID RICARDO.

SIR JOHN SINCLAIR, Bart.

XXXVII [1].

[TO MACVEY NAPIER.]

SIR, LONDON, 15 *May* 1820.

I return the *Proof* of the article on the Sinking Fund which you sent me; I wish it was more worthy of insertion in your valuable publication.

The Table at the end has little to do with the subject, it contains some information and may be omitted or inserted as you think best.

I will be obliged to you for 2 or 3 separate copies of the article.

I am Sir with great esteem
Faithfully yours
DAVID RICARDO.

[1] From vol. ii of the Correspondence of Macvey Napier, in the British Museum.

XXXVIII [1].

MY DEAR TROWER   BRIGHTON 21 *July* 1820

I have been here above a week, and ought, before this time, to have acknowledged the receipt of your kind letter of the 5th inst. All business of consequence had been dispatched in the House of Commons before I quitted London, and as my family had left me alone in my large house, I was anxious to join them in this place, which they had chosen for their residence for a few weeks, previous to our journey into Gloucestershire. They are much more partial to Brighton than I am, and are much more persuaded also of the beneficial effects of sea air to all persons, and to all constitutions, than I ever shall be.—I should have preferred going straight to Gatcomb as soon as I could quit London. It does not appear likely that public business will allow me to stay long in Gloucestershire this year. The enquiry into the charge against the Queen [2], will, no doubt, make a very early meeting of the House of Commons necessary, and when we meet we shall not, I think, be very soon discharged from our attendance. I am sorry that this unfortunate business was not settled without an appeal to Parliament. Under all the circumstances of the case I do not think that ministers were justified in making it an affair of state. It can have no other effect but to bring royalty itself into disgrace, and to weaken the attachment of the people to monarchical Government. If these proceedings should lead to a change of ministers I am very far from expecting that the proceedings of the whigs when in administration will be essentially different from those of the men they will displace—something they must do to preserve an appearance of consistency, but it

---

[1] Addressed on back of last half sheet, and franked by 'David Ricardo.'
[2] Compare Letters to Malthus, pp. 172, 173, 177.

will be very little indeed—they are in their hearts as little friendly to any real reform as the tories.

You say more than I deserve in my praise for asserting the true principles of Political Economy in my place in Parliament. I feel that I am quite unequal to do what a better speaker might do, and I am more than usually daunted by observing that on every point where an abuse is to be got rid of there are such powerful interests to oppose, who never fail of making the worse appear the better reason.

I have not met with many persons who have yet read Malthus' book [1]. I am pleased however with the observations you make on what he has said respecting my doctrine, of price being ultimately regulated by cost of production [2]. By the very definition of natural price, it is wholly dependent on cost of production, and has nothing to do with demand and supply. The terms on which a commodity can be produced, so as to remunerate the producer, will remain the same altho' the demand should be for five times the quantity produced. We all acknowledge the effect of such a demand on market price.

Mr. Malthus pays me a very unmerited compliment at the end of his chapter on the rent of land [3], but he is very unjust to me in his comments on my doctrine of rent and profit, in that same chapter. He represents me as holding the landlords up to reproach, because I have said that their interests are opposed to those of the rest of the community, and that the rise of their rents are at the expence of the gains of the other classes. The whole tenor of my book shews how I mean to apply those observations. I have

---

[1] 'Principles of Political Economy considered with a View to their Practical Application.' London, 1820.
[2] Ibid., ch. ii, sections ii, iii, iv.
[3] 'Principles of Political Economy,' p. 238, note. 'A more honourable and excellent man I could not point out in the whole circle of landholders.'

said that the community would not benefit if the landlords gave up all their rent—such a sacrifice would not make corn cheaper, but would only benefit the farmers [1].—Does not this shew that I do not consider landlords as enemies to the public good? They are in possession of machines of various productive powers, and it is their interest that the least productive machine should be called into action [2]—such is not the interest of the public—*they* must desire to employ the foreign greater productive machine rather than the English less productive one. Mr. M. charges me too with denying the benefits of improvements in Agriculture to Landlords.—I do not acknowledge the justice of this charge, I have more than once said, what is obvious, that they must ultimately benefit by the land becoming more productive. Perhaps I have not expressed myself so strongly on this point as I ought to have done, but it was evident that I acknowledged the principle. I refer you to the last Chap. of my book, and particularly to the paragraph beginning 'Another cause of the rise of rent, according to Mr. Malthus, &c. &c.,' [3] for the truth of my assertion. Pray look at Page 237 of Mr. M's book, and you will see an instance of a great (unintentional I am sure) misrepresentation of an adversary's argument. I contend for free trade in corn on the ground that while trade is free, and corn cheap, profits will not fall however great be the accumulation of capital. If [4] you confine yourself to the resources of your own soil, I say, rent will

---

[1] Ricardo, 'Principles of Political Economy,' (2nd ed.), p. 59, in Works (ed. McCulloch), p. 39.

[2] Cf. Malthus, 'Inquiry into the Nature and Progress of Rent,' pp. 38, 39.

[3] Ch. xxix. of 1st ed., headed 'Mr. Malthus's Opinions on Rent,' pp. 549 seq.; Works, p. 243 seq., esp. 251. The immediate effect is more food than is wanted, the remote effect is higher rents. In the text Trower has added in pencil '571,' the reference to the 1st edition, though more exactly it should be 570.

[4] Underlined by Trower in pencil.

in time absorb the greatest part of that produce which remains after paying wages, and consequently profits will be low. Not only individual profits but the aggregate amount of profits will be diminished, notwithstanding an increase of capital. The whole net produce will be increased, but less will be enjoyed by capitalists (see Chap. on Profits, Pages 128-129, 2nd edition)[1]. Now how does Mr. M. apply my arguments? 'Do not let cheap corn be imported,' says he, 'because if you do you will lose a part of that portion of your surplus produce which now appears in the form of rent.' I agree that this would be the consequence, but then it is known that I contend this would be more than compensated by increased profits, but Mr. M. was my authority for the very opposite conclusion: you will have no compensation in increased profits, he says[2], and I appeal to Mr. Ricardo for the correctness of this opinion, who has admitted that not only each individual capital in the progress of society will yield a continually diminishing revenue, but the whole amount of the revenue derived from profits will be diminished. I admit it! yes I do but in the case of high rents and a high price of corn, not in the opposite case to which he applies it of low rents, and a low price of corn.

Pray look to Section 6—Page 192, and you will observe that all the points on which my theory is raised are admitted. There are only two causes for a high price of corn. A fall in the value of money. An increase in the quantity of labour and capital necessary to produce corn[3]. After this admission is it not wonderful that anything should be said in *favor* of a rise in what Mr. M. calls

---

[1] In Works (ed. McCulloch), pp. 68, 69.

[2] Malthus, 'Pol. Ec.' (1820), p. 237: 'According to Mr. Ricardo, not only will each individual capital in the progress of society yield a continually diminishing revenue, but the whole amount of the revenue derived from profits will be diminished.'

[3] Malthus, 'Pol. Ec.' (1820), p. 193.

real rent when it is caused by an increase in the quantity of labour and capital necessary to produce corn? and yet this I consider to be Mr. M's argument, for according to him high rent is in itself a good, independently of its being a sign of wealth and power. Is it not a good to obtain all your productions by the least sacrifice of labour and capital? I could fill sheet after sheet with what appears to me to be false reasoning and inconsistencies in this book, but I will spare you.

You have no doubt observed that Hume[1] has undergone the ordeal of an election committee with success. The ministers have not a more formidable opponent. He never speaks without a formidable array of figures to back his assertions, and he pores over documents with persevering zeal and attention, which most other men fly from with disgust and terror. His manner of speaking is I think improved—he is however generally too diffuse—speaks too often—and sometimes wastes his own strength, and his hearer[']s patience, on matters too trifling for notice. He justifies this indeed by saying that he contends for sound principles, which are as much outraged by an unjust expenditure of a few hundred pounds, as of a million. He is I think a most useful member of parliament,—always at his post and governed I believe by an ardent desire to be useful to his country.

I hope Mrs. Trower and your girls are well. Mrs. Ricardo joins me in kind remembrances to them.

   Believe me ever My dear Trower
      Very truly yrs
        DAVID RICARDO.

I have seen no account of the Savings Bank Fund on the table of the House, but I believe one is ordered to be presented.

---

[1] Joseph Hume, then member for the Border burghs.

XXXIX[1].

I have been here since the 9th of Aug.   GATCOMB PARK
15 *Septr.*, 1820.

MY DEAR TROWER,

I learnt with great concern that you had had the misfortune to dislocate your knee. Besides the pain which you must have endured, it was a cruel grievance to one so fond of moving about as you are to be confined for so great a length of time, as you already had been when you wrote on the sopha. I hope you were able to resume your accustomed pursuits before that interesting day to most country gentlemen, the 1st of Septr., and that the next account I receive from you will be that you are quite recovered, and looking after your plantations and improvements with the same interest and enjoyment as her[e]tofore[2].

I have suffered too long a time to elapse without writing to you, but Mr. Mill is partly to blame. He has been staying with me for more than three weeks, and as he is fond of exercise we have taken advantage of the fineness of the weather, and have been pretty constantly on the move. Our last excursion was down the Wye from Ross to Chepstow. From Chepstow we went to Malvern and passed a few days with my son who is settled in that neighbourhood[3]. Mill speaks well of my house and grounds at Gatcomb, but he greatly prefers those of my son. The soil about us is poor; the trees are chiefly beech, which grow very luxuriantly, but we have few oaks. In the country where my son lives, the soil is good, and oaks flourish better than any other tree ; the ground too is beautifully diversified. I wish you would come to see me, and let me shew you the various beautiful spot[s] within a

---

[1] Cover wanting.
[2] Written 'hertofore,' as our forefathers used often to pronounce it.
[3] Osman Ricardo, of Bromesberrow Place, Ledbury.

moderate circuit of us. We were greatly delighted with the scenery on the Banks of the Wye. Report has not exaggerated its beauty—my expectations were at any rate surpassed. We travelled in a low phaeton which I have lately bought, and to save a few miles in our journey, and also to see some country which we had not before visited, we resolved to cross the Severn in a boat instead of going over the bridge at Gloucester. When we arrived at the Ferry, opposite Newnham, it was low water, and by the direction of the boatman I drove first over the dry sand, and then into the water alongside the boat which was ready to receive us. I proceeded with perfect safety till I got within three or four feet of the boat, when the carriage began to sink in the sand, and the horses to plunge violently in their efforts to extricate themselves from the place where they also were sinking. The men became greatly alarmed at our awkward situation, in a moment half a dozen of them, besides my servant, were in the water, and if they had not united their strength to support us on the side which was sinking fastest, Mr. Mill, two young ladies who were behind, and myself, would have been all overturned into the water. The first object was to disengage the horses from the carriage, the next to carry us into the boat. The poor horses were so exhausted with their struggles that they lay on the ground with their heads just above the water without making any further effort to get out, and for a short time I thought I should lose them both. At length however they got on their legs and reached firmer ground, but it was nearly an hour before the carriage was lifted up from the sand in which it had sunk. By the aid of levers and the united strength of the men this was at last effected. With the utmost difficulty the horses were made to get into the boat. The carriage was put in after them, and we all at length landed in safety at Newnham, with the very slightest damage to the harness and the horses quite uninjured. Our two young ladies behaved like heroines.

I am glad that you have been employing your leisure time in reading Malthus, and examining the grounds of his difference with me[1]. I have turned to p. 125 of his work as you requested and I think it must be admitted that when corn rises from difficulty of producing it, manufactures will generally fall from facility of producing them, which will make a rise of wages on account of a rise in the price of corn often unnecessary. I quite agree with you that the passage in 128 is inconsistent with this doctrine, for in [the] one place he says when corn is high, labour will command a great quantity of other things besides corn, and in the other he says that under the same circumstances it will command only a small quantity of them. The passage in 128 is very faulty and proceeds on the supposition that 'when *corn* compared with labour is *dear*, *la'our* compared with *corn* must necessarily be *cheap*.' But to say that *corn rises* and will therefore command *more labour*, is a very different thing from saying that *labour falls* and therefore will command *less corn*; for when we talk of a thing rising or falling we always mean in reference to something which we suppose does not move. Because labour falls in reference to corn, it does not necessarily undergo any variation in reference to *other things*, and therefore in fact *labour* does *not fall*—it is improper to say it does, the truth being that labour is of the same value, but one of the commodities on which wages are expended has risen in value, not only in reference to labour, but in reference to every thing else. Now if we suppose that the same circumstances which are favorable to a rise of corn are also favorable to a fall of manufactures, which was Mr. Malthus['] doctrine, Page 12[5] —not only will labour not fall in reference to manufactured

---

[1] There are several pages of notes on Malthus among the Trower MSS.

commodities, when it falls in reference to corn, but it will do exactly the contrary; it will rise in reference to those commodities while it falls relatively to corn. This however would not be the correct way of explaining what was taking place. I should say that labour continued *uniformly* of the *same value*, but that corn one of the objects on which wages were expended rose in value, while manufactured goods, the other objects on which wages were expended, fell in value.

Mr. Malthus['] argument for using a mean between corn and labour as a standard and measure of value is full of fallacy when patiently examined. Corn rises because it is more difficult to produce it. In consequence of the rise of this prime necessary, labour rises also but not in the same degree in which corn rises. Now here are two things which rise in value, and Mr. Malthus chuses a mean between the two as a good measure of value. Altho' they both rise in value, yet comparing them with each other and making each the measure of the other, one will appear to fall. Here then says Mr. M[.] I have two commodities which vary in opposite directions, and therefore a mean between them is an admirable measure of value. Suppose corn to rise from 80 to 100 p^r quarter, and labour from 10/- to 11/- p^r week, nobody would deny that they both rose. Now compare corn and labour, a quarter of corn at 8o/- would command 8 weeks labour, at 100/— it will command more than 9 weeks labour. Corn has risen as compared to labour and is therefore dear, but if corn is dear compared with labour, labour must be cheap as compared with corn. 8 weeks labour would command a quarter of corn, 9 weeks labour must now be given for it—who can doubt that labour is cheap? Do you not observe that the whole argument from beginning to end is completely fallacious? and that a commodity really become dear is stated to be cheap?

I do not think that Mr. Malthus is wrong in Page 145[1]. I think he means to say that if you diminish the fertility of the land so much that the whole produce must go to the cultivator there can neither be surplus produce to afford profit or rent. If it should be even enough to afford a trifling profit there could be no rent because no worse land could be taken into cultivation. Now says Mr. Malthus if you diminish the fertility of the land one half you will place us in this condition. This is a question of fact and degree, not of principle, and it is one of my complaints against him that he does not answer your principle but wishes to shew that you have taken your case so wide, that it could under no circumstances exist; but however limited might be your case, the same principle is involved, and it is that which should be answered.

No commodity is raised unless there is a demand for it. If it were raised without a demand, it would sink in value, and not afford the price necessary to remunerate the labour bestowed upon it, and to afford the usual profits of stock. If this be true, in what respect is corn different from silk, wine or sugar? Those who manufacture, or grow these commodities, will be losers if they produce more than is equal to the demand at a certain price, but is not the producer of corn in the same condition? He will not raise corn if there be no demand for it at the remunerating price.

---

[1] 'If the fertility of all the lands in the world were to be diminished one-half... the largest portion of the lands in most countries would be thrown completely out of cultivation, and wages, profits, and rents, particularly the latter, would be greatly diminished on all the rest. I believe there is hardly any land in this country employed in producing corn which yields a rent equal in value to the wages of the labour and the profits of the stock necessary to its cultivation. If this be so, then, in the case supposed, the quantity of produce being only one-half of what was before obtained by the same labour and capital, it may be doubted whether any land in England could be kept in tillage' ('Pol. E.,' 1820, pp. 145, 146).

If any man wishes to increase his capital he produces that which he has good reason to think he can sell at a remunerative price. It is with money he is to pay labour, and it is money which he seeks to obtain. He may indeed anticipate that the commodity which will be immediately demanded in greater quantity than before will be corn, but then he will produce that as a means to an end, in the same way as he would produce any other commodity. Corn is produced because it is immediately demanded, or an additional demand for it is reasonably anticipated, but we should not on that account be justified in saying that corn raises up its own demanders, or that its plenty bribes people to come into existence, because that always supposes a price of corn below the natural or remunerating price, and it is no man's interest to produce it on such terms. An increased demand for labour is not immediately supplied by an additional number of people—higher wages induce the same number of people to do more work. An increase of capital, then, and a demand for labour, does not necessarily produce an increased demand for food, but an increased demand for other things agreeable to the labourer. It is those things which will be produced in the first instance, and corn will not be demanded, in any unusual quantity, till the number of children are increased, then the commodities demanded in the first instance will be relinquished[.] and an increased demand will take place for corn. I hope you will think this a justification of the opinion which I have given that corn does not raise up demanders, any more than coats raise up wearers, or wine, wine drinkers. A producer has a right to demand either his own commodity or some other. If he intends to add to his capital he naturally seeks to possess himself of that commodity which will be in demand by those whose labour he wishes to dispose of: it may be corn, but there is no more necessity for its being corn than cloth, shoes, stockings, tea, sugar, iron, or any other thing. I do not think then with you, that a demand for labour is the same thing as a supply of necessaries. Labour and necessaries may come in additional quantity into the market at the same time, in which case neither of them will fall[1]; they will both be supplied and demanded in greater abundance. Suppose the necessaries only to come into the market in additional quantity, that will not occasion any greater demand for labour than if an additional quantity of iron was brought to market, for no one wishes to consume it. The way most effectually to increase capital is to produce a commodity that you know will be demanded and consequently will not fall in value, not one that will not be demanded and will fall in value. Pray understand that I am answering Mr. Malthus who contends that there is something peculiar about corn which gives it a character of being able to raise up demanders different from all other things—I contend on the contrary, that there is no difference between them, that nothing is produced until it is wanted unless from mistake and miscalculation.

You must be tired of reading this long letter. One word only about the Queen. Whatever her conduct may have been can ministers shew that the real interests of the country required a bill of pains and penalties under the circumstances of the cruel usage she has received? Every one must answer this question in the negative.

Mrs. Ricardo unites with me in kind compts to Mrs. Trower.

Very truly yours
David Ricardo.

There is nothing new in the second edition of my book.

[1] Word a little doubtful, being bound up.

XL[1].

GATCOMB PARK
MY DEAR TROWER　　26 *Septr* 1820.

You see that I follow your good example, and while the subject is fresh in my memory offer the best reasons I have in vindication of the view which I take of it.

The point in dispute is this, Does the supply of corn precede the demand for it, or does it follow such demand? You are of the former—I of the latter opinion. You have not answered one important objection I made to you, namely, that if the supply of corn preceded the demand it must be at a lower price than the grower could afford to produce it—this is the inevitable consequence of supply exceeding demand—who under such circumstances would be induced to grow the surplus quantity of corn? Your mistake appears to me to proceed from considering the case too generally. It is undoubtedly true that if production were wholly under the control of one individual, whose object it was to increase population, he could not better effect his object than by growing more corn in the country than the existing community consume—it would in that case be at a low price, and the greatest stimulus would be given to population. We might indeed then justly say that it was the abundance of corn which raised up consumers, and that in this respect corn differed from iron, silk or any other commodity, but this is not the question under consideration—what we want to know is, whether, in the present distribution of property, and under the influence of the motives which invite to production, corn is produced for any other reason than that iron, silk, wine &c. &c., are produced—whether they are not all produced on account of an actual or expected demand for them, and whether this demand is not always indicated by the relation

[1] Cover wanting.

of the market price to the natural price? If the supply existed one moment previously to the demand, the market price must sink below the natural price, and the manufacturers of the commodity or the grower of the corn, whichever it might be, would not get the usual and general rate of profits, and would therefore be unwilling to produce such a commodity [1].

What all producers look steadily at is market price, and its relation to natural price. Suppose you to be disposed to add from your revenue to capital this year, it would not induce you to change the nature of your production, for whether you spent your revenue, or employed it as capital, the next year, your immediate object would be to realize it in money. But with your increased capital what would you produce next year? Corn, undoubtedly, if the price indicated that the supply did not equal the demand, or if you have good reason to expect that but for your production the supply would not equal the demand. Now what I ask is would not the same motives induce you to employ your additional capital in the manufacture of cloth, iron, silk, &c., if you answer it would not, then I request you to give me your reasons why you, or any other producer, would so obviously neglect your best interest. If you answer that the motives for the production of either of these commodities are the same, then there is an end to the dispute, for this is all that I am contending

---

[1] Compare the tract on Protection to Agriculture (1822, sect. iv. p. 21), Works, p. 467 : 'If we lived in one of Mr. Owen's parallelograms, and enjoyed all our productions in common, then no one could suffer in consequence of abundance ; but, as long as society is constituted as it now is, abundance will often be injurious to producers, and scarcity beneficial to them.'

The speech reported in Hansard (March 5, 1822), N. S. vol. vi, 919, is probably to be amended in the light of these passages : 'Mr. Ricardo said it was true that, if the produce of the land was divided into certain proportions, every party would be benefitted by an abundant crop.' Instead of 'certain' we should probably read 'equal.'

for. Suppose a man intent on saving were to employ his savings in producing corn—he would do unwisely if he did not expect the price of corn to be at least as high as its natural price,—in this you must agree—he will not then produce corn. But corn is as high as its natural price? then there is an end of the argument, for it can not be so if the supply preceded the demand. You will not say that he may as well produce corn as any other commodity, because it is possible that corn and all other commodities may be under their natural price, for that would be to adopt the great and fundamental error of Mr. Malthus, who contends that there may be at one and the same time a glut of all commodities, and that it may arise from a want of demand for all—he indeed argues that this is the specific evil under which we are at present suffering. This is I think the only defence you can make for your opinion, and if you do make it, I shall know how to deal with you in a subsequent letter—at present I shall content myself with saying that I have no conception of any man knowingly and wilfully producing a commodity which will sell under its natural price. I do not deny that it is often done, but then I say it is from error and miscalculation, and cannot continue for more than one or two years.

You say that 'the surplus produce of necessaries must in the first instance have preceded the surplus produce of conveniences,' but did the surplus produce of necessaries precede the demand for them?—this is the question. I say they did not, for the men who had their labour to offer in exchange for them were effective demanders of this surplus produce, and the conveniences are the result of this demand.

A man first produces necessaries because he himself has a want or demand for them—he produces more of these necessaries because he wants conveniences, and he can obtain them by other men's labour which his necessaries will command. Hitherto he has produced nothing for which there is not a demand. But he wants to increase his possessions, and it can be done only by having the power to employ more people; must not his first step be to provide necessaries for such additional number of people? Not absolutely, because he may have the power of employing more people, and others may have the means of employing fewer—his capital will increase whilst that of another man diminishes. But no other man[']s capital diminishes! The aggregate capital will be increased! If labour cannot be procured at the usual price no more work will be done with the additional capital, but wages will rise, and the distribution of the produce will be favorable to the workmen. In this case no more food will be produced if the workmen were well fed before, their demand will be for conveniences, and luxuries. But the number of labourers are increased, or the children of labourers! Then indeed the demand for food will increase, and *food will be produced in consequence of such demand*. It would be wrong to infer always that an increase of capital will procure an increased quantity of work to be done, it will be followed by no such effect, if the labourers happen to be in a position to enable them to command the whole addition to the fund for the maintenance of labour, without doing any more work *

I thought of leaving off half an hour ago but my pen runs on. I cannot even now conclude without expressing my satisfaction at the improvement in your knee—I hope all traces of your late accident will soon be lost.

Ever yrs
DAVID RICARDO.

* It is on this ground that I dispute your position that a demand for labour is the same thing as a supply of necessaries.

There is a part of your letter I have not noticed, I mean that part which refers to M. Say's doctrine of demand being only limited by production[1]. His doctrine appears to me to be correct. You say it must be limited by the due distribution of capital. Undoubtedly you are right, but M. Say would answer that private interest would always lead to such a due distribution. He would not deny that errors might be made and more of one, two, three or of 50 commodities be produced than what there was any effective demand for, but he would not agree with you that for any length of time there could be high profits on manufactures and low profits on land. High profits are the consequence of high price—high price of increased demand—increased demand of an imperfect distribution of capital, it is the remedy and not the grievance.

XLI[2].

My Dear Trower

Gatcomb Park
3 *Octr.* 1820.

We are agreed upon so many points, connected with the subject under discussion, that I do not think we can long differ upon that on which there is now a contrariety of opinion. You are perfectly right in estimating profits in the way you do. If the expenditure of 1000 qrs. of corn would procure 1200 qrs., 1200 qrs. would be the gross income, and 200 the net income, or profit. If the expenditure of 1000 lbs. of iron would ensure a return of 1200 lbs., 200 lbs. would also be the net profit; but your mistake,

---

[1] 'Traité d'Économie Politique,' livre i. chap. 15 (" Des Débouchés "). In the Preface to the first edition of the 'Principles of Political Economy and Taxation,' Ricardo alluded to this section of Say's treatise as containing 'some very important principles, which I believe were first explained by this distinguished writer.'

[2] Franked by himself, and dated, 'Minchinhampton, October four, 1820.' Back of last sheet used as cover, and addressed, 'Hutches Trower, Esq., Unsted Wood, Godalming, Surrey.'

I think, is this, you suppose that because when 1200 qrs. of corn are produced, and by the same expenditure 500 cwt. of iron and 100 pieces of cloth, and consequently they are all of the same value, therefore when the quantity of each of these commodities is doubled they will still be of the same value:—it may affect the division of the gross produce you think between the capitalist and the labourer [1], but as this will affect all commodities alike, their relative values will remain the same. If one is below, for a time, its natural price, all will be so. Now on the truth of this doctrine depends the whole question. I contend that in all ordinary cases some commodities will under the circumstances supposed be very much below their natural price, that is to say below the relation which they should bear to other commodities. If 1200 qrs. of corn be of the same value as 500 cwt. of iron, and 100 pieces of cloth, as before supposed, those are the relations which should be preserved between them to keep them all at their natural value, and to afford equal profits to the producer of each, however their quantity may be multiplied. But the market price of every commodity depends on the relation between demand and supply, and it is the interest of all the suppliers of commodities to cease producing them when they fall below their natural value. The demand for corn, with a given population, is limited; no man can have a desire to consume more than a certain quantity of bread, if therefore more than that quantity is produced, it will fall in relative value to those commodities which are produced only in such quantity as is required. But the demand for commodities such as luxuries; or for services, such as are performed by gardeners, menial servants, builders &c. &c. is unlimited, or rather it is only limited by the means of the demanders. Under these circumstances it is not necessary

[1] He first wrote 'producer.'

to produce any thing for which there is not a demand, and therefore it is not necessary that any thing should be under its natural price. If the demand for corn were for 1000 qrs. it would be absurd to employ 1000 qrs. when we knew that the result would be 1200 qrs. for 200 qrs. would be unnecessary, and it would be much better policy to employ 833 qrs. to obtain 1000 and the remaining 166 to obtain some convenience or luxury the demand for which could be positively anticipated. The same remark applies to iron, cloth &c. &c. If we were under any obligation to produce them, or to produce nothing, there might be an universal glut, and the glutted market of one commodity might continue in its former relations to the glutted market of another commodity, but there would be no glut of any commodity, because the capital of the country could always be employed in producing commodities for which there would be a demand. If in the division of the gross produce, the labourers commanded a great proportion, the demand would be for one set of commodities—if the masters had more than a usual share, the demand would be for another set. Suppose the labourers were so well off, they would not demand more corn than they wanted for themselves, but yet none of their revenue would remain unexpended, an unusual quantity of the luxuries and conveniences of the labourer would be demanded. When would the demand for an additional quantity of corn commence? then only when an unusual number of children were born, and this would eventually take place for it never fails to follow the easy and happy situation of the labourer. Before this there would be no demand, and before this there would be no supply. It follows I think irresistibly from your own doctrine. 'Profit is the mighty hinge, upon which all productive capital turns[1].' In every state

---

[1] Malthus uses the metaphor, Edinr. Rev. Feb. 1811, p. 341 ('the main hinge on which the principles of circulation must necessarily turn').

of society there will be a demand for some commodities, and it is these which it will be the interest of capitalists to produce. If they produced corn before there was a population to consume it, they would produce more of that commodity than could be consumed, and consequently it would fall in relative value to those things which would be demanded. If I satisfy you on this point the argument must be at an end. The capitalist says, 'if I produce corn, I shall lose; for it will fall in relative value.' 'If I produce iron in greater quantity, that may perhaps not be wanted, but if I produce those luxuries required by the labourer I am sure I shall find a market for them, and their price will afford me a better profit than if I produced more corn or more iron.' If all commodities were on a par, and whichever I produced would glut the market, then I should agree with you, but being perfectly sure that there would be a demand for commodities of some description—on the part of the capitalists if profits were high—on the part of the labourers if wages were high—I feel confident that the production of no commodity except from miscalculation, precedes the demand or anticipated demand for it. Our difference then [is] you say that if corn and all other commodities be increased in [the] same proportion, they will continue at the same relative value to [each ot]her [1]. To which I answer If the population do not immediately increase, there will [be no] additional demand for corn, but there will be an additional [dem]and—for other things, consequently corn cannot be produced without affording less profits than can be obtained by the production of those other things. It is most true that 'if this growing produce is not accompanied by a proportionate growth of population it alters the relative proportion of capital and labor, and the exchangeable value of com-

[1] MS. defective.

modities in reference to labor' but the labourers will chuse what commodities they shall buy with their additional wages, we are quite sure that corn will not be one of them, and as sure that some convenience or luxury will be chosen. I recollect that if the production of corn costs more, on account of the rise of labour, so will also the production of other things, and therefore if they bore the same relation to each other, there could be no motive for producing one rather than the other; they might all then be in great abundance. But I say they will not continue in the same relation to each other, one will be demanded the other will not. It is not a question of cost of production, but of the relation of market price when produced, to cost of production. Look into your own household and tell me what would be the effect of doubling your income. You would spend it all, but would you double your demand for every commodity you now consume in your family? Should you purchase twice the number of loaves, twice the quantity [of] meat, poultry, horses, carriages &c. &c.? No; you would con[sume] more bread—you would probably have a little more m[eat] and fish because you would keep more company, but you [would] spend much more than double what you now do on pictures and many other [things] [1] to please yourself and Mrs. Trower. No mistake can be greater than to suppose that the demand for every thing increases in the same proportion. You say the labourer is not a consumer of conveniences. Is this true? If he is not, must we not impute it to his poverty? Give him the means, and do you think he wants the inclination? Will he not improve his house and furniture, his clothing, and that of his wife and children—will he not purchase more fuel, and indulge himself in the enjoyment of better beer, tea, tobacco and snuff?

---

[1] MS. defective.

I forget what I said about M. Say's doctrine, but whatever it was I agree with you that a great inequality in the profits afforded by productive capital may produce much individual suffering, by the inducement which it offers to the change of employments. This evil however generally follows from bad legislation. If free trade were now established, how many individuals would suffer! Political Economy would teach us to guard ourselves from every other revulsion, but that which arises from the rise and fall of states—from the progress of improvement in other countries [than] our own, and from the caprices of fashion; —against these [we can]not guard, but we are not permanently to deprive our country [of many] & important benefits because the adopting of a good instead of [a bad syst]em, will be attended with loss to individuals—I would make [the]ir fall easy, but I would not to support them, perpetuate abuse, and countenance bad laws. It is a safe rule to legislate for the public benefit only, and not to attend to the interests of any particular class. In these sentiments I have no doubt I shall have your concurrence.

I have answered your letter without delay, because I expect a few friends[1] to-morrow, and my time will for some time be fully engaged.

Mrs. Ricardo unites with me in kind remembrances [to] Mrs. Trower.

Yours very truly,
DAVID RICARDO.

---

[1] Henry Warburton, and the Smiths of Easton Grey; see Letters to Malthus, p. 173.

XLII [1].

My Dear Trower,   Gatcomb, 26 Novr, 1820.

Hardly a day passes, without some new and extraordinary circumstance occurring, to keep up the agitation in the public mind, respecting the Queen. What could induce ministers to prorogue parliament without finally concluding their proceedings against this persecuted woman? If they thought the bill expedient, why did they not send it to the commons? If they thought a vote of censure necessary, as appears to be your opinion, why not now propose it to parliament? What good can be expected from putting off this question, which so engrosses the public attention, for two months longer, and put it off too in such a manner, by proroguing the parliament without a speech from the throne? Can the Queen do otherwise than court the mob? Has she any hopes of safety from the malignancy of her enemies but in the support of the people? To that she has hitherto been indebted for protection;—without it she would have been crushed by her enemies; and while these proceedings are hanging over her head she will be greatly to blame if she suffers the spirit which has been raised in her favor to subside.

I am glad that you are pleased with the proceedings in the House of Lords stopping where they did. For my part I think they should never have commenced, and never can I consent to hold up my hand to censure or degrade the Queen, with the knowledge I have of the means which have been used to ruin her. If she has had an adulterous connection with Bergami, which I think is by no means

---

[1] Franked by himself. The reverse of the last sheet is used as the cover, and addressed, 'Hutches Trower, Esq., Unsted Wood, Godalming'; dated, 'Minchinhampton, November Twenty Seven.'

proved, never had woman so many reasons of justification to urge an extenuation of her fault. Considering all the circumstances, a veil of oblivion should have been thrown over her conduct, instead of employing the basest means for detecting and proving her guilt. I most heartily join in feelings of indignation against all the Queen's persecutors, and of compassion for her. Though it is to be lamented that she is the rallying point of the discontented and disaffected—she is absolutely driven to such an alliance, and the only way of detaching her from her present connections is to cease to persecute her [1].

I very much fear that we shall have no change of ministers, and I am not sanguine, if we have, in my hopes of their adopting the wise measures which you think so essential to our safety, and future prosperity. What ministers, with the present constitution of the House of Commons, can succeed in sweeping away many of our commercial restraints, particularly the greatest, the restraints on the importation of corn? What ministers will dare to encounter our financial difficulties, in the only way in which they should be met, or will seriously commence the work of retrenchment in our expences? We may probably find men who will remove the disabilities from the Roman catholics, and make some amendments in our criminal laws, but this will be all, we must not expect much more improvement, and when we are involved in another war, then will come the time for those efforts which, if we were wise, we ought to make now.

I am glad to find that you do not think our differences great on the question which we have lately been discussing. —I fully expected that we should approximate in our opinions when we came fully to understand each other.

---

[1] See 'Proceedings in the House of Lords upon the Bill of Pains and Penalties against Her Majesty.' Hansard, Parliamentary Debates, vols. ii, iii (N. S.).

I have been lately employed in writing notes on Mr. Malthus' work, with a view to defend my opinions, when fairly attacked—to place them in a true light, when unintentionally mis[s]tated—and to detect the fallacies which appeared to me to lurk under the author's arguments[1]. My task is now ended, but with what success must be left to the judgment of others. The whole might occupy about 150 pages if printed. It is not however probable that I shall publish them, because they are not in an inviting form, and would consequently have few readers. Wherever I have met a passage against which I have an objection to make I have quoted the few first words of it, and then written my comments—in this way for example Page 103 "If we were determined &c. &c.[2]' ['] If equal capitals yielded commodities of nearly equal value, there might be some grounds for this argument; but, as from a capital employed in valuable machinery, such as steam engines &c. a commodity of a very different value is obtained, than from a capital of the same value, employed chiefly in the support of labour, it is at once obvious that the one term thought to be the more correct by Mr. Malthus, would be the most incorrect that could be imagined.' This being a short comment I have copied it as a specimen, and you will from it be able to judge how little interest general readers would take in such a performance. I have also

---

[1] Cf. Letters to McCulloch, p. 84, note, Letters to Malthus, p. 172, and Ricardo's Works, p. xxxi, where McCulloch writes of Ricardo: 'He also left "Notes" on Mr. Malthus's "Principles of Political Economy," containing a vindication of his own doctrines from the objections of Mr. Malthus, and showing the mistakes into which he conceives Mr. M. had fallen. But we doubt whether they have sufficient interest to warrant their publication.'

[2] 'If we were determined to use only one term, it would certainly be more correct to refer to capital rather than to labour, because the advances which are called capital generally include the other two [wages and rent].' From the Chapter (ii) on the Nature and Measures of Value, section iv: Of the Labour which a Commodity has Cost considered as a Measure of Exchangeable Value.

added a few comments on M. Say's letter to Malthus, which I think is written with more self satisfaction than its merit deserves[1]. I remember a remark of yours on a passage, Page 128 of Malthus['] work, and as I fully agree with you in your comments, and you will only have the trouble of reading what I write, I am tempted though it is long to copy what I have said as another specimen of my labours. Page 128. ' Though neither of these two objects &c. &c.'[2] 'A complete fallacy seems to me to be involved in the whole of this argument. Corn is a variable commodity, says Mr. Malthus, and so is labour variable, but they always vary in different directions: if therefore I take a mean between the two, I shall probably obtain a measure of value approaching to the character of invariability. Now is it true? do corn and labour vary in different directions? When corn rises in relative value to labour, labour falls in relative value to corn, and this is called varying in different directions. When cloth rises in price, it rises as compared with gold, and gold falls as compared with cloth; but this does not prove that they vary in different directions; for at the same time gold may have risen as compared with iron, hats, leather and every other commodity except cloth. What then would be the fact? that they had varied in the same direction;—gold may have risen 10 pc. in value compared with all things but cloth, and cloth may have risen 25 pc. compared with all things, excepting with gold, relatively to which it would have risen only 15 pc. We should think it

---

[1] 'Lettres à M. Malthus sur différens sujets d'économie politique, notamment sur les causes de la stagnation générale du commerce.' Paris, 1820. Say had sent Ricardo a copy of the work, with an accompanying letter; see Letters to McCulloch, pp. 84, 85. For Ricardo's acknowledgment, see Say, Mélanges et Correspondance, p. 108; Letters to Malthus, p. 181.

[2] 'Though neither of these two objects, however, [corn and labour], taken singly, can be considered as a satisfactory measure of value, yet by combining the two we may perhaps approach to greater accuracy.' Ch. ii. sect. vii.

strange in these circumstances to say that we should in chusing a measure of value take a mean between cloth and gold because they varied different ways, when it is absolutely demonstrable that they have varied the same way. This is however what Mr. Malthus has done in respect to corn and labour. A country finds increasing difficulties in supplying the corn necessary for a continually increasing population, and in consequence corn rises as compared with all other commodities. As corn rises, which forms so material an article of consumption to the labourer, though not the only one, labour also rises, but not so much as corn;—if corn rises 20 pc. labour may probably rise 10 pc. In these circumstances, estimated in corn, labour appears to have fallen—estimated in labour corn appears to have risen, but it is evident that they have both risen though in different degrees for they will both be more valuable estimated in all other commodities. A mean then is taken between two commodities which are confessedly variable, and it is taken on the principle that the variation of on. corrects the effects of the variation in the other; as however I have proved that they vary in the same direction, I hope Mr. Malthus will see the expediency of relinquishing so imperfect, and so variable a standard. From Mr. Malthus' argument in this place, one would suppose that labour fell when corn rose, and consequently that with a given quantity of iron, leather, cloth &c. &c., more labour would be obtained; the contrary is the fact: labour as well as corn rises as compared with these commodities. Mr. Malthus says so himself in Page 125 "In the progress of improvement and civilization it generally happens, that when labour commands the smallest quantity of food, it commands the greatest quantity of other commodities," what is this but saying that when a great quantity of other commodities is given for food, a great quantity of other things is also given for labour; or in other words that when food rises labour rises?' I would not h[ave][1] troubled you with this if it imposed any heavier task on yo[u than][1] reading it.

I have not seen Godwin's answer to Malthus[2]. Mill writes to me that it is a most contemptible performance.

I send you my article on the Sinking Fund[3]. Tell me freely your opinion of it.

I believe they have lowered the price of labour here, but I, as a gentleman I suppose always pay the same. Mrs. Ricardo unites with me in kind regards to Mrs. Trower.

Believe me
Ever, my dr Trower
Yrs truly
DAVID RICARDO.

My man filled my lamp too full of oil. I have let 3 drops fall on the first sheet; pray take it with all its imperfections.

XLIII [4]

GATCOMB PARK
MINCHINHAMPTON,
Jan. 14—1821.

MY DEAR TROWER,

I am sorry that so long a time has elapsed without my returning an answer to your last kind letter, but since I received it I have not only been a great deal employed at home, but I have been to Gloucester; to my sons near Malvern, and to my daughters near Bath [5].

You give me great pleasure by the favorable opinion

---

[1] MS. defective.
[2] 'Of Population: An Enquiry concerning the Power of Increase in the Numbers of Mankind, being an Answer to Mr. Malthus's Essay on that subject.' London, 1820.
[3] 'Supplement to the Fourth, Fifth, and Sixth Editions of the Encyclopaedia Britannica' (Edinburgh, 1815-1824), vol. iv. pp. 410-426; reprinted in Works (ed. McCulloch), pp. 515-548. Cf. Letters to McCulloch, p. 46.
[4] Cover wanting.
[5] See above, pp. 14, 117.

you give of my Essay on the Funding System; I am glad to have your sanction to the view which I have taken of that subject and that you condemn equally with myself the breach of faith to the Stockholder which is so hypocritically defended by our present Chancellor of the Exchequer, who really would have us imagine he performs all that was engaged to be done, by his nominal sinking fund of £16,000,000, while he is every year borrowing 12 millions and adding that sum with 2 or 3 more millions to the public debt. What you say about the market of 5 pcts. becoming more expanded by frequent repetition of funding large sums in that stock is most true, but as the capital of 3 pcts. was already so large at the commencement of the late war, I doubt whether it would not have been an exceedingly difficult thing to give the same currency to the 5 pc. Stock which has been so long possessed by the 3 pc^{ts}. Probably Dr. Price and Dr. Hamilton have over-rated the advantage one way [1], and I have under-rated it the other. At some future time perhaps, I may try whether I can say any thing worth publication in the shape of a pamphlet on the subject of the policy and practicability of paying off the debt.

My remarks on Malthus's work have been sometime with M[']Culloch, who long ago requested me to shew him any observations I might make on Malthus's book. I am desirous of having his opinion on the remarks themselves as well as on the expediency of publishing them [2]. I expect

---

[1] See Ricardo's 'Works' (ed. McCulloch), p. 538 (Essay on the Funding System, from Suppl. to Encycl. Brit.): 'Dr. Hamilton has followed Dr. Price in insisting much on the disadvantage of raising loans during war in a 3 per cent. stock, and not in a 5 per cent. stock. In the former, a great addition is made to the nominal capital, which is generally redeemed during peace at a greatly advanced price,' &c. See also Ricardo to Malthus, p. 157 seq., and the two letters to Place above, pp. 85 seq.

[2] Cf. Letters to McCulloch, pp. 89, 90; for McCulloch's unfavourable opinion, ibid., pp. 93, 94.

soon to hear from him and to have my papers returned to me. Although they are in a very rough form you shall see them if they possess the least interest in your estimation. Your opinion, I perceive, is in favor of publishing them as an appendix to a new edition of my 'Principles of Political Economy.' That was the form in which I at first had an idea of giving them to the public, but I was strongly dissuaded from it by Mill, who thought I ought by all means to avoid giving too controversial a character to my book, and indeed he advises me not to notice any of the attacks which have been made upon me, in my third edition, which will I apprehend be printed soon after I get to London. I shall not urge the objection which you appear to anticipate, that the new modelling of my book is a work of time and labor—I should not grudge however much of these [I] should be called upon to bestow on it, if I thought I could give it a better chance of success, either with the present race, or any future race of Political Economists. I have carefully looked over every part of it, and with my limited powers of composition I am convinced I can do very little to improve it. When Mill, M[']Culloch, Malthus, and you have seen these notes of mine, and have given me your opinions of them, I shall know what to resolve upon respecting the mode of disposing of them. Perhaps the fire will be the proper place to which to consign them.

I have lately had a visit here from Malthus—he came with the expectation of seeing my notes and he would have seen them had he not after engaging to come to me, been detained in town by the illness of his sister[1], which made him think that his visit to me must be put off altogether. Before I knew of his coming I had engaged to send the notes to M[']Culloch, and detained them when

[1] Mary Catherine Harriet, born 1764, died 13th March, 1821 (J. O. Payne, 'Family of Malthus,' priv. pr. 1890).

I had reason to expect him, but finally sent them off when I despaired of seeing him. While here he was as good-natured and agreeable as ever. We spent many hours of each day in discussion, the result of which was only to understand more clearly the points of difference between us. He must be as well acquainted with my objections to his work as if he had read my notes themselves, for I believe there was not one which I forgot to urge, but he is still desirous of seeing the notes. I have promised to pay him a visit, with them, as soon as they are returned to me.

You are mistaken in supposing that it is possible I may th[ink] you a very idle fellow, by the apology with which I accompanied the long quotation I sent to you. I know you are something very different from an idle fellow, and I insist that you had no right to come to any such conclusion because I hesitated about sending you a long winded performance of mine. If you never studied at all, I should not call you an idle fellow, I know that much of your time is very usefully employed. I hope now I have appeased your irascible spirit.

It was not one of the acts of the late Bishop of Landaff[1] which has contributed much to his fame, his selling his library when he retired into the country. It surely must have arisen from a sordid passion for money, for he could not fail to have preserved his relish for books.

I leave the country on thursday next, and expect to feel a great deal of interest in the approaching session of parliament. I hear that Ministers are relaxing a little in their severe measures respecting the Queen. I am told that they will propose £50,000 p^r Ann. for her, and a suitable sum for the . .

[The conclusion of the letter is missing. At the bottom of the last sheet is written, in red ink and by another hand, a note:

[1] Richard Watson. See p. 52.

'The rest wanting. Ch. A. Secy, May 12.' The writer was probably Charles C. Atkinson, who was secretary of the Council of University College in 1843-44.]

XLIV [1].

MY DEAR TROWER,   LONDON 2 *March* 1821.

Before I address you on any other subject, I must express the great pleasure I have felt from hearing from all quarters, and from all parties, commendations of your impartiality and talents, on the occasion of the County meeting in Surrey at which you presided [2]. Before the meeting I was sure that the part to perform would be done in a way to reflect credit on you, but I confess I did not expect that the opportunity would have been so favourable for the display of the good temper, moderation and talents which so certainly belong to you.

I was disappointed in not seeing you on your late short visit to London. I hope that you will soon be disposed to take another trip to this busy scene, and that then you will not forget the satisfaction you will afford me by giving me your company as often as you may find it convenient.

Mr. Malthus has now had my notes for five weeks—he has been interrupted in the examination of them by the death of Mr. Dalton, a friend of his in Lincolnshire, to whose funeral he was obliged to go [3]. I expect to see him in London next week at which time he will no doubt return me my MS. I am glad that you speak with appro-

---

[1] Cover wanting.   [2] See note below.
[3] Sydenham (son of a Daniel Malthus and father of the Daniel Malthus whose son was Thomas Robert) married Anne Dalton; and Daniel, father of the economist, bequeathed the botanical collections that he had from Rousseau to 'Mrs. Jane Dalton.' See J. O. Payne's 'Family of Malthus,' pp. 88, 100.

bation of the spirit in which I carry on the contest with Mr. Malthus—I always wish him to see what I have to say against his opinions before I publish them [sic], that I may be sure that I have not misunderstood him, and therefore not misrepresented him. He certainly has not done the same thing to me, and has, I am sure, without intending it, misrepresented me in many important particulars.

A writer in the Times of this morning appears to have adopted some of Malthus' principles, and the conclusions he draws from them are so wild and extravagant, that if we had no other reason for suspecting their fallacy, these would afford them. This writer recommends that we should raise loans now instead of the taxes with which we are burthened, and for this sagacious reason, because it will promote expenditure and take off the superfluity of our productions[1].

In my dispute with Baring the House listened to me with great attention[2]. The subject of the two standards will again come under discussion, and I shall be prepared to shew from Baring's evidence that there are insuperable objections to the alterations which he proposes. He, I am sure, ascribes too much to the rise in the value of money, and I am prepared to shew that even measured by silver, that is to say by the exchange with France, or Hamburgh, the rise in our currency has not been more than 10 pc. in five years,—he may answer that silver itself has risen in value,—that may be, but then it is common

---

[1] The letter, which occupies two and a half columns in The *Times* of March 2, 1821, is the fourth of a series 'On the Revenue and Taxation,' and is signed 'Abraham Tudela.'

[2] On February 8, 1821, in the debate upon the Birmingham merchants' petition for an inquiry into the causes of national distress; see Hansard, Parliamentary Debates, vol. iv. (N. S.) 530 et seq. Alexander Baring testified before both the Lords and the Commons Committees of 1819 on the Resumption of Cash Payments. See Commons' Reports: Minutes of Evidence, p. 180 et seq.; Lords' Report: Minutes of Evidence, p. 101 et seq.

to all countries that use silver as a standard, and I should be glad to know what security we can have against such an inconvenience, whilst we use the metals as a standard, and by what means he would guard us against it. Would he give us the paper system again unchecked by a fixed standard?

I am sorry that no security can be found against the forging of Bank notes [1],—the recalling of the one pound notes cannot fail to enhance the value of the currency.

You speak of the landholder most justly—he is an interested being seeking unjustly to load the other classes of the community with his share of the public burthens. I am however disposed to concede that if we are to have restrictions on the importation of foreign corn the most eligible mode would be by a fixed duty, not more operative in excluding corn than the present restrictions; for I think it is better to have a steady price of corn, rather than one which must alternate from low to high and then from high prices to low ones again. On the present plan we are either overwhelmed with foreign corn, or totally deprived of it.

Mr. Plunkett's speech the other evening was a very fine one [2]—I thought Peel tame and feeble [3]. Surely no reasonable man can apprehend danger to the United Kingdom from according the catholic claims in Ireland—I believe that the church establishment in Ireland would be more secure, but I should not see much to regret if Ireland had a catholic establishment, in the same way as Scotland has a presbyterian one. If there be an established religion it

[1] See the 'Report of the Committee of the Society of Arts, together with the approved communications and evidence upon the same, relative to the mode of preventing the forgery of Bank Notes' (London, 1819).

[2] On his own motion for the consideration, in the Committee of the whole House, of the Roman Catholic Claims; see Hansard, Parliamentary Debates, vol. iv. (N. S.) 961 et seq.

[3] Ibid., 988 et seq.

should be that of the greatest number. In this I do not expect you to agree with me. Fare you well, my dear Trower, and believe me ever y^{rs}

DAVID RICARDO

Mrs. Ricardo begs to join with me in kind remembrances to Mrs. Trower.

NOTE.—A meeting of the nobility, gentry, clergy, and freeholders of the county of Surrey, was held at the Spread Eagle Inn, Epsom, February 2, 1821 :—
'to take into consideration the propriety of petitioning the two houses of Parliament to adopt such measures as will prevent all further proceedings against the Queen, secure the country against the revival of discussions injurious to the morals and painful to the feelings of the people, and thereby enable the great council of the nation to attend to the various and important questions of foreign and domestic policy, which in the present distressed state of the country, urgently call for the immediate consideration of Parliament.'

Hutches Trower, Esq. as High Sheriff of the County presided. The Meeting, after animated debate—over which the chairman seems to have presided with skill and tact—adopted resolutions (1) Supporting the reigning House of Brunswick, (2) Urging economy in expenditure, (3) Deprecating the Bill of Pains and Penalties against the Queen, urging the restoration of the Queen to her former status, and the reinsertion of her name in the Liturgy.

For a full account of the meeting, see *Times*, February 3, 1821.

XLV[1].

UPPER BROOK STREET
21 *April* 1821

MY DEAR TROWER

I was very much concerned to hear of the accident you had met with; and yet considering how very near you were to a result much more serious I ought rather to congratulate you on your narrow escape, than condole

---
[1] Cover wanting.

with you on the slight injury you have received. Since receiving your letter I have heard of you twice; once from Mrs. Trower, when you were in town for a day, and another time from your brother, whom I accidentally met in the street. I am glad to find that you are getting well.

Our discussions in the House on the currency question, are I hope now closed[1]—I trust that we shall have no more proposals to deviate from the course which after due consideration has been determined on.

Your view of Godwin's book exactly agrees with mine. The real question at issue is not whether under favorable circumstances population will double in 25 or in 50 years, but whether it has not a tendency to increase faster than the capital which is to employ it, and if so what measures of legislation should be pursued. It must be manifest that the principle of population is strong enough for human happiness, and it neither wants poor laws nor any other laws to encourage it.

Mr. Mill's book is not yet quite finished, though in a state of great forwardness. His object is to give a clear exposition of all the elementary principles of Political Economy as they are at present understood. He does not mean to notice any other writer, nor to attempt to controvert the errors into which he may think they have fallen. It may probably be a month or two before his book will be published[2].

The catholic bill is lost[3]. I am sorry for it, though

---

[1] On February 13, 1821, the House of Commons passed the bill (1 and 2 Geo. IV. c. 26) permitting the Bank of England to begin to pay its notes in coin on May 1, 1821, instead of a year later as provided by the Resumption Act of 1819 (59 Geo. III, c. 49); see Hansard, Parliamentary Debates, vol. v. (N. S.) 208.

[2] 'Elements of Political Economy' (London, 1821). In July the work was passing through the press; Bain, 'James Mill,' p. 194.

[3] Defeated in the House of Lords on the second reading, by a vote of 159 to 120; see Hansard, Parliamentary Debates, vol. v. (N. S.) 356.

I cannot but think that it is only delayed. You are undoubtedly right, 'the real fear is the ultimate consequences of that spirit of cession in which the measure originates. Test and Corporation Acts, Tithes, Church Establishments — these are the real foundation of the alarms.' If by good legislation the resources of Ireland were fairly brought forth, they would contribute greatly to the wealth of the United Kingdom. What a quantity of capital might be advantageously employed in that country, and no doubt would be if there were not fears for its security in so disturbed a region. This resource is however in store for us. We landholders have formidable rivals in the landholders of that country. Our alarm is excited by the rivalship and competition of Poland, Russia and America, but we never think of Ireland the most formidable of them all. The tillage of Ireland continues uniformly to increase and will I have no doubt for many years to come. When the improvements in husbandry so well followed in England are introduced into that country the effects must be very marked on the price of corn, and on the interests of English landlords.

I have worked very hard in the Agricultural Committee and I hope not without effect in correcting mistaken principles. We have had many farmers before us who have given a sad but I believe a true picture of the great prevalence of distress. These farmers were questioned as to remedies, and were all for protecting duties, amounting almost to the prohibition of foreign corn. It was my business to shew how little they were qualified to be advisers on this important question, by exposing their ignorance of the first principles which should guide our judgments[1].

[1] See Ricardo to McCulloch, pp. 97, 104, and notes.

Mr. Attwood[1], a great publisher of Essays on the currency, was called before us, and if he were to be believed, there is no other cause for a fall of prices but an increase in the value of money. His claims to infallibility have been sifted by Huskisson and myself, and I believe it will appear that he is no great master of the science. Mr. Hodgson[2] and Mr. Tooke have been our best informed witnesses. Mr. Hodgson is a merchant and corn dealer of Liverpool, who expends annually a large sum of money in sending people about the country to examine into the state of the crop just before it is reaped[3]. They do so by going from field to field at two or three miles distance from each other, and actually counting the ears, and weighing the grains in a square foot or yard; by which means they are enabled to compare it with the crops of former years. The last appears to have been an unusually abundant crop, greater than for many years before. This evidence is confirmed by more than one land surveyor. Mr. Tooke who is a good political economist gave us some valuable information of the effect of abundance on price, particularly with such a corn law as is now established, when we are deprived of the markets of other countries until our prices are below theirs.

This is in fact the present cause of the great depression in the price of corn. A little effect may be ascribed to the currency but abundance is the great operating cause.

[1] Thomas Attwood, the bitter opponent of resumption, has been already mentioned, above p. 34; for a sketch of his life, and a list of his writings, see Palgrave, Dictionary of Political Economy, *sub nom*. For his examination see 'Evidence,' 1821, pp. 242-263. He attributed Depression to Resumption, considering that Resumption had lowered prices 30 p. c. (252).

[2] David Hodgson of Cropper, Benson, and Co., large corn merchants and importers in Liverpool. The survey was meant in the first place to serve their business, and in the printed evidence Hodgson is chary of details as to the way it was carried out.

[3] 'Minutes of Evidence,' 1821, pp. 263-283. Compare Cobbett's 'Rural Rides,' (London, 1830), p. 127; and his Weekly Register, 1821, pp. 582, 734).

You will have seen that we made a stand for good principles on the question of the Timber duties, without success at the present moment, but not I hope without making some impression. The debate was very briefly and very badly reported [1].

Mrs. Ricardo joins with me in kind remembrances to Mrs. Trower.

Ever y^{rs}

DAVID RICARDO.

XLVI [2].

[TO SIR JOHN SINCLAIR.]

DEAR SIR,   56 UPPER BROOK STREET, 15th *June* 1821.

Your plan is neither more nor less than a proposal to depreciate the currency 20 *per cent*. If I could consent to such a measure, I should propose to do it openly, without disguise; but I do not think such a plan necessary or expedient, and confidently expect, that in no long time, we shall surmount all our difficulties. I remain your obedient servant,

DAVID RICARDO.

XLVII [3].

GATCOMB PARK, MINCHINHAMPTON,

MY DEAR TROWER,   4 *July* 1821.

Before I left London I gave directions to Mr. Mitchell, at the Vote Office, to send you a copy of the printed Minutes of Evidence of the Agricultural Committee as soon as it should be obtainable, which I have no doubt

---

[1] Hansard, Parliamentary Debates, vol. v. (N. S.) 264. Cf. Mr. Cannan on Ricardo in Parliament, Econ. Journal, 1894, p. 410.

[2] 'Sinclair's Correspondence,' pp. 374, 375.

[3] Franked by himself; dated 'Minchinhampton, July fourth, 1821,' and addressed, 'Hutches Trower, Esq., Unsted Wood, Godalming, Surry.'

he will do. I hope that you are satisfied with a great part of the Report[1], there are some absurdities and contradictions in it, but considering how the committee was formed, and the opposition which was given to sound principles by the landed gentlemen, I think it on the whole creditable to the Committee.

I am glad that you think I have vindicated my book against Malthus's attacks, in my notes—if I have not, it is owing to my weakness, and not to his strength, for I am quite sure that his book abounds with inconsistencies and contradictions.

I am not surprised that you should not agree with me in my definition of exchangeable value, but when you say that 'the labour expended upon a commodity is the measure by which the accuracy of its exchangeable value is ascertained and constantly regulated' you admit all I contend for. I do not, I think, say that the labour expended on a commodity is a measure of its exchangeable value, but of its positive value. I then add that exchangeable value is regulated by positive value and therefore is regulated by the quantity of labour expended.

You say if there were no exchange of commodities they could have no value, and I agree with you, if you mean exchangeable value, but if I am obliged to devote one month's labour to make me a coat, and only one week's labour to make a hat, although I should never exchange either of them, the coat would be four times the value of the hat; and if a robber were to break into my house and take part of my property, I would rather that he

---

[1] 'Report from the Select Committee, to whom the several Petitions complaining of the Depressed State of the Agriculture of the United Kingdom were referred; Minutes of Evidence; Appendix.' London, 1821. A Summary is given in the Annual Register 1821, Appendix to *Chronicle*, pp. 506 seq. Spencer Walpole (History of England, vol. ii) gives a spirited account of the Committee and its treatment of and by the farmers' friends.

took three hats than one coat. It is in the early stages of society, when few exchanges are made, that the value of commodities is most peculiarly estimated by the quantity of labour necessary to produce them, as stated by Adam Smith[1].

I confess I do not rightly understand what meaning you attach to the words 'exchangeable value,' when you say that 'the labour which a commodity can command is what actually constitutes its exchangeable value.' A yard of superfine cloth we will suppose can command a month's labour of one man, but in the course of a year, from some cause, it commands only a fortnight's labour of one man, you are bound to say that the exchangeable value of cloth has fallen one half. You are bound to say this whether the cloth be produced with a great deal less labour in consequence of the discovery of improved machinery, or the food and some of the other necessaries of the labourer be produced with so much difficulty that wages rise and therefore labour rises as compared with cloth and many other things. You would say then cloth has fallen one half in exchangeable value although it should exchange for precisely the same quantity of gold, silver, iron, lead, hats, tea, sugar and a thousand other things, and you would use precisely the same language if, by the discovery of machinery cloth was produced with great additional facility and consequently would exchange for only one-half the same quantity of gold, silver, iron, lead, hats, tea, sugar and a thousand other things. Now the difference between you and me is this: in the latter case I should say with you that cloth had fallen to half its former exchangeable value and my proof would be that it would exchange for only half the former quantity of labour and of *all other*

---

[1] W. of N., i. ch. vi. (beginning): 'Of the Component Parts of the Price of Commodities.'

things[1], but in the other case I should say cloth has not altered in exchangeable value, because it will exchange for precisely the same quantity of all other things. It is true it will exchange for more labour, and why? because labour has fallen in exchange value, and the proof is it will exchange for only half the quantity of gold, silver, lead, iron and all other things, excepting perhaps corn and some other necessaries, which have also fallen in value. I cannot approve of your saying that cloth has fallen in exchangeable value merely because it will exchange for less labour, no more than I can approve of the same terms being applied to the fact of its exchanging for less salt, or for less sugar. Surely such a use of the words exchangeable value tends to perplex and mislead. Labour rising in value is one thing, commodities falling in value is another, but once admit your language and these two different things are confounded. It would be quite accurate to say in both cases that cloth had fallen in exchangeable value estimated in labour, as it would be to say it had fallen in value estimated in salt if such should be the fact, but then the medium by which you measure exchangeable value is named and you only express a fact—this is very different however from saying that cloth has fallen in exchangeable value without mentioning the medium in which [*sic*] its alteration in value is specifically confined.

In what I have said respecting natural and market price I have obviated your objections in regard to the difference between cost and value. Cost is an ambiguous word and sometimes includes the profit of stock, and sometimes excludes it. In the way you use it, and I think properly use it, there is no ambiguity, you include in it the profits of stock.

I cannot but flatter myself with the hopes of a continuance

---

[1] Words in italics are underlined in the original.

of peace in Europe—the agitations which at present exist will I think subside, and we shall witness a general course of prosperity. When our purses are again filled indeed, we may as usual become quarrelsome, but I hope nations are becoming wiser, and are every day more convinced that the prosperity of one country is not promoted by the distress of another—that restrictions on commerce are not favorable to wealth, and that the individual particular welfare of each country, as well as the general welfare of all, is best encouraged by unbounded freedom of trade, and the establishment of the most liberal policy. I must do our ministers the justice to say that I believe they view these questions in their true light and would make great improvements in our commercial code if they were not thwarted and opposed by the narrow and selfish policy of the particular interests which are so powerfully exerted in the H. of Commons to check improvement and support monopolies.—

Mrs. Ricardo unites with me in best regards to Mrs. Trower and yourself.

Ever Truly y^{rs}
David Ricardo.

XLVIII [1].

My Dear Trower

Gatcomb Park
22 *Aug* 1821

It is nearly a month since your letter to me was written, and it ought long before this to have been answered; but the fact is that in proportion to my time being unoccupied by business I become more and more idle, and feel more and more disposed to indulge in excursions of pleasure and amusement. Since I have been here I have always had some friend with me, and a great deal of my

---

[1] Franked by himself; cover dated 'Minchinhampton, August twenty-two, 1821'; addressed 'Hutches Trower, Esq., Unsted Wood, Godalming, Surrey.'

time has been passed in visits to my son, who lives in a beautiful country, which I always shew to my friends, and to other places within a moderate distance of my own habitation [1].

I am glad you approve on the whole of the Report of the Agricultural Committee. I had no other hand in its construction than using the best arguments I could in support of those doctrines which I thought correct, and never sparing the doctrines of my opponents when I thought they were unsound and could be shewn to be so. When the Committee broke up there were very few points on which Mr. Huskisson and I differed.

The Committee has done, and will, I think, do good, by giving information to the House itself. The agricultural gentlemen will soon have enough of committees. I feel quite sure that if we had a committee every year, the restrictions on the trade of corn, instead of being increased, would be after a very few years wholly abolished. Mr. Huskisson justly observed to me that the landed gentlemen entered the committee as plaintiffs and left as defendants. I am quite astonished that the evidence is not yet published—it must appear soon, and when it does a copy of it shall be sent to you.

With respect to our difference of opinion on the subject of exchangeable value, it is more an apparent difference than a real one. In speaking of exchangeable value you have not any idea of real value in your mind—I invariably have. Your criticisms on passages in my book are I have little doubt correct, because they are also the criticisms of others on the same passages. A pamphlet has appeared 'On certain verbal disputes in Polit. Econ.' where the same ground of objection is taken as you take [2]; the fault

---

[1] See above, p. 117.
[2] 'Observations on Certain Verbal Disputes in Political Economy, particularly relating to Demand and Supply.' London, 1821. [Anon.]

lies not in the doctrine itself, but in my faulty manner of explaining it. The exchangeable value of a commodity cannot alter, I say, unless either its real value, or the real value of the things it is exchanged for, alter. This cannot be disputed. If a coat would purchase four hats and will afterwards purchase five, I admit that both the coat and the hats have varied in exchangeable value, but they have done so in consequence of one or other of them varying in real value, and therefore if I use the word value without prefixing the word exchangeable to it, it will be correct for me to say that the coat has risen in value whilst hats have not varied, or that hats have fallen in value while coats have remained stationary. With this explanation look at the passage (Pages 3/4 and 12 [1]) which you quote and tell me why they are objectionable.

The troubles of the poor Queen are now at an end, and if ministers had not grossly mismanaged the business she might have been carried to her grave, with the sympathy of the people indeed, but without any increased odium to the Government [2]. Her will, directing where her body should be buried, had removed all difficulty from the question of her interment—why then should not ministers have humored the people in any wish they might have formed respecting the course of the procession? Can there be the least doubt that the public tranquil[l]ity would not have been disturbed if the strongly expressed opinion that the Queen's remains should go through the city had been complied with.

From the high price of the English and French funds we are I suppose to conclude that the peace of Europe is not to be disturbed by the disputes between Turkey and her

---

[1] Pp. 3, 4, and 12 of 'Political Economy and Taxation,' third ed., 1821.

[2] Queen Caroline died on August 7, 1821. At her funeral there was a riot resulting in the death of two persons.

greek subjects[1]. I hope that peace will be maintained, but considering the great effect which war would have at the present moment on the price of the public securities, I think it quite astonishing that with such appearances of angry discussions being likely to take place between Turkey and Russia they keep at their present elevation.

Mushet has published a curious set of tables, to prove that the Stockholder has, on the whole, derived no advantage, first from the depreciation, and then from the restoration in the value of money. He has in his methodical manner, and with great labour calculated the advantage or disadvantage from year to year, has considered each loan separately, and shewn what ought to have been, and what actually has been paid to the public creditor. The result is, and I believe it is a correct one, that the Stockholders as a body if they had received uniformly what was really due to them, might now have been entitled to £72,704 pr. ann. more than they actually receive, in money of the standard value [2].

You ask me how I should value tithes—whether I should value them in reference to monied or landed capital. I differ with you, and think in reference to the latter. I think Tithes at 28 years purchase is [sic] a much cheaper purchase than Land at 28 years purchase, particularly if you contemplate the increasing prosperity and population of the country. In an improving country Tithes always increase in a greater proportion than rent, because they are always the same proportion of the gross produce of the

---

[1] The Greeks rose in insurrection, March, 1821.

[2] 'A Series of Tables Exhibiting the Gain and Loss to a Fundholder arising from the Fluctuations in the Value of the Currency from 1800 to 1821.' By Robert Mushet, Esq. London, 1821.

As originally published the work contained certain fundamental errors which were pointed out by Ricardo, and corrected by Mushet in a 'Second edition, corrected,' published in the same year (cf. Letters to McCulloch, pp. 111-113). Ricardo's reference, above, is to this corrected edition.

land; rent, even when it increases, is probably always a diminished proportion of the gross produce. Should the rent of your land in 50 or a hundred years rise 50 pc, I have no doubt whatever that the Tithes on the same land will rise very considerably more than 50 pc. If your Tithes are at a fair valuation, and not unusually high, you would do well I think to purchase them at 28 years purchase.

Matters are bad enough in this part of the country. Rents are falling, and tenants much distressed. Poor-rates, wages, and tradesmen's bills also fall, but tithes I believe keep up. Labourers appear to be well off, no scarcity of work, and wages fully adequate to obtain for them more than the usual quantity of necessaries and comforts. Manufacturing labour is also fully employed, but the masters say they do not get their usual profits—by usual I suppose they mean unusual and exorbitant profits.

I did not know that your brother was a country gentleman, or rather that he resided in the country. I should not expect that he could enter much into country amusements; but what enjoyment can be greater to a man fond of Books than a good library in a beautiful and healthy retirement—particularly if it be varied with the pleasure of society in London for 2 or 3 months in the year. I hope your brother[']s eldest son will realise the expectations which he has raised—it will be very gratifying to his father.

Mrs. Ricardo joins with me in kind remembrances to Mrs. Trower.

Ever truly y^{rs}

DAVID RICARDO.

XLIX[1].

[TO JOHN WHEATLEY.]

GATCOMB PARK
MINCHINHAMPTON
18 *Sept* 1821

SIR

I received your letter and the pamphlet[2] which accompanied it yesterday. Although I agree in principle with you, on the evils of a variable currency and the impolicy of a country's using measures to raise the price of its corn as compared with its manufactures, yet I do not agree with many of the arguments and conclusions in the pamphlet. My opinions on these subjects are before the public, and therefore I shall only now say that I think it an error to suppose that the price of corn is regulated by supply and demand, only, without reference to the cost of producing it.

In manufacturing goods and exporting them for corn, the cost of that corn is the cost of production of the goods, and if by restricting the importation of corn we, instead of making the goods, raise the corn at home, the only loss we sustain is the greater cost of producing it. From the tenor of your pamphlet I should think you estimated the loss much higher, and attributed the high price of corn to the diminished quantity and not to the greater difficulty of producing it.

---

[1] British Museum, Add. MSS., Autograph Letters of Sheridan, &c, 29,764, f. 44. Franked by himself. The last sheet is used as the cover, addressed, 'John Wheatley, Esq., Shrewsbury,' and dated 'Minchinhampton, September Eighteen, 1821.'

[2] The pamphlet referred to is doubtless vol. ii of Wheatley's 'Essay on the Theory of Money and Principles of Commerce.' The title-page is dated 1822, and probably advance sheets were sent to Ricardo. The first volume of Wheatley's interesting though neglected work appeared in 1807.

On the question of the currency, your calculations would lead us to infer that the nation had been great losers by restoring it to a fixed and increased value:—now I will agree that in some cases such a measure might be very unjust, but I do not see how it can affect the interests of a country as a whole. You say that the *farmers and manufacturers* have lost £230,000,000 millions [1] a year by the reduction of prices [2]. I ask has no one gained these £230,000,000? and if you say some have, I again ask who have, if they be not *farmers and manufacturers*? You will not say that the stockholder has gained this immense sum, for the whole of his annual interest amounts only to £29,000,000,—you will not say that the stockholders and public officers together have gained it, for the whole public revenue of the country from which they are paid amounts only to £54,000,000—the fact is that some manufacturers, and some farmers, have been gainers, and others losers, as always is the case when the currency is tampered with—the only injury which these classes have sustained, as classes, is the real increase of taxation, which may probably amount to 5 or 6 millions pr. ann. on the depreciation of 1813.

I perceive that you rather misconceive my opinions on this question—I never should advise a government to restore a currency, which was depreciated 30 p.c., to par; I should recommend, as you propose, but not in the same manner, that the currency should be fixed at the depreciated value by [lowerin]g the standard, and that no further deviations should [take] place. It was without any legislation that the cu[rrency] from 1813 to 1819 became an increased value, and within 5 p.c. of the value of gold,—it was in this state of things, and not with a currency depreciated

---

[1] So in the original, by an evident oversight.
[2] 'Essay on the Theory of Money and Principles of Commerce,' vol. ii. p. 128 (a reference kindly supplied by Professor H. S. Foxwell).

30 p.c., that I advised a recurrence to the old standard. The advice might have been bad, and the measure unwise, but in judging of it, injustice would be done to me, and those who agreed with me, by referring to a state of things, which had ceased to exist, for more than 4 years.

I am Sir
Your obed. Serv.
DAVID RICARDO.

L[1].

MY DEAR TROWER

BROMESBERROW PLACE, LEDBURY
4 *Octr.*, 1821

I was much pleased to find by your last letter, that you thought well of the information contained in the minutes of Evidence, which accompanied our Report from the Agricultural Committee, and that in your criticisms on the evidence of the different individuals called before the committee, your opinion coincides so nearly with my own. The only part of Mr. Tooke's evidence in which I cannot agree with him, is that in which he says, that if the trade in Corn were left perfectly free, the growers of corn in the United Kingdom would be able to compete with the corn growers of other countries, meaning thereby, as he explained himself, there would be as much probability of our exporting corn to other countries, on an average of years, as of importing it from those countries [2]. This I do not believe—our manufacturing superiority—our greater riches—our dense population, all have a tendency to make us importers of corn, and although the quantity we should import would be only a few weeks['] consumption, yet I think we should be habitually and constantly an importing

---

[1] Franked by himself; cover dated 'Ledbury, October Four, 1821,' and addressed, 'Hutches Trower, Esq., Unsted Wood, Godalming, Surrey.'

[2] Cf. 'Minutes of Evidence,' pp. 288, 289.

country. In the Committee the great holders of land went to the other extreme of Mr. Tooke's opinion, they thought that with a free trade in Corn we should import almost all our corn, and in that case they asked what was to become of the aristocracy—if they were ruined, they wanted to know what class in the community would perform the important services which they rendered as magistrates, grand jurors, &c., &c. If indeed all our land was to go out of cultivation, as these alarmists anticipated, then the question of importation would be a serious one indeed, and we should be obliged to give due consideration to the important political consequences which might result from it. Mr. Jacob[']s facts [1] are interesting, but on the scientific part of the subject I thought him quite wild, and persevered in my questions to him till I believe he thought me rude. I knew by his publications [2] that he had taken a very prejudiced and unskilful view of the subject.

On the subject of 'Real value' and 'Exchangeable value' you ask why should not these two ideas be kept perfectly distinct, and be expressed by distinct terms? Why indeed should they not? I reply, but I ask in my turn whether they are not kept distinct by prefixing the word 'real' to one, and 'exchangeable' to the other?

I have neither seen Torrens' publication [3], nor Lord

[1] Probably in support of the statement that, 'none of the countries from which England derives supplies of corn, were able to export much more than three days of their own consumption.' See 'Minutes of Evidence,' 1821, 368 et seq.; cf. 355.

[2] William Jacob, F.R.S., of Chelsham Lodge, Surrey, had written: Considerations on the Protection required by British Agriculture and on the influence of the price of corn on exportable productions (1814). A Letter to Samuel Whitbread, Esq., M.P. [on the same subject, with remarks on West, Ricardo, and Torrens] (1815). See Cannan, 'Production and Distribution' (1893), p. 320.

[3] 'An Essay on the Production of Wealth; with an Appendix, in which the Principles of Political Economy are applied to the Actual Circumstances of this Country.' London, 1820. The promised 'Appendix' was never published.

Stourton's letter to Lord Liverpool[1]. Of the last I have heard nothing, but of Torrens' book I have heard a favorable account from Malthus—he says it is well and clearly written, and on the whole he thinks it makes as much for his (Malthus's) view of the question, as for mine. I do not know why Mill's book does not appear, I believe he has finished it[2].

I, as well as you, would like to seé an application of the Principles of Political Economy, as now understood, to the practical operation of taxation, and I hope it will not be long before such a work appears. Ministers will always look more to the facility with which they can raise money by a tax, and the produce they can obtain from it, than to its consequences on the prosperity and future resources of the country (witness the legacy duty); this however is no argument against the general dissemination of good doctrines, for if a minister was not restrained by an honest legislature, he would receive no inconsiderable check from an enlightened public. You make a great mistake in supposing me capable of producing so important a work.

About Gatcomb, we have not lost a great deal of corn from the badness of the weather, though it has suffered some damage, but I hear great complaints made by the farmers in the part of the country where I am now writing —their crops are entirely spoiled.

The proceedings of the Coroner's Inquest on the late affray at the Queen's funeral[3] have a better chance than

---

[1] In the British Museum, 1027. b. 22 (10) is a tract of Stourton's: 'Two Letters to the Right Hon. the Earl of Liverpool . . . on the Distresses of Agriculture . . . with Observations on Cash Payments and a Free Trade.' Second edition, with additions. London, 1821. In the following year, a third letter was written, and the work republished as 'A New Edition, with Additions,' with the title 'Three Letters.' &c. It states that the 'First Letter' was published in the summer of 1820.

[2] See above, p. 147, and below, 173.

[3] During the funeral procession, on 14th August, 1821, the troops fired on the mob, and two men (Honey and Francis) were killed. See Hansard,

ever of being made the subject of discussion in Parliament, since they have ended in the dismissal of Sir R. Wilson from the army. According to what we at present know, I think he has been very harshly used [1].

I cannot agree with you that in the investment of one's money it is necessary to take a much more limited view than what would include the probable variation of half a century. Although *we* shall not be alive then, our children or our children's children will, and in investments of money we never fail to estimate a future and contingent benefit at its just value, accordingly as it may be near or distant. In comparing the purchases of land and of tithes it is quite right to estimate the advantages of the former, in the shape of influence, enjoyment and amusement at its just value; but the objection you make, that in buying tithes you only make the common rate of interest and you would have made as much if you had employed the same amount of capital in improving your land, or else you would not so employ it, is not a good one, and entirely changes the question in dispute.

What we were discussing was whether it would be more advantageous to buy land, or buy tithes; but the proposition as stated by you would be, whether it was more advantageous to employ a capital in improving land, or in buying tithes. I have no doubt that in an improving country the

---

N. S. vi, March 6, 1822; Cobbett, Weekly Register, 1821, p. 289 seq., 534 seq. The straight road between Hammersmith and Harwich, where the body was to be shipped for Brunswick, would have taken the procession through the heart of the City. By diverting it to the north to avoid the City, the Government excited the wrath of the people, who, by barricades of waggons and stones, forced the procession back into the direct route through the City to Whitechapel and Mile End. Cobbett deals with the dismissal of Wilson, ib., 890, 942, 1059, 1131. Cf. Brougham, 'Life and Times,' written by himself, vol. ii. 425 seq., and (as to Wilson) 439.

[1] The debate on his removal took place on 13th Feb., 1822. See Hansard, *sub dato*. He was dismissed from the army as having, when present in a private capacity, interfered with the soldiers in the discharge of their duty.

latter would be most advantageous but it is essentially a different question from that which we were before discussing—if you buy land you have no capital with which to improve land, you obtain only the rent and that rent will improve in proportion as it becomes the interest of your tenant to expend a greater capital on that land, even although he should not in the least improve it. By such expenditure he may derive more from it, and of that increased quantity he may be constrained to give you a portion—you will have a larger portion, and each portion will be of a greater value, but I contend the tithe holder will be still better off—his proportion of the whole produce will be as before—he will not only have a larger portion, but the same proportion [;] the landlord[']s *proportion* of the whole produce will be probably diminished.

Sydney Smith and his family passed a couple of days with me on their way from Taunton to York [1]. He was in his usual good spirits and we were sorry to lose him so soon. His articles in the Edin. Review on Spring Guns, and Prisons, are I think both very good [2]—he is a good reasoner, and has much the best of the argument with the Judges. I like the article on Godwin[']s book, I have not heard who the writer is but I have no doubt whatever that it was written by Malthus himself [3]. His doctrines are very fairly vindicated against the calumny by which they are usually assailed, and I think the principles themselves most successfully established. In Malthus[']

---

[1] 'I have travelled all across the country with my family to see my father, now 82 years of age.' Letter of Syd. Smith to Jeffrey, written from Taunton, 7th August, 1821. Memoir &c. by Lady Holland, ii. 217. He was back at Foston, his Yorkshire parsonage, by 16th Sept. (ib. 219).

[2] Edinburgh Review, July, 1821 (No. LXX), Art. ii and viii.

[3] Edinburgh Review, July, 1821 (No. LXX). See Letters to Malthus, pp. 198, 206: 'I have mentioned my suspicions respecting the writer of the article on population in the Edinburgh Review to several persons. I will not utter them from this time.'

book there is much attackable matter, but he is very unfairly used by his antagonists, and his leading principle is studiously kept out of view.

I am passing a few days with my son, who is living in a fertile and beautiful country. A walk of ten minutes takes one to the summit of the first and lowest of the Malvern Hills from whence there is an extensive prospect, and a good view of Eastnor Castle (Lord Somers') and Park. I dare say you know the country.

Mrs. Ricardo unites with me in compliments to Mrs. Trower.
    Believe me
      My dear Trower,
        Ever truly yours
          DAVID RICARDO.

Sydney Smith when a youth lived in this very spot[1].

LI[2].

BROMESBERROW PLACE
11 Decr. 1821.

MY DEAR TROWER

It appears to be your fate to receive letters from me dated from this place. I intended writing to you before I left home, but I had various things to do which obliged me to defer it till this moment. I came here on Wednesday last on my way to Hereford, to which place I was invited, by the admirers of Mr. Hume, to attend a public dinner, which they meant to give him in that town, on the occasion of presenting him with a hogshead of Cider, and

---

[1] The Memoir by Lady Holland is silent on this sojourn.
[2] Addressed and franked on back :—

    Gloucester December Twelve 1821
     Hutches Trower Esq[re]
        Unsted Wood
         Godalming
  David Ricardo

a silver tankard, which had been purchased from a fund created by subscriptions of one shilling. I went to Hereford on friday, and soon after my arrival there, saw my friend Hume arrive in a carriage drawn by the people, and preceded by a great number of horsemen and banners. The whole population of the town appeared to be in the streets, and the windows were crowded with women. He was greeted with that portion of noisy acclamations which is usually bestowed on popular favorites. In a moment he was in the balcony of the Inn, next to a window which I occupied, and from thence made a long speech to the gentlemen in the street which was constantly interrupted with cheering. At 3 o'Clock we sat down to dinner. Our number was 250 mostly consisting, I should think, of farmers and trades-men; perhaps there were about 50 of the higher class of gentlemen of fortune in the neighbourhood. After dinner we had plenty of speaking—Hume performed for an hour and a half, the rest who were called upon, of which number I was one, spoke for a very moderate time[1]. The day went off well and a large party of us went, as was previously agreed on, to Mr. Price[']s, the member for the County (whose father is the author of a work on the Picturesque)[2] where we were handsomely entertained for 2 days.

Hume as you may believe is highly gratified. He was to be yesterday at Monmouth, and he will to day join me here, and return with me to Gatcomb. You will call all these proceedings by the name of 'Radical,' but I believe they are calculated to do much good—to increase the

[1] See Letters to Malthus, p. 208, but especially Letters to McCulloch, pp. 122-125.
[2] Sir Uvedale Price, of whom Sir Walter Scott wrote that 'he had converted the age to his views.' The work here mentioned, 'An Essay on the Picturesque, as compared with the Sublime and the Beautiful, and on the use of studying Pictures for the purpose of improving real Landscape,' first appeared in 1794; it was translated into German at Leipsic in 1798.

interest of the people in the affairs of government, and to make them better judges of what constitutes good and what bad government — at the same time this will be useful to our governors, and incline them to economy and forbearance.

Your remarks on the article in the Quarterly Review, on the Agricultural Report, appear to me to be very just [1]. I am glad I have got so good an ally, for what I think the correct principles, and you must partake of the pleasure which I feel in observing that they are every day making way. Mrs. Marcet's last edition is a very improved one,— in it she recognizes much of which her former editions did not speak at all, or of which they spoke doubtingly [2]. The Champion has given a series of papers on Rent, Wages, Taxes, &c. &c. all of which appear to me sound [3]. Mill has just published his book too in which all the good doctrines are advocated. So that we ought to be satisfied with the progress we are making. In the country I find much error prevailing on the subject of the currency, every ill which befals the country is by some ascribed to Peel's Bill, and Peel's Bill is as invariably ascribed to me. The whole fall in the value of corn and cattle is by such persons said to be merely nominal, these things they say have not in fact fallen, it is money which has risen, — they will not hear of a variation in the value of money of 10 pc. which I am very willing to allow them, nor will they listen to my defence of myself against their unjust accusation. I proposed a scheme by the adoption of which there

---

[1] Quarterly Review, July, 1821 (No. L), art. ix. Nominally a review of the 'Report on Agricultural Depression,' and of Sir Edward West's 'Essay on the Application of Capital to Land.'

[2] 'Conversations on Political Economy, in which the Elements of that Science are familiarly Explained.' Fourth edition. London, 1821.

[3] 'The Champion: Weekly Review of Politics and Political Economy.' The head-piece of the paper was a printing-press with Horne Tooke's sentence as a motto: 'The liberty of the Press is like the air we breathe, when we have it not—we die.' Cf. Letters to Malthus, p. 208.

would not have been a demand for one ounce of gold, either on the part of the Bank, or of any one else, and another is adopted by which both the Bank and individuals are obliged to demand a great quantity of gold and I am held responsible for the consequences [1]. If I had been a bank director, and had had the management of this currency question, I maintain that I could have reverted to a metallic standard by raising money (only) 5 pc., I do not say that having a metallic standard I could protect it from the usual fluctuations to which standards have at all times been subject. Cobbet[t] says [2] I am little better than a fool in speaking of gold as a standard, that the only fair standard is corn. He shews his ignorance in saying so, but supposing it true, can he tell me what is to secure us from variations in his standard,—it would perhaps be more variable than any other. But it is useless to say all this to you who know it so well.

Hume says Ministers cannot make out anything of a case against Sir Rob. Wilson [3], that they thought they had a case against him, but that they were wholly deceived by false statements.

What think you of the late changes in the Administration? [4] Is not Peel very much elevated? Do his talents entitle him to fill so prominent a situation? Will things be arranged finally without some provision being made for Canning? He is a formidable opponent, but I suppose he cannot under any circumstances fairly come over to our side.

---

[1] Cf. Letters to McCulloch, pp. 118-121 (xxix, 3rd Jan., 1822), which go more fully into the matter.

[2] 'To refer to the market price of gold as a standard is exactly what the Oracle did.' 'This queer, this 'Change Alley, this Jew-like notion of the price of gold being the standard.' Cobbett, Weekly Register, Oct. 20, 1821, pp. 925, 926. Ricardo goes a little beyond the words of Cobbett when he passes judgment on him.

[3] See preceding letter.

[4] Robinson in place of Vansittart; Peel in place of Sidmouth.

There will be many interesting questions brought before Parliament next Session. Economy and Retrenchment will be a standing dish. We shall have the question of the Corn Laws, the disturbance in Ireland—Sir Rob. Wilson's case—the criminal law and many others—I like business.

Pray give my kind remembrances to Mrs. Trower, and believe me ever my dear Trower

yrs truly

DAVID RICARDO.

LII [1].

GATCOMB PARK
25 *Jany* 1822

MY DEAR TROWER

This day week I shall leave Gatcomb for London, and shall soon after enter with all my energies on my parliamentary duties. I expect that the Agricultural question will occupy a great deal of attention, and I am not without my fears that some injudicious measures may be adopted, in consequence of the general prevalence of error on that important subject. I have read with attention all that has been said at the different meetings, and although I think I see a decided improvement in the public mind on the policy of corn laws, yet it appears to me that very few take a rational and scientific view of the origin of the distress, and of the true means of remedying it. They all concur in attributing the want of a remunerating price to enormous taxation, in which opinion I cannot agree; although I am willing to allow that an immediate repeal of some of the taxes which affect agricultural produce, would materially relieve the farmer. There is an interval between

---

[1] Franked by himself; dated, 'Minchinhampton, January Twenty-four, 1822,' and addressed, 'Hutches Trower, Esq., Unsted Wood, Godalming, Surrey.'

the repeal of a tax which falls indirectly on a commodity, and the fall of the price of such commodity, that is favorable to the producer, and the benefit of this interval would be enjoyed by farmers. It might, if the distress is owing to temporary causes, be sufficiently long to enable them to surmount the difficulty which immediately presses upon them, it would however be quite unscientific therefore to say that it was the burthen of taxation which was the cause of the low price of corn. The cause of the low price is nothing else but the supply exceeding the demand. Why it should do so now, and why it should have done so for two years back is an interesting enquiry, and many may have their different theories to account for it. When I say the cause of the low price is nothing else than the supply exceeding the demand, I am not quite correct, for I appear to exclude the alteration in the value of the currency as one of the causes, which I am not desirous of doing. To that cause I ascribe an effect of 10 pc. and in so doing I am making a liberal allowance. I perceive that a meeting of your county is called to consider this subject—I hope you will do what you are so well able to do, express your own correct views on this most important question, and not let the reveries of a Webb Hall[1], and the exaggerated, and often wicked, statements of a Cobbett[2], pass every where uncontradicted[3]. I shall look to the public papers with great interest for a full and correct account of your speech.

I agree with much of what you say about Ireland, but on some points we differ. I think it desirable that small farms, and small tenancies, should be got rid of, but I do not look upon these, and many other things which might

---

[1] Of Sneed Park, Gloucester. See Ricardo's 'Protection to Agriculture,' Works, p. 479, and 'Agricultural Comm., Evidence,' 1821, pp. 163-175.
[2] Cf. Letters to McCulloch, p. 119, note 2.
[3] In place of 'unrefuted,' struck out.

be advantageously corrected in Ireland, as the cause of the evils under which that unfortunate country groans, but as the effect of those evils. If Ireland had a good system of law—if property was secure—if an Englishman lending money to an Irishman could by some easy process oblige him to fulfil his contract, and not be set at defiance by the chicanery of sheriff[']s agents in Ireland, capital would flow into Ireland, and an accumulation of capital would lead to all the beneficial results which every where follows [*sic*] from it. The most economical processes would be adopted—small farms would be laid into large—there would be an abundant demand for labour, and thus would Ireland take her just rank among nations. The evils of Ireland, I, in my conscience believe, arise from misrule, and I hope that during the administration of Lord Wellesley a commencement will be made in the reformation of the enormous abuses under which that country labours. Hume I believe means to attack the Tithe System of Ireland in the House of Commons. I do not know whether he is sufficiently skilful to meddle with so intricate a subject advantageously, but he will not fail I think to do some good. The oftener that abuses of all kinds are stated and discussed the better; it sets able heads to work, and the people become informed as to their real interests. This reacts on the Government, and thus abuses, even on our present imperfect system, are often finally redressed.

You will have received Mill's article on Government, which I sent you many days ago.—You will not approve of it, but I think it an excellent article, and well reasoned throughout. Since writing that article he has written two others for the Supplement to the Encyclopedia, which are I think both very good—one is on Jurisprudence, the other on the Liberty of the Press. If you cannot conveniently get the Encyclopedia, I can lend you the articles, as I have one copy of each in London, and I think you will like to read them¹.

I am not a good judge of his book on Political Economy, I have thought so much on the subject myself, that I can form a very inadequate idea of the impression which his work is calculated to make on one who is a learner, but I am told by learners that it is very clear, and fully accomplishes the object which he professes to have in view.

I received some months ago a letter from M[.] Say in answer to my last observations on his book, to which I intend very shortly to send him my reply. You will probably like to see both his letter and my answer—I will shew them to you when I see you in London².

The reviews of Godwin's work both in the Quarterly and Edinburgh were I think very good;—surely in the minds of all reasonable men the principle for which Malthus contends is fully established.

I continue to hear, from time to time, from Mr. M'Culloch; he is a zealous advocate for the correct principles of Polit. Economy and is more actively employed in their dissemination than any individual I know. Besides the excellent articles which he wrote in the Supp^t to the Encyclopedia, in the Edinburgh Review, and the Scotsman, he gives lectures on Polit. Economy in Edinburgh, and contemplates the extending them next year to a general instead of a private class—this is as it should be, notwithstanding the wise observations of Lord John Russell on the

---

[1] 'Supplement to the Fourth, Fifth, and Sixth Editions of the Encyclopaedia Britannica,' 6 vols. (Edinburgh, 1815 1824). For Mill's other contributions to the 'Supplement,' see Bain, 'James Mill,' pp. 215 259. The more important articles were reprinted for private circulation, as intimated above, ibid., p. 191.

[2] See 'Mélanges et Correspondance d'Économie Politique : Ouvrage posthume de J.-B. Say ; publié par Charles Comte' (Paris, 1833), pp. 112-130. Both letters and reply are summarized in Letters to Malthus, pp. 182, 183, 209.

little advantages to be derived from a knowledge of this science, in his letter to the Electors of Huntingdon [1].

Mrs. Ricardo joins with me in kind remembrances to Mrs. Trower. Believe me, My dear Trower

Ever most truly yours,

DAVID RICARDO.

I hope we shall see you very soon in London.

LIII [2].

[To SIR J. SINCLAIR]

DEAR SIR,   GATCOMB PARK, MINCHIN-HAMPTON, 29th January, 1822

You are fully aware that you and I do not agree in our opinion of the causes of the present agricultural distress, nor in our views of the remedies which it would be expedient to apply to it. We agree still less on the disadvantage which you suppose to have resulted to the importer of corn, from the increased value of the currency. The question you put to Mr. Attwood is not a fair one; for the same cause which would elevate the exchange from 18 to 25, would lower corn from 40/ to 28/9 *per* quarter, and it would be a matter of indifference to the foreign exporter of corn to England if he sold it at 40/, and negociated his bill at 18 francs *per* pound Sterling, or sold it at 28/9, and negociated his bill at 25 francs. Is it not a fallacy to suppose money so to rise in value that gold should appear to fall from £5:10/ to £3:17:10½, the exchange rise from 18 to 25, and yet suppose wheat to remain steadily at 40/ *per* quarter?

I remain, Dear Sir, your faithful and obedient servant,

DAVID RICARDO.

---

[1] In the letter (dated from Woburn Abbey, 14th Jan. 1822) he speaks of 'a party among us distinguished in what is called the *science* of Political Economy' as wishing to 'substitute the corn of Poland and Russia for our own,' to the ruin of our farmers. See Morning Chronicle 18th Jan. 1822 and Cobbett, Weekly Register, Feb. 2, 1822, pp. 274, 287.

[2] Sinclair's 'Correspondence,' i. 375.

LIV[1].

20 Feb. 1822
My dear Trower   London

I thank you for the account you have given me of your proceedings at the County meeting[2]. I was sorry to find, before I received your letter, that your speech had been cut short by the impatience and clamor of your audience. I wish you had not ventured on the delicate topic of the repeal of taxes having been the cause of Agricultural distress, for if that doctrine be true, which I very much doubt, it was one which could not be successfully handled in such an assembly. They would not perhaps have been more civil to you if you had supported the less unpalatable doctrine of which I profess myself to be the advocate, that taxation is not the cause of Agricultural distress, and that a repeal of taxes will lighten the burthens of all, but will not afford particular relief to the Agricultural class.—

This doctrine I was advancing in the H. of Commons on the same day you had been speaking at Epsom, and as I had a more polite, and a less numerous audience, the expression of my opinions was listened to with patience and attention[3]. I flatter myself that in the progress of the debates on this subject many will be found to advocate the same doctrines.—I wish that the Table[4] you gave the

[1] Franked by himself; dated, 'London, February Twenty, 1822,' and addressed, 'Hutches Trower, Esq., Unsted Wood, Godalming.'
[2] See Note following this Letter.
[3] February 18, 1822, on the Marquis of Londonderry's motion for the appointment of a new Agricultural Committee, to consider further petitions on agricultural distress, and the report of the earlier Committee. Ricardo attacked the Sinking Fund, argued that taxation was not responsible for the prevailing depression, and vindicated his estimate of a five per cent. fall in prices, resulting from the resumption of specie payments. See Hansard, Parliamentary Debates, vol. vi. (N. S.) 479.
[4] Statistics of quantities and prices of grain, &c. after harvest, for 1820-1, and 1821-2. They are unfortunately not complete in the MSS. The letter given below (note, p. 178) has a bearing on the matter.

reporters may be published—if it is not, send it to me, and I will endeavor to get it into some of the papers. Every thing which tends to shew the excessive quantity at market, whether of corn, of cattle, or of sheep, will be highly useful towards the establishing of correct notions on this important subject. Cobbett and his followers contend that the alteration in the value of money has been of inestimable advantage to the working classes[1], they contend therefore that it has increased the demand for provisions, and yet he as well as others give us constant accounts of the quantities of corn remaining at market unsold, and of cattle and sheep penned at fairs for which there is no adequate demand—can we have a stronger proof of increased supply? An alteration in the value of money is a sufficient reason for an altered price of commodities, but it can have no effect on quantity. If it plunges the farmer and landlord into distress, why are the other classes of producers exempted from its effects? Is not taxation from the same cause increased to the merchant, the manufacturer, &c., &c.? Never was there a greater fallacy than that of ascribing the present distress either to taxation, or to the altered value of money[2]. Cobbett is a mischievous scoundrel[3]; he ascribes the evils

[1] This is hardly Cobbett's position. He contends that 'a paper system is never prosperity. There has been an *appearance* of it; and the return to cash payments intensifies distress' e.g. Weekly Register, 1820. pp. 706, 737); but he says, 'Peel's Bill ought not to be repealed. I was half dead with fear when it was a matter of doubt' (Weekly Register, 27th Oct., 1821, p. 970). It would be no easy task to prove Cobbett consistent throughout; but Ricardo, wincing a little under Cobbett's rudeness, seems unwilling to allow that he is ever in the right.

[2] These views were developed in Ricardo's tract, 'On Protection to Agriculture' (8vo., London, 1822, in 'Works,' ed. McCulloch, pp. 455-498), published two months later (Letters to McCulloch, p. 133). McCulloch stated that the tract was written because Ricardo did not choose 'to have his opinions identified with those of the Report'; he added, 'Had Mr. Ricardo never written anything else, this pamphlet would have placed him in the very first rank of political economists' ('Literature of Political Economy,' p. 78).

[3] The genial Sydney Smith calls Cobbett 'that consummate villain'—

under which the country is laboring to the altered value of money, and yet recommends the people to hoard gold[1], which he knows will increase the value of money still more. It is confusion he wants, and he cares not what means he takes to produce it. But in spite of him the country will get over its difficulties, and when it is again prosperous he will have the insolence to say that he foretold it.—

What say you to Brougham's speech[2]? What a falling off was there! I have not heard for a long time from any man who pretends to know anything of Political Economy so many absurd opinions as were delivered by him on Monday sen'night,—they will be a standing dish for the remainder of the Session.—

    Believe me ever
      Most truly yrs
        DAVID RICARDO.

NOTE (1).—A detailed account of the meeting of the freeholders of the county of Surrey, held at Epsom on February 18, 1822, and mentioned above, is contained in 'The Times' of February 19, 1822. The purpose of the meeting was 'to take the sense of the county upon the propriety of petitioning Parliament for a reduction of taxation, and a reform in the representation of the people in the Common[s] House.' In the course of the meeting, ' Mr. Trower expressed his regret that the important questions of agricultural distress and parliamentary reform had been mixed up together on the present occasion. It was not so much to Mr. Peel's bill, as to that lamentable corn bill which was passed in 1815 that the present low prices of agricultural products were to be attributed. In saying this he did not intend to advocate the fooleries of Mr. Webb Hall. He thought that much of the present agricultural distress was attributable to the late abundant harvests. The hon. gentleman proceeded in this position at some length amidst general outcries from the meeting; in the midst of it he was interrupted by some

adding, 'he is still a great deal read.' (See the letter dated 12th January, 1819, in the Memoir by Lady Holland, ii. 168.)
 [1] See below, 182.   [2] See Note (3).

person asking him whether he thought taxation to be among the probable causes of the distress now existing among the farmers. Upon his answering that the farmers had suffered most from the taxes that had been taken off, so great a confusion was created in the multitude, that the speaker found it impossible to proceed. Having made two or three ineffectual attempts to obtain a farther hearing, he gave way to Mr. Grey Bennet, who stated that he was not surprised that the startling proposition of Mr. Trower, that the country was too little taxed, had caused the commotion which had just taken place. After ridiculing the strange sophistry which could have led a gentleman of his sound understanding to patronize such a delusive statement, Mr. Bennet,' &c.

NOTE (2).—The following letter is among the Trower MSS. :—

London, 15: feby. 1822.
MY DEAR SIR,

I take the earliest opportunity of handing you a statement, which will I believe, answer your Enquiry and which shews that the low Price of Wheat is in some degree occasioned by a surplus quantity received last quarter, and which I take to be the consequence of the superabundant harvest of 1820—of which we still feel the Effects—

The returns are published weekly and quarterly—at 4.4. P.an. [sic]. Those that we take are for friends in the Country, but our Clerk keeps a Copy of them—which for the last week or two having been ill, he has neglected—but which we can easily get a friend to supply us with—therefore if you wish any further Information, I beg you will not hesitate to ask for it at this or any future time—there is no Account kept of Corn coming from the Western Counties by the Thames or by Canals—last year the quantity of Wheat and Barley brought thence was considerable, this season the Western Counties send us none, but require occasional supplies from hence—In the autumn of 1819, Barley was sent into Hertfordshire from hence—

An Account of Corn Imported into the Port of London (including Foreign).

From Sepr 27th 1819 to Jan. 1st 1820

	Wheat	Barley	Oats	Beans		Flour
qrs.	150,712	111,907	208,256	22,164	sacks	128,269

From Oct. 2ᵈ 1820 to Decʳ 30 1820

	Wheat	Barley	Oats	Beans		Flour
[qrs.]	145,858	71,882	342,862	28,594	[sacks]	107,417
[1820-21?]	188,378	78,970	221,776	31,635		130,761

qrs

Malt about 50,000 ⎱ in each of the above Quarters with
and Peas — 22,000 ⎰ scarcely any Variation.
This season, the Hertfordshire farmers can almost supply our Distillers, so abundant is their crop of Barley—You will see by these Instances that the supplies by shipping are regulated in some degree by the probable Demand or superabundance of the inland Counties—

I remain

my dear Sir

Yours very truly

JOHN GRENSIDE[1].

NOTE (3).—On Monday, Feb. 11th, 1822, Brougham concluded a long speech on the 'Distressed State of the Country' by moving 'That it is the bounden duty of this House, well-considering the pressure of Public Burthens upon all, but especially the Agricultural Classes, to obtain for the suffering People of these Realms such a reduction of the taxes as may be suited to the change in the value of money, and may afford an immediate relief to the distresses of the Country.' (Hansard, Parl. Deb., New Series, vi. 220-259).

The motion was lost by 104 votes (108 for, 212 against). Ricardo voted in favour of the motion but made a speech against the arguments of the mover. Taxation, he said, was not the cause of the present agricultural distress. A country might be without taxes and yet in the same distress as England at present. The restoration of the currency had not made so great a change in its value as was thought. The change was not 50 per cent. and if Peel's Act had been judiciously managed might only have been 5. His honourable and learned friend had proved too much when he

---

[1] Probably of the firm of Grenside and King, Corn Factors, 26, Mark Lane. Cover addressed to 'Hutches Trower Esq., Unsted Wood, Godalming, Surry.'

said that manufacturers could defeat taxation by raising prices; if they could do so, so could the agriculturists. The cause of distress was really the abundance of produce, through the late good harvest, the quantity of land lately brought into cultivation, the importations from Ireland, and other causes. The remedy would be that much land would be thrown out of tillage. It was unfair, too, to suppose any of us were anxious to transfer the land to the stockholders, though it would as a matter of fact be advisable for the landholder to part with a portion of his property to the stockholder in liquidation of the debt, and indeed a portion did in a sense belong to the stockholder at that moment as a receiver of interest.

Brougham in reply defended the statement about manufacturers;—the tax on leather keeps the large manufacturer free from the competition of smaller men, but there are no agriculturists with capitals so large that they can drive out the small capitalists.

LV[1].

My Dear Trower   London 5 *March* 1822

I have not been able to examine your plan of paying off a considerable portion of debt[2], by allowing persons to compound for their assessed taxes; but on a cursory view I should conclude that it contained some fallacy which would be detected on a close examination. You propose to allow at the rate of 5 pc: to those who purchase their life interest in the assessed taxes, and the money obtained is to be employed at 4 pc. in paying off debt. You do not add to the whole burden of taxation, and yet with the disadvantage I have stated you think the debt will be much more diminished on your plan, than if the present mode be persevered in. I might possibly agree that yours was the safest plan because it left little or nothing in the power of ministers, but it is impossible, I should think, to be so economical as the one now in operation. One error is immediately observable; you suppose that a 5 million

[1] Cover wanting.   [2] See Note.

sinking fund will only pay off 60 millions in 12 years, but you forget that it operates at compound interest, and therefore that its effect will be very greatly increased. Perhaps I may be wrong, and if I am you will be kind to set me right.

Sir H. Parnell[1] mentioned a plan to me which would have the effect of making the sinking fund available, and at the same time of placing it out of the grasp of ministers. It is as follows: Employ your 5 millions in making your perpetual annuities terminable ones, and you secure the object of extinguishing a large portion of debt in a period of short duration in the existence of a nation. Long ann^s are at 20 years purchase and 4 pr^{cts} are at 25 years purchase in the market. Give 5 millions p^r Ann to the holders of 500 millions of 4 pc^{ts} and they will agree to accept 25 million p^r Ann^m (instead of 20 million p^r Ann^m) on the condition that the interest should cease altogether in 1860, the period at which the Long Ann^y terminates. In 1860 then our debt would be reduced to 300 millions, and indeed might be altogether extinguished if in the meantime by a surplus of revenue a larger sum could be diverted to the above purpose. This will explain the principle: it might be desirable to extinguish a smaller sum in fewer years, by devoting the 5 millions to that purpose, or you might extinguish different amounts of debt at differently determinate periods—this you will easily understand.

I am glad you approved of the sentiments I expressed in my speech in Parliament[2]. It is a great disadvantage to me that the reporters not understanding the subject cannot

---

[1] See his speeches on the subject in 1823 (Hansard, viii. 536, 548), and his 'Financial Reform,' 1829. He was a member of the Agric. Comm. of 1821 and 1822.

[2] Probably the speech of February 18, 1822, noted above (p. 175). Just before writing the present letter, Ricardo had again spoken in the House on Agricultural Distress, and urged that the prevailing low prices were caused by excessive harvests. Hansard, Parliamentary Debates, vol. vi. (N. S.) 919.

readily follow me—they often represent me as uttering perfect nonsense.

The country circulation is I believe very much reduced, and I trust it is issued by bankers of character and property. I have not much fear of their being shaken by a return to specie payments. If Cobbett's recommendation [1] should again endanger the safety of the Bank of England in consequence of an extensive practice of hoarding sovereigns, which I by no means apprehend, it might become necessary to adopt the Ingot plan of payment once more [2]. I should however be very sorry if the present system were not persevered in as long as it was practicable. Cobbett's aim is mischief, but he will not be able to succeed in it, if the Bank manage their affairs with common discretion. The Directors are very ill calculated to regulate a currency situated as ours now is, and if there is anything to fear it is from their incapacity. I shall not fail to repeat my cautions to them from time to time when the subject comes under discussion.—Huskisson must have great influence in the situation which he fills, and he cannot fail to direct it usefully and scientifically.

I do not think that we shall examine evidence in the Agricultural Committee [3]. We have got rid, after a long discussion, of a proposal made by Mr. Banks to devote a million of the public money to the purchase of corn—we negatived it. Some more absurd proposals are before us, but they I trust will meet with the same fate. The present corn law will I think be repealed, and another less objectionable, but still a bad one, will be substituted in its place.

[1] E. g., Weekly Register, Nov. 17, 1821. 'To Money Hoarders,' p. 1188, 'There is absolutely no safety but in hoarding.' 'There is no risk in hoarding. Gold will not, cannot lose in value.'

[2] Ricardo's 'Economical and secure currency.'

[3] A few witnesses were examined (April 24 to May 6) on proposed alterations in the warehouse and distillery laws, and their evidence was appended to the Second Report, ordered by the House of Commons to be printed on May 20, 1822.

I have gained an important and powerful ally, in the Committee, by the nomination of Mr. Whitmore[1], who is a zealous advocate for the correct doctrines. On the other hand I have lost the assistance of Huskisson, who absents himself on the plea that Wodehouse made an attack on him in the House, but I think his real reason is that he cannot approve, and will not oppose, the plan recommended by the Government[2].

The House broke up early this evening, which has given me an opportunity of scribbling to you. My letter is a strange jumble, compounded much in the same manner as my speeches. You must treat me as the House of Commons does; try to make out what I mean and excuse the manner of my expressing my meaning.—

With kind regards to Mrs. Trower, in which I am joined by Mrs. Ricardo, I remain very truly Yours

DAVID RICARDO.

NOTE.—Hutches Trower's proposal as to the assessed taxes is set forth in one of his MSS. as follows:—

'Assessed Taxes, say £6,000,000, Suppose *life interest* in these Taxes to be purchased.

Calculation of Lives as follows—*for example*

From 20–30 years old—14 years' purchase ⎫
    30–40 ——— 13 do   ⎬ at
    40–50 ——— 12 do   ⎬ 5 p Ct
    50–60 ——— 11 do   ⎭

$$4 \,|\, \underline{50}$$
$$12\tfrac{1}{2}$$

---

[1] See Miss Martineau, 'History of the Peace,' Bk. II. ch. i. (Bohn's ed.), vol. i. p. 449.

[2] For an account of this Agricultural Committee and Ricardo's part in it, see Letters to McCulloch, pp. 130, 131. It had the same Chairman as the previous Committee (Thomas Sherlock Gooch), and was composed for the most part of the same persons. The names are given in Hansard, (N. S.) vol. vi, Feb. 1822, p. 509. Huskisson's name and that of Wodehouse both appear on the list.

and suppose the average 12 years' purchase. The value of the Assessed taxes would then be £72,000,000. Suppose this to be applied to the paying off of £4 p. C^t Stock at *par*.—It would redeem say £70,000,000. The annual interest upon this sum is £2,800,000, which would cease; but annual Taxes to the amount of £6,000,000 will have ceased; How then is the difference, vizt. £3,200,000 to be supplied? This deficiency can be taken out of the £5,000,000 surplus, appropriated to the purchase of the Debt.

In addition to the original purchase money, received at first, there would be coming in *annually*, a sum in further reduction of the Debt, arising from persons attaining to manhood, and others newly liable to the assessed Taxes. Thus a constant Fund would be established in aid of the discharge of the debt.

The Annuities being calculated at the rate of 5 *pC.* whilst the Current Interest is £4 pC. would make it worth while for the payers of Assessed Taxes to purchase out the Tax.

The *Principle* was adopted in the purchase of the Land Tax, and the recent practice of compounding for Assessed Taxes, for several years *certain*, seems to evince a disposition to accede to any arrangement that would fix that burthen upon reasonable terms.

The *Assessed Taxes* are fixed upon as the only Taxes, upon the *regular amount* of the payment of which any *certainty* can be ascertained.

Probably not more than a *moiety* would be purchased, at first: but if peace should continue, and the rate of interest should diminish, additional purchases would be made.—The value of the *Lives* purchasing would, of course, be accurately ascertained from the Annuity Tables. The purchase might be made in money, or in 4 p. C. Stock. It is difficult to say what may be the *average lives* of the larger portion of the payers of Assessed Taxes; but supposing them to be, generally, between the ages of *30 and 50*, the average purchase of the life interest would be about *12 years*, as it has been stated before in the first page. Supposing, then, the whole amount of the Assessed Taxes purchased at that rate, there would be, during those 12 years, an annual deficiency to supply, out of the £5,000,000 (set apart for the Sinking Fund) arising from the difference between the annual amount of the assessed Taxes redeemed, and the annual amount of interest on the Four p. C. Stock redeemed; but this difference would be annually diminishing, from the growing amount annually receiving from the new payers of Assessed Taxes, who either would redeem their interest in the Tax, or continue its annual payment. In the *former case* funds would be furnished for the further reduction of the Debt, with the assistance of the unappropriated portion of the £5,000,000; in the latter case these new assessed Taxes would be annually added to amount of Sinking Fund for purchase of Stock.

A purchase of Taxes upon these conditions appears to hold out sufficient inducement to the payers of these Taxes to redeem them. It would be a relief at the present period of distress; in as much as it would diminish the *annual expenditure* of the purchaser of his Taxes.

Suppose the annual amount of his Assessed Taxes to be £50; this, at 12 years' purchase, would cost £600, the interest of which at £4 pC. (the present rate of interest) is £24—whereas he would be relieved from the payment of an annual sum equal to the interest upon £1,250 (at the same rate of interest) vzt £50. It would be a *popular measure*, in as much as it would be bringing the £5,000,000 Sinking Fund in aid of the present distresses, to the extent of the difference between the annual amount of Assessed Taxes purchased, and the annual interest of the Four pC. Stock redeemed.'

LVI[1].

MY DEAR TROWER   LONDON 25 *March* 1822

I should very much like to accept your kind invitation to pass a few days with you during the short vacation of Parliament, but it will not be in my power. I have various engagements which I am bound to fulfil,

---

[1] Franked by himself; the last page is used as the cover, and addressed, 'Hutches Trower, Esq., Unsted Wood, Godalming,' with date of 'London, March Twenty-four, 1822.'

and which will render my absence from London very inconvenient. I very much regret being obliged to deny myself the pleasure which a visit to you would have given me.

I saw Mr. Mill yesterday and gave him your message. He requested me to say to you that his occupations at the India House will prevent him from being absent during the holidays. It is the period at which the election for Directors takes place, when there are frequent Court days which he is expected to attend. He desired to be kindly remembered to you.

I should be neglecting my duty if with my opinions of the Sinking Fund I did not do every thing in my power to get rid of it. Of what use can it be to diminish the debt in time of peace, if you leave in the hands of ministers a fund which experience shews will be used only for the purpose of ultimately further increasing the debt? While ministers have this fund virtually at their disposal they will on the slightest occasion be disposed for war. To keep them peaceable you must keep them poor.

The answer to every proposal for the adoption of good measures in the Agricultural Committee, is that the Agriculture of the country is in a state of unparall[el]ed distress, and that the Committee was appointed for the purpose of affording it relief. I had no idea of being able to do any good now, in the way of making better laws, but I hoped to lay the foundation of a better system in future. In that hope I shall probably be disappointed, for the regulations which you mention as too restrictive [1], are protested against most vehemently by the country gentlemen, who form themselves into a compact body determined to yield no point which has the least semblance to diminished protection. We meet today to hear

---

[1] Probably his 'Resolutions.' See Note to this letter. They certainly show that Ricardo was not averse to compromise.

Resolutions on the Corn Trade

the Report[1] read, which was to be prepared by our chairman.

I was obliged to withdraw my motion for the return of Corn sold in Mark Lane, because I was waited on by the officer to whom the order was directed to say that he had no means of complying with it. I then moved for a return of the corn imported into the Port of London, which has not yet been laid on the table of the House— I will send it to you when it is printed. The return which the officer told me could not be prepared has however been laid before [the] Committee[2], and if I can get a copy I will send it to you.

I know of no Poor Rate returns made to the House this Session, neither have I seen Mr. Chetwynd's Vagrant Bill[3]. I will enquire for them at the Vote Office this day, and if you do not receive them by the Post, you may conclude that they are not yet in the hands of members.

Mrs. Ricardo unites with me in kind remembrances to Mrs. Trower.

Ever Truly Y^{rs}

DAVID RICARDO.

Mr. Chetwynd's bill has been this moment left at my house—I send it by this day's post.

NOTE.—Among the Proposed Resolutions for Regulation of the Corn Trade, printed uniformly with the Report of the Select Committee on Agriculture, are Resolutions proposed by Ricardo, and dated 29th April, 1822 (paper 245) (a single sheet).

---

[1] First Report presented 1st April, 1822; Second Report, 20th May.
[2] See Appendix to Second Report of Select Committee (1822) on Petitions complaining of the Depressed State of Agriculture, p. 52. The return is dated 25th March.
[3] 'A Bill for consolidating into one Act, and amending the Laws relating to Rogues, Vagabonds, Vagrants, and idle and disorderly Persons,' presented in the House of Commons on March 20, 1822.

They are:—' 1. That it is expedient to provide that the Foreign Corn now under bond in the United Kingdom, may be taken out for home consumption, whenever the average price of Wheat, ascertained in the usual mode, shall exceed 65/ per quarter, upon the payment of the following duties; viz.

Wheat 15/	per quarter.
Rye, Pease and Beans . 9/6	per quarter.
Barley, Bear or Bigg . . 7/6	per quarter.
Oats 5/	per quarter.

2. That whenever the average price of Wheat, ascertained in the usual mode, shall exceed 70/ per quarter, the trade in Corn shall thenceforth be permanently free, but subject to the following Duties upon importation; viz.

Wheat 20/	per quarter.
Rye, Pease and Beans . 13/3	per quarter.
Barley, Bear or Bigg . . 10/	per quarter.
Oats 6 8	per quarter.

3. That at the expiration of one year from the time at which the above duties on Corn imported shall be in operation, they be reduced as follows; viz.

On Wheat 1	per quarter.
Rye, Pease and Beans . /8	per quarter.
Barley, Bear or Bigg . /6	per quarter.
Oats . . . . /4	per quarter.

4. That a like reduction of duties be made in every subsequent year, until the duty on the importation of

Wheat . . . . . be 10/	per quarter.
Rye, Pease and Beans 6/7	per quarter.
Barley, Bear or Bigg . 5/	per quarter.
Oats 3/4	per quarter.

At which Rates they shall thenceforth be fixed.

5. That a drawback or bounty be allowed on the exportation of Corn to Foreign countries,—

On Wheat 7/	per quarter.
Rye, Pease and Beans . 4/6	per quarter.
Barley, Bear or Bigg . . 3 6	per quarter.
Oats 2/4	per quarter.

And that such drawback or bounty, in like manner as the Importation duty, be fixed.'

The substance of these resolutions is given in a Note to the Letters to McCulloch, pp. 130, 131.

LVII [1].

My Dear Trower,   London 20 May 1822.

I will follow your advice and take care not to expose myself to the resentment of the Farmers when Parliament breaks up. If they knew their own interest well they would feel no resentment against me, because the measures which I have proposed would make their trade a much more secure one than it can be under the operation of the present, or of the amended, law. I believe it will be a good time at the end of the Session to put in execution a project which I have long entertained, of making a short tour with my family on the Continent. I shall probably go as far as Switzerland, and after an absence of a couple of months seek my own retirement in Gloucestershire. My constant attendance in the House, and the little anxiety which the part I have taken on the Corn question naturally has excited makes a little rest and recreation necessary—I think I shall enjoy my journey, and shall improve my health by it.

Mr. Huskisson and I did not exactly join our forces; he abandoned his resolutions in the Committee, and I adopted those of them which laid down the correct principles, and added to them my own practical measure, which I argued was more consonant with his principles than the one which he recommended. Lord Althorp proposed a permanent duty of 20/- on the importation of Wheat, and a permanent drawback of 18/- on the exportation of Wheat, which was supported by Brougham. On what principle either the proposer or supporter of such resolutions could

· Cover wanting.

proceed I know not, nor have either of them ventured to expound it to the House.

You, have no doubt seen Mr. Turner's Pamphlet[1]—he sent it to me with a very kind note, hoping he said that it was written in the fair spirit of criticism. On that score I have nothing to complain of, but he has failed to convince me of a single error in principle in the work which he attacks. Is it not strange that a writer in the present day should say that rent is a cause of high price and not the effect of it?

'The extra rents to the landlord are not the measure of the whole loss sustained by the public in consequence of the Corn law,' says M'Culloch[2], and to this doctrine you demur. I apprehend he means to say that the loss to the country is a real one. It must not be supposed that because the landlords get a high price, which is paid by the consumer, the whole inconvenience to the country is an improper and unjustifiable transfer of property—it is much more than this, the landlord does not gain what the consumer loses—there is a real diminution of production, and the real loss is to be measured by such diminution of production, without any regard to price or value.

---

[1] 'Considerations upon the Agriculture, Commerce, and Manufactures of the British Empire, with Observations on the Practical Effect of the Bill of the Right Hon. Robert Peel, for the Resumption of Cash Payments by the Bank of England'; and also upon the Pamphlet lately published by David Ricardo, Esq., entitled, 'Protection to Agriculture.' By Samuel Turner, Esq.. F.R.S. London, 1822.

[2] The reference is to McCulloch's article in the Edinburgh Review of February, 1822, on the Report of the Committee on Agricultural Distress, pp. 452-482. (For proof of his authorship, see 'Catalogue of Books the Property of a Political Economist' (edition of 1862), and 'Notes and Queries,' 5th Oct., 1878.) McCulloch contends that 'of every *five* millions drawn by them [the Corn Laws] from the pockets of the consumers, scarcely *one* finds its way into the pockets of the landlords! The other *four* are absolutely and totally lost to the country' (474). By forcing recourse to poor soils we increase the value of that portion of the produce required to indemnify the farmer for his expenses, a portion much greater than the landlord's (475); we increase the cost of producing corn (480).

I sent you a copy of Mr. Scarlett's bill[1]—that of Mr. Courtenay is not yet printed[2].

Mrs. Ricardo and I were sorry not to see you on the last evening you were in London, but we acknowledge that your charge was too important to be neglected.

The South Sea Plan[3] has failed so I need say nothing on that point. We shall see what ministers will do to raise the £2,200,000 p^r ann^m.—

I wish you were in the House to give me support in attacking the fallacious arguments for monopolies and restricted trade which are daily brought forward. I do my best, but that is bad enough;—it is difficult to express oneself in terms sufficiently familiar to be understood by those who either understand nothing on these subjects, or who have imbibed prejudices to which they obstinately adhere. I am a very bad speaker, and am sorry to say I do not improve—I have not one good supporter; there are some who understand the subject, but they are on the ministerial bench, and dare not always speak as they think.

Very truly yrs

DAVID RICARDO.

LVIII[4].

MY DEAR TROWER,

I am told that nothing has been laid before the H. of Commons in the present Session, respecting the Poor Rates. There is a committee sitting on Poor Rates Returns, but they have not yet made their Report.

Mr. Mill is acquainted with the Editor of the Chronicle[5]

---

[1] 'To Amend the Laws relating to the Poor of England.'
[2] 'A Bill for consolidating and amending the Laws relating to the building, repairing, and regulating of certain Gaols, Bridewells, and Houses of Correction in England'; presented in the House of Commons on May 13, 1822.
[3] A loan from the South Sea House.   [4] Cover wanting.
[5] In 1817 John Black became principal editor, though he had not

—I have given your letter to him with a view to get it inserted in the above paper; he will speak to the Editor on the subject, but he has doubts whether so long a letter can be inserted, at the present time, when the Parliamentary proceedings engross so large a portion of the paper.—I have read your letter, and agree with the greatest part of it. I am much flattered by the approbation you express of my plan of bullion payments. You estimate the coin in circulation previous to 1797 higher than I think it really was. The whole amount of circulation, at the present moment, both in London and the country, does not probably much exceed 32 millions, of which there are nearly 16 millions of Bank of England notes of 5 pounds and above, 7,500,000 of sovereigns, and nine millions of country Bank notes. If this be true there has been little or no falling off in the amount of Bank of England notes and coin together since 1819, but country Bank notes have diminished to the amount of 7,500,000£, and if we could get returns it would I think be found to be confined chiefly to the Agricultural districts;—it is nevertheless a great reduction.

If paper money displaced 20 millions of notes the whole profit from the interest of 20 millions was not enjoyed by the Bank of England, the country Banks participated in the advantage.—By a return laid before the H. of Commons more than 19 millions of sovereigns have been coined since 1817. During the period that the Bank so foolishly issued coin, when it was advantageous to export it, they got rid of 5 millions of sovereigns; so that if these were all exported more than 14 millions of sovereigns must now be in the country. Besides this quantity of gold it is probable

entire management of the paper till Perry's death in 1823. (Bain's Life of James Mill, 1882, p. 164.) Perry had been editor for nearly 20 years, and was in a sense the maker of the Chronicle. See Edinburgh Review, May, 1823, 'The Periodical Press,' p. 361.

the Bank may have a tolerable supply of bullion, and perhaps also some guineas. How badly has this business been managed! We might safely, even with payments in coin, dispense with 3 millions of gold since we are to maintain the 1 and 2 £ circulation in the country.—

On tuesday Mr. Western brings forward his motion respecting Mr. Peel's bill[1], I am very much interested in that discussion.

Mrs. Ricardo unites with me in begging our kind remembrances to Mrs. Trower.

Yrs very truly

DAVID RICARDO.

London 9 June, 1822.

If your letter is inserted I will send you the paper.

LIX[2].

BROMESBERROW PLACE LEDBURY
14 *Decr.* 1822.

MY DEAR TROWER,

Your letter of the 11th July did not reach me till sunday last, on which day I arrived in Brook Street from Dover. I left London for the Continent very early on the 12th July, and proceeded by the Steam Packet from the Tower-Stairs to Calais: this voyage was performed in about 13 or 14 hours. I was accompanied in my tour by Mrs. Ricardo, my two youngest daughters, Miss Lancey (the governess), Mrs. Ricardo's female servant, and a courier. As I could not comply with your request contained in the

---

[1] It was the occasion of one of Ricardo's longest and most important speeches in Parliament; see Hansard, Parliamentary Debates, vol. vii. (N. S.), 938 (June 12, 1822). The speech was reprinted in pamphlet form with the title: 'Mr. Ricardo's Speech on Mr. Western's Motion, for a Committee to consider the Effects produced by the Resumption of Cash Payments, delivered the 12th of June, 1822.' London, 1822.

[2] Franked by himself, cover dated, 'Ledbury December Fifteen 1822,' and addressed, 'Hutches Trower, Esq., Unsted Wood, Godalming, Surry.'

letter of the 11th, mentioned above, to give you an account of the journey I intended to make, I will, now that it is over, lay before you the route we followed. From Calais we went to the principal towns in the Netherlands ; then to Holland, where we visited Rotterdam, The Hague, Amsterdam, Sardam [sic], Utrecht, &c., &c. From Holland we followed, in an opposite direction, the course of the Rhine, and saw all the beautiful country on the banks of that noble river. We halted for a day or two at Coblentz and Frankfort. From Frankfort we went to Heidelberg, Carlsruhe, Baden, &c., &c., and entered Switzerland at Bale. From Bale our course was to Schaffhausen, Zurich, Wallenstadt, Zug, Art, Lucerne, Meyringhen, Interlachen, Grindlewald, Lauterbrun, Berne, Lausanne, Geneva, and Chamouny. From Chamouny we returned to Geneva, and from thence went to Mt. St. Bernard, Martigny, Bryg, and then across the Simplon, to Como. From Como we proceeded to Milan, Verona, Venice, Bologna, and Florence. Florence was the extreme point of my tour. We then went to Leghorn, Pisa. Genoa, and Turin. From Turin we crossed Mount Cenis, made the best of our way, through Lyons, to Paris. At Paris I stayed 3 weeks, arrived in London on the 8th of this month, and here on the 12th. I have given you a hasty sketch of the countries through which we have passed and shall only add that we met with scarcely any difficulty worth mentioning ; were all very much pleased with the beauties of nature and of art which we have seen ; and have been uniformly in good health.

At Geneva I was most hospitably received by my old friend Dumont, who is universally esteemed and respected by his countrymen—he accompanied us to Chamouny, and was adventurous enough to go up the Montanvert with me and my girls. At Coppet, which is near Geneva, I found the Duke de Broglie, whose acquaintance I had had the pleasure of making last autumn in London. I do not know whether I ever mentioned him to you—he is married to Madme de Stael's daughter. He and the Baron de Stael, his brother-in-law, paid rather a long visit in England, and employed their time in seeing every thing worthy of notice. They are both clever men, but the Duke is particularly so. Political Economy is his favorite study, and I am happy to say that he is one of the best defenders of those principles which I think the correct ones I ever met with. I knew this before I went abroad, but at Coppet I had an opportunity of hearing him to great advantage, for on the day that I dined with him there, M. Sismondi, who has published a work on Political Economy, and whose views are quite opposed to mine, was on a visit at the Duke's house. M. Sismondi advanced his peculiar opinions, which were combated by the Duke and me—but the difficult part of the contest fell chiefly on the Duke, who defended our common principles so well that it appeared to me Monsr Sismondi had no chance with him. Mons. S. indeed once or twice confessed he could not answer the points objected to him, but he would never agree that they could not be answered. Mr. Dumont, and Madme de Broglie, sat by as umpires, but they only interfered to see fair play. Madme is a very pleasing lady—she on this occasion, as well as on a subsequent one, for I met them again at Paris, left a very pleasing impression of herself on my mind.

Notwithstanding my differences with Mons. Sismondi, on the doctrines of Political Economy, I am a great admirer of his talents, and I was very favorably impressed by his manners—I did not expect from what I had seen of his controversial writings to find him so candid and agreeable. M. Sismondi's [*sic*] takes enlarged views, and is sincerely desirous of establishing principles which he conceives to be most conducive to the happiness of mankind. He holds that the great cause of the misery of the bulk of the people in all countries is the unequal distribution of property, which tends to brutalize and degrade the lower classes. The way to elevate man, to prevent him from making inconsiderate marriages, is to give him property and an interest in the general welfare;—thus far we should pretty well agree, but when he contends that the abundance of production caused by machinery, and by other means, is the cause of the unequal distribution of property, and that the end he has in view cannot be accomplished while this abundant production continues, he, I think, entirely misconceives the subject, and does not succeed in shewing the connection of his premises with his conclusion [1].

At Paris I saw M. Say several times, but never found him much inclined to talk on the points of difference between us. I believe M. Say finds it difficult to converse on these subjects; his ideas do not flow in a sufficiently rapid course for conversation. Speaking to the Duke de Broglie of M[.] Say he observed that he did not appear to him to have the least notion of the doctrines of the New School,—that his notes in the French translation of my book shewed clearly that he did not know what the subject in dispute was. In France very little is understood about Political Economy, altho' they have some good writers on that subject. M. Garnier, the translator of Adam Smith, had completed an additional volume of notes for a new edition of Smith's work when he died. This new edition has just been published, and I had an opportunity while in Paris, of seeing the additional volume, and of reading the lengthened remarks, which he makes on my opinions. M[.] Garnier is in every instance opposed to me when I attack his favorite author, but I am sure that the obser-

---

[1] Professor Bain says ('Life of Mill,' p. 203): 'In one of Mrs. Grote's letters to which I have had access, dated 14th October [1822], there are a few references to Mill and his friends. [She says:—] "I read a few days ago an interesting and long letter from Mr. Ricardo to Mr. Mill, a good part of which related to the conversations he had maintained with the great men at Geneva."'

vations of the D[.] de Broglie on Mr Say's knowledge of my principles are equally applicable to M. Garnier. M. Say's brother, Louis Say, has written a thick volume of criticism on Adam Smith's, Malthus', his brother's, and my doctrines;—he quarrels with all our opinions, but shews pretty evidently that he knows very little about them. M. Ganilh, a deputy, has also made remarks on my work, but I have not seen them—the Duke gave me no encouragement to read them. At Geneva the 1st number of a review has been lately published [1], with the names of the writers of the different articles signed to them. There is one article, on two houses being better than one, by M. Rossi—another on law, by Dumont, one on Polit. Econ., by Sismondi, and several others. The Duke de Broglie told me that he had half promised to write an article on my book—if he does, I shall be eager to see it. Besides the gentlemen I have mentioned I met some very clever men, but had too little time to improve my very slight acquaintance with them.

In all the countries through which I travelled the people appeared to be enjoying ease and plenty. Provisions are everyw[here] uncommonly cheap, and nothing prevents those fine countries from making a most rap[id] progress in wealth and population, but the unsettled state of the governments. Nobody seems to think that the present order of things will continue long on its present footing, which damps all enterprise and speculation that requires a few years to reap the fruits from them.

---

[1] Possibly the Annales de Législation et d'Économie Politique. For a description of the distinguished group assembled at this time at Geneva, see 'Dictionnaire de l'Économie Politique,' Art. 'Rossi.'

For notes on the subject of this letter, see Letters to Malthus, pp. 210-214, and to McCulloch, pp. 138-144, where will be found extracts from the 'Letters written by David Ricardo during a Tour on the Continent,' priv. pr. Gloucester, 1891. We may add the reference 'p. 8 to travellers smuggling Continental goods into England. He forbids it to his party, and regards it as 'dishonest and immoral.'

When I go to town I will make some inquiry after your papers, I ought to have done so before I left England, but my time was so taken up that I never thought of it.— I wish you had expanded the subject into a pamphlet[;] it is not too late now, and I hope you will undertake it [1].

We shall I suppose have an active session of Parliament;—the continued distress of the agricultural class will make the country gentlemen clamorous for some measures to relieve them. They do not see that no relief can be afforded them, but at the expense of the other classes of the community—they must either withhold a part of the dividend of the stockholder, or pay a fewer number of pounds than that which they have contracted to pay, to their mortgagees and other creditors. I do not wonder that a depreciation of the currency is a popular measure with landed gentlemen[,] for it at once enables them to effect those two darling objects. Many of them conscientiously believe that there would be no injustice in it, and here I am at issue with them. In this county they are very favorable to an income tax, because, they say, it would reach the Stockholders, as if the stockholder was now exempted from his just share of the taxes. They talk of calling a county meeting at Hereford, where some such measure is to be recommended as a fit object for a petition to Parliament—if I am here I shall attend it, and shall be induced perhaps to try to prove the insufficiency of the proposed remedy [2].

I have not yet read O'Meara's book [3]—I do not wonder at its having been read with great interest.

[1] Whether the matter was Currency or Poor Relief we have no means of discovering. See preceding letter.
[2] See following letter.
[3] 'Napoleon in Exile, or a Voice from St. Helena: the Opinions and Reflections of Napoleon on the most Important Events of his Life and Government, in his own words.' By Barry Edwards O'Meara. 2 vols. London, 1822. The author was confidential medical attendant of Napoleon at St. Helena.

I hope Mrs. Trower and your family are well, pray make Mrs. Ricardo's kind regards to her.

Ever My dear Trower,
Yrs truly
DAVID RICARDO.

LX [1].

MY DEAR TROWER

WEDCOMB HOUSE BATH
30 Jany 1823

Before Parliament meets it will be wise in me to discharge my debt to you, and to assure you that I felt great gratification at the receipt of your letter. It was very kind of you to write to me so soon after the receipt of mine. I was very desirous of hearing from you, and am glad to find that you are well, and as usual in the road of improvement, storing your mind with useful knowledge.

In my last I told you I intended to go to the Hereford meeting, but I could not be at it on account of the late period to which it was postponed. Cobbett as usual asserted falsehoods respecting my opinions; and the landed gentlemen being strongly inclined to confiscate a part of the property of the fundholder sought to cover their project with a shew of justice [2]—they of course will magnify the effects of Mr. Peel's bill, and will admit no other cause for their distress but the augmented value of the currency. I am rather singularly circumstanced—agreeing as I do with the reformers, on the subject of parliamentary reform, I can not agree with them that taxation and bad government has been the cause of our present difficulties: I believe that under the best possible government, and without taxes, we might have been involved in similar troubles. Still less can I support the doctrines of the new converts to

---

[1] Franked by himself; cover addressed, 'Hutches Trower, Esq., Unsted Wood, Godalming,' and dated, 'Bath, January 30, 1823.'

[2] See Note following this letter.

reform, who attribute our distress to every cause but the right one, and who not being governed by principle will quit the cause of reform the moment that the times mend. I on the contrary am a reformer on principle, and whether we get rid of our difficulties or continue to struggle under them shall advocate a reform of the house of commons, because I think it would very materially contribute to good government and to the happiness of the people. I am sorry that you do not agree with me on this subject,—the objection you make, that reformers are not agreed in what they want, is not I think a weighty one,—all real reformers are agreed on the principle: they want a house of commons which shall speak the sentiments of the people, and are willing to agree to any details which shall not interfere with that important principle. Lord Folkestone[1] has become a staunch reformer, and more nearly agrees with the views which I think correct than any man in the H. of Commons, Burdett and Hobhouse not excepted. You will soon have an opportunity of giving your opinion on this interesting question at the County meeting of Surry—I hope you will speak there—I know beforehand that I shall applaud every thing you shall say on Agricultural distress, but I shall condemn your opinions on Reform. Strange that you should like a House of Commons which represents only the interests of a very small fraction of the people!

Thinking as you do that much service would be done to the science of Political Economy by an examination at some length of the different systems advocated by Malthus and me, why do you not undertake it? I cannot help thinking that you have already prepared the materials for such a work, because you have given a great deal of con-

---

[1] Afterwards Earl Radnor. Folkestone had joined Brougham and the rest in vigorous opposition to the Income Tax in 1816, spoken on the Radical side in the debates on Oliver the Spy in 1818, and opposed the grant to the Earl of Kent in the same year.

sideration to the subject and are in the habit of making
notes and remarks on every book which greatly interests
you [1]. You ought to let us have such a work from your pen.
Without half the pretensions which you have to offer,
I boldly ventured, and as I have had no reason to repent
it, why are you not encouraged to follow my example?

The die appears to be cast and war will immediately
commence in Europe. One would have thought it impossible that France would have exposed herself to so much
risk, as a war with Spain, against principles of freedom,
must involve her in. I hope her defeat will follow, and that
the consequences of this rash step may be the establishing
of *real* representative Governments all over Europe. I wish
to approve of the conduct of our ministers, and as far as it
is yet known it appears to have been firm and judicious. I
hope we shall keep out of the contest, but it will be a difficult task to do so if the war should be of long duration.

You have I conclude read the pamphlet [2] in defence of
Government. Many of the points are well put, but how
miserably the question of the Sinking fund is handled.
A tolerably good case may be made out in favor of the
Sinking fund, but the author of this pamphlet has taken
up untenable ground, and is constantly contradicting himself, and exposing his ignorance. What sort of a Chancellor of the Exchequer will Robinson make? He is a
good tempered man, a tolerable political economist, and
well inclined to liberal principles of trade, but he is a very
timid man. He will not, I fear, dare to act on enlarged
views of policy, but will like his predecessors be always
for conciliating particular interests. I did not like what
he and Lord Liverpool said lately at a dinner in the city

[1] Trower's MSS. bear out this statement.
[2] Probably the anonymous 'State of the Nation at the Commencement
of the year 1822, considered under the four departments of the Finance,
Foreign Relations, Home Department, Colonies and Board of Trade,' &c.
Hatchard, London, 1822; see esp. pp. 24-26.

given by the Shipping interest—I am sure they did not speak their real sentiments. I am surprised that Huskisson was not appointed to the office of Chancellor of the Exchequer, every body expected that he would be Van's successor [1].

There has been a talk, I believe nothing more, amongst ministers about restoring the two standards, but I am assured all thoughts of it are relinquished.—Lord Liverpool is very decidedly against it. I am sorry to hear that Huskisson is not much disinclined to it. I have lately seen a letter from Lord Grenville on this subject to one of his friends, in which he expresses himself strongly and ably in favor of the single standard. His Lordship's opinions on the subject of the currency appear to me to be very sound. Lord Lansdowne I have been informed is inclined to the two standards—Baring I suspect is the ringleader in this conspiracy.

I leave Bath on Saturday next—I hope I shall soon see you in London.

Pray give Mrs. Ricardo's and my kind remembrances to Mrs. Trower and believe me My dear Trower

Yrs truly

DAVID RICARDO.

NOTE.—On January 17, 1823 a meeting attended by some five thousand persons was held at Hereford 'for the purpose of taking into consideration the propriety of representing to both Houses of Parliament, the unparalleled and daily increasing distress of the agricultural interest of the country, and the several causes thereof; of petitioning them to adopt such measures as they in their wisdom may deem best calculated for its relief—and of expressing to them our apprehensions of the awful consequences of further delay in affording aid in difficulties so overwhelming.'

Cobbett made one of the early speeches, in the course of which

---

[1] Huskisson was soon after appointed President of the Board of Trade and Treasurer of the Navy. Within the same year a vacancy was made in the Board of Trade, to which he was immediately called. See 'Biographical Memoir,' prefixed to 'Speeches' (London, 1831), p. 87.

he said 'It was Mr. Ricardo who had persuaded the ministers that the landlords and tenants were doing so well—it was he who repeated the old Scotch doctrine of Adam Smith, that all taxes fell on the consumer; this doctrine might be very well as applied in several instances to persons in trade, but not so to real property. The error was in laying down the proposition at all in an extensive way, for it nowhere universally applied. This he could illustrate in the simplest manner. Suppose a maker of candles—the duty upon them at first is 6*d.* per pound, but afterwards the Government laid on 1*s.*—will the consumer pay this? Yes so far as he buys; but will he buy the same quantity? No, he won't; and what is the result? that the chandler to get rid of his stock must induce a sale, by reducing the price partially, and selling some beneath the cost. So it was with the landlords and farmers. If all went on smooth with the landlord and tenant, then the consumer undoubtedly paid the taxes; but if, as was the fact, the case was the reverse, then who paid them?—not the consumer, but the farmer and landlord in the depreciation of their share of the prices. Out of the gross error that the consumer paid the taxes, arose the whole evil. Ministers, proceeding on this false foundation, were resolved not to alter the currency—not to make bank-notes a legal tender; but they had, without any premeditated intention, driven the former to the brink of ruin, and the time of resistance must come, if they pressed matters to extremities.'

The general tenor of the meeting was hostile to Cobbett and his proposals, but a subsequent speaker (Rev. Mr. Smithies) said: 'He agreed that much of the existing evil might be traced to the calculating economy of Mr. Ricardo, and the cold-blooded sophistry of Mr. Peregrine Courtenay; and also that, in its consequences, an adherence to the system would transfer their estates to the Jew-jobbers of Change-alley.'

The Petition finally adopted attributed existing distress to extravagant and corrupt expenditures, debased paper currency and transition to metallic payments at the old standard without regard to contracts made in the interval, and prayed that an investigation be instituted as to variations in currency with reference to the adjustment of debts, etc., desiring greater economy in expenditure, revision of Civil List, etc., etc.

See The Times (London) of January 20, 1823.

LXI [1].

[TO ISAAC LYON GOLDSMID.]

UPPER BROOK STREET,
April 4, 1823.

MY DEAR SIR,

The approbation which you express of the sentiments I endeavoured to deliver in the House a few evenings ago [2], in favor of religious liberty, gives me great satisfaction. It appears to me a disgrace to the age we live in, that many of the inhabitants of this country are still suffering under disabilities, imposed on them in less enlightened times. The Jews have most reason to complain, for they are frequently reproached with following callings which are the natural effects of the political degradation in which they are kept. I cannot help thinking that the time is approaching when these ill-founded prejudices against men on account of their religious opinions will disappear, and I should be happy if I could be an humble instrument in accelerating their fall.

I carry my principles of toleration very far. I do not know how, or why, any line should be drawn, and I am prepared to maintain that we have no more justifiable ground for shutting the mouth of the atheist than that of any other man. I am sure it will be shut, for no man will persevere in avowing opinions which bring on him the hatred and ill-will of a great majority of his fellow men.

With best wishes,
Yours very truly,
DAVID RICARDO.

[1] Memoir of Sir Francis Henry Goldsmid (1879), p. 91. Sir Isaac Goldsmid ' was meditating the question of emancipating the Jews from their disabilities as early as the year 1823.' A letter of Ricardo to Geo. Grote, dated ' March, 1823 ' (Personal Life of G. Grote, pp. 42, 43), thanks Grote for a similar commendation to Goldsmid's.

[2] Probably on March 26, 1823, in the debate on Mary Ann Carlile's petition for release, Hansard, Parliamentary Debates, vol. viii. (N. S.) 722.

MY DEAR TROWER

GATCOMB PARK
24 July 1823

The latter part of my residence in London was so taken up by parliamentary business that I had not really time to write to you. Besides the regular attendance which I always give to the House I was obliged to be every day on some committee, which, altogether, entirely occupied my time; but now that I am once more settled in my peaceable retreat in the country, I remember my debt to you, and hasten to discharge it.

I regret that I did not see you oftener in London during my six months['] campaign, particularly as you give me no hope of a visit here. I know you are usefully employed as a country gentleman;—equitably settling differences between your poorer neighbours, and arresting as far as you can the diffusion of erroneous principles amongst your richer ones, yet I would wish to see you more in London, for that is the place in which we meet a succession of clever men in all branches of knowledge, and in which we gain instruction by the active opposition which all our speculations whether right or wrong encounter. If you had been there lately you would have met Mr. MCulloch of Edinburgh, the writer of many able articles in the Edinburgh Review, and in the Encyclopedia, on Political Economy[2]. Mr. MCulloch is an agreeable, well-informed man, a sincere lover and seeker of truth, and I think you would have been pleased with him. He had a great deal of

[1] Franked by himself. The last sheet is used as the cover; addressed. 'Hutches Trower, Esqr., Unsted Wood, Godalming,' and dated, 'Minchinhampton July Twenty four 1823.'
This letter is misplaced in the collection at University College, where Letter LXIII comes before it. Letter LXIII was written *after* and Letter LXII written *before* receipt of a letter from Trower.

[2] It was in the course of this visit of McCulloch to London, and later to Gatcomb Park, that he first actually met with Ricardo. The two had been in correspondence for some years before.

discussion with Blake but did not succeed in weaning him from his newly published opinions [1]. With Malthus, as you know, he greatly differs, and their conferences have not been attended with the effect of reconciling them to each other's views. He attended the last meeting of our Political Economy Club and the result of our discussions on that day convinced him, as we all had been long before convinced, that the progress of the science is very much impeded by the contrary ideas which men attach to the word value [2]. When Malthus speaks of the rise or fall in the value of a commodity he is estimating it in the particular measure of value which he himself recommends [3]; MCulloch, Mill and I are thinking of quite a different measure. Torrens and Warburton again have their particular view of a proper measure; and therefore until we can agree as to some common measure by which to estimate the variations in the value of the commodities of which we speak, altho' it be not, as it appears impossible any can be, an accurate measure of value, we cannot understand each other. To this task several good understandings are I hope at this time devoted, for all appear to acknowledge the necessity of adopting some general measure. I know MCulloch's attention is turned to the subject and I expect much from his accuracy and precision.—Malthus is I know quite full of the subject but then his views run in a particular direction from which nothing can make him swerve.—As for myself I mean also to turn my thoughts to the subject,

[1] 'Observations on the Effects produced by the Expenditure of Government during the Restriction of Cash Payments.' By William Blake, Esq., F.R.S. 8vo. London, 1823.

[2] The meeting occurred on June 2, 1823, with Mr. Basevi in the chair. One of the four questions discussed was the query, propounded by N. W. Senior, 'Can there be an increase of Riches without an increase of Value?' See 'Minutes of Proceedings' of Political Economy Club, vol. iv. (London, 1882).

[3] Malthus' tract on the 'Measure of Value' had appeared in the Spring of this year, 1823. As to Warburton, see Letters to Malthus, p. 96, note.

but I fear I cannot arrive at any sounder conclusions than the acknowledgedly imperfect ones which I have already published.

In one of the Committees, which I have lately attended, we were directed by the House to inquire into the cause of the want of employment of the poor in Ireland, and into the best means of remedying the evil which all agree exists[1]. It is a favorite plan, with many, for Government to lend capital to Ireland, in order that the people may be employed. Against such a scheme I have the most decided objections, which I never fail to urge. If the greater part of the Irish members could have their way, we should not only grant a vast number of charitable loans but we should encourage all sorts of manufactures by bounties and premiums. Amongst other schemes we have listened with great attention to Mr. Owen, who assures us that if we give him 8 millions of money he will make Ireland now and for ever happy. The Irish appear to me to differ from the rest of the inhabitants of the United Kingdom, and not to take a commonly enlightened view of their own interest. They have no idea of waiting patiently for the profitable result of a well considered speculation. An English landlord knows that it is not his interest to make his tenant a beggar by exacting the very hardest terms from him if he had the power of dictating the rent, not so the Irish landlords—they not only do not see the benefits which would result to themselves from encouraging a spirit of industry and accumulation in their

[1] A select Committee was appointed on June 20, 1823, 'to inquire into the condition of the labouring poor in that part of the United Kingdom called Ireland, with a view to facilitate the application of the funds of private individuals and associations for their employment in useful and productive labour; and to report their observations and opinion thereon to the House.' Ricardo was added to the Committee some days after its original appointment. The Report and Minutes of Evidence were presented to the House and ordered to be printed on July 16, 1823.

tenants, but appear to consider the people as beings of a different race who are habituated to all species of oppression—they will for the sake of a little present rent, divide and sub-divide their farms till they receive from each tenant the merest trifle of rent, altho' the aggregate is considerable. They consider as nothing the severe [1] means to which they are obliged to resort to collect these rents, nor to the individual suffering which it occasions. Ireland is an oppressed country—not oppressed by England, but by the aristocracy which rules with a rod of Iron within it; England could redress many of her wrongs, but stands itself in awe of the faction which governs.

What say you to Agriculture and its prospects? Is the distress over? Shall we have a short crop? If we have, will the ports be opened? If the ports be opened how will the future prospects of landlords and tenants be affected by it? These are interesting topics. You have no doubt seen Tooke's publications [2]—they are I think very clever. What is your opinion of that theory of his on which he lays so much stress: the continuance, for a succession of years, alternately, of good and bad seasons. Out of twenty successive years he contends you will frequently find only 2 or 3 good crops, and then perhaps for the same number of years only 2 or 3 bad ones. He makes the scientific part of the subject very difficult, for he will not allow you to reason with a view to practice from an observation of the produce for 10 years; according to him you must look to the a[vera]ge result of a period of from 30 to 50 years.

The country about me is looking beautiful, but it is n[ot] possible to enjoy it amidst the incessant rain which at present prevails; a great quantity of hay will be spoiled.

---

[1] He wrote first 'painful.'

[2] 'Thoughts and Details on the High and Low Prices of the last Thirty Years.' 4 pts. London, 1823.

Will the war in Spain soon be at an end to be renewed at some future opportunity by the friends of liberty there, with greater effect, or will they yet offer so much resistance to the French, as to prolong the contest, and have a chance of ultimately prevailing over their formidable enemy? I fear their case is for the present hopeless, but I trust might will not long continue to subdue right.

Mrs. Ricardo unites with me in kind remembrances to Mrs. Trower.

Ever Yours
DAVID RICARDO.

LXIII[1].

MY DEAR TROWER   24th *July* 1823

Just as I was about sending my letter to the Post yours of the 20th. was delivered to me, it came with a weekly dispatch and parcel by the coach from my house in London. I am glad that I wrote before I received it, as you will see I had you in my recollection.

You have answered some of my questions respecting the approaching crop—I quite agree with you that a price neither too high nor too low is what we now want, but can we long have it with the present corn law? I think not, and must use my best efforts to get it amended.

We are deserving of some of the praise you bestow on us for a more liberal spirit than heretofore in Parliament. We shall I hope go on from Session to Session getting rid of some of the absurd regulations which fetter commerce till all shackles are removed. Huskisson behaved very well after I left London in refusing to have anything to do with the Lords' amended bill respecting the magistrates['] interference with wages in Spitalfields—the bill was quite spoiled, there was nothing left in it worth retaining[2].

[1] Probably enclosed in No. LXII.
[2] See Mr. Cannan, 'Ricardo in Parliament,' *Economic Journal*, 1894, pp. 411, 412, and *Letters to Malthus*, Introd. p. xi.

You ask me what I think of Malthus['] 'measure of value[1]'[.] I have in some degree answered your question in my letter, for I have told you that a good measure of value is among the things of which we know little. Malthus's is objectionable because his measure is not invariable which a measure of value should be.

Suppose an epidemic disorder were to carry off one-fourth of our people[;] labour would rise as compared with all commodities—Malthus would call this a fall in the value of commodities, whereas nothing would have altered except the supply of labour. Malthus objects to my measure of value, and justly, because it is not itself produced under the very same circumstances as the commodities whose value it is to measure. 'Your money' he says 'is produced with certain [pro-]portions of fixed and circulating capital, and with it you would measure the variations of commodities produced with other and very different proportions of fixed and circulating capital.' Does he not fall into the same error?—his money is produced with labour alone and he makes it a measure of the value of commodities produced under all the varieties of mixed proportions of capital and labour. In a country where the people feed on rice or potatoes a great deal of labour may be commanded with a small proportion of the whole produce of labour; instead of saying as the fact would appear to be that labour was cheap in those countries and dear in England we should be bound to say commodities were dear in those countries and cheap in England although their money price was the same. Surely this cannot be right.

Ever Yrs
D R

[1] 'The Measure of Value stated and illustrated, with an application of it to the alterations in the value of the English Currency since 1790.' London, 1823.

LXIV [1].

MY DEAR TROWER

GATCOMB PARK
31 *Aug.* 1823

To make up for my former omissions I lose no time in replying to your last kind letter, and I am the more induced to do so from a hope I entertain that you may not find it inconvenient to pay me a visit here in Gloucestershire. You say in your letter that you feel a great desire to become acquainted with my residence, and to take a peep at the beautiful country that surrounds me. Let me ask you then what hinders you from doing so? Travelling is now so easy all over England that it is no undertaking to go from your house to mine, and I beg seriously to call upon you to do it. I have some temptation too to offer you. I know you are pleased with Mill's company, and although you do not quite agree in opinion with him I am certain that you derive both pleasure and instruction from his conversation. Mill is coming to me in the middle of the next month (September), and you cannot do better than come at the same time—we shall all enjoy ourselves together—we shall walk and ride, we will converse on politics, on Political Economy, and on Moral Philosophy, and neither of us will be the worse for the exercise of our colloquial powers. I entreat you to take this matter into your serious consideration, and to assure Mrs. Trower that we will take great care of you if she will join us in promoting this little scheme.

Several letters have passed between Malthus and me on the subject of value, and one or two between MCulloch and me[2]. We none of us exactly agree. MCulloch says he is

---

[1] Franked by himself. The last sheet of the letter is used as the cover; addressed, 'Hutches Trower, Esqr. Unsted Wood Godalming' and dated, 'Minchinhampton August Thirty-one 1823.'

[2] See Letters to Malthus, pp. 214-240; Letters to McCulloch, pp. 154 179, where a letter of Malthus to Ricardo is given, pp. 161-167.

not in search of a measure of value, his only object is to know what it is which regulates the relative value of commodities one to another, and that, he insists, is the quantity of labour necessary to produce them. But MCulloch uses the word labour in a sense somewhat different to Political Economists in general, and he does not appear to me to see that if we were in possession of the knowledge of the law which regulates the exchangeable value of commodities, we should be only one step from the discovery of a measure of absolute value.

Malthus avows that he is in search of a measure of absolute value, he does more, he contends that he has found it, and that it is the value of daily labour which is the only permanent and unalterable measure of value. The reasons indeed by which he supports this opinion are far from satisfactory to me[:] they seem so little convincing that I am sure h[e] has not aided us in the search for this important measure. I will mention only one contradiction as it seems to me of his[.] He says that my measure would be a perfect one if all commodities were produced under the same circumstances as my proposed measure, and that it is a perfect one for commodities so produced. Should not then my measure be as applicable to this description of commodities as his? and should not the commodities so particularised vary equally in his measure as in mine? they do not, therefore either my measure or his is not a correct one, or equally good measures will give different results.

The rain has given us a little respite here for two or three days, and we live in hopes that we shall be able to house the harvest from our fields.—The crop is said to be a good one. It is quite wonderful to me that corn has continued at so steady a price with the prospect which we have lately had. Can any thing more strongly prove that the supply in the country must have been very abundant than that corn should have risen no higher with so dismal a prospect as has lately been p[resen]ted to us. Your maxim of 'whatever is, is right' [is in other] words [sayi]ng that what is inevitable must be patiently borne.

The preservation of the peace of Europe is a grand object, yet I cannot help regretting that the Spanish cause has not been better supported by the Spaniards themselves. If the French had been driven out of Spain, I do not see why the peace of Europe wd have been disturbed. Other powers might indeed have joined in the attack, and the war would have probably ended as soon as the contest between liberty and despotism had been decided. I fear that Despotism will reign triumphantly for a time in consequence of the result of the present contest. I have sold my Spanish stock, I got for it rather a better price than that at which I purchased it.

I suppose that you continue to plant and improve at Unsted Wood and that you are now seeing in full beauty the effects of your former efforts in the same line. I forget whether your land is of a very good description, its being so or not makes a great difference in the progress of trees. I am living in a country where the soil is very poor. Beech flourishes with us, and larch and fir get on very well. I scarcely saw the place last year and therefore see the improvement of my small plantations more marked now than at any former period. As for improvements I attempt very few and am very much disposed to be satisfied with things as they are—Mrs. Ricardo on the contrary, would always like to have a dozen men active in her employment for the mere purpose of altering and improving.

Mrs. Ricardo and my family join with me in kind remembrances [to] Mrs. Trower.

Ever, My Dear Trower,
Truly yrs
DAVID RICARDO.

LXV[1].

GATCOMB PARK
6 *Septr* 1823

MY DEAR SIR,

I am grieved to tell you that Mr. Ricardo is at this moment confined to his bed by an Illness originating from [a] cold in the ear. The Ladies have been in constant attendance at his bedside for the last 2 days [;] it has therefore devolved on me to write to you.

There is at present every appearance that a day or two will restore our Friend to health and that he will be able to enjoy your society on the 30th Inst. when he hopes to have the pleasure of seeing you here.

Should he contrary to all our expectations have a relapse you shall hear again [;] the information I have been able to obtain about the stage coaches is that there is one daily to Stroud (5 miles from h[ere]) and one 3 times a week to Minchin Hampton (one mile from h[ere]), the latter travels by night.

I am
My Dear Sir
Yours very truly
ANTHY AUSTIN [2].

LXVI[3].

MY DEAR SIR

to correspond with you, one of my earliest friends, would be a pleasing occupation if the nature of the com-

---

[1] This and the following letter, from the pen of Anthony Austin, a son-in-law of Ricardo, are included in the University College collection of Ricardo's letters to Trower. For similar details of Ricardo's unexpected death, see Letters to McCulloch, pp. 179–182, and to Malthus, p. 240, also Life of James Mill, p. 209.

[2] Cover addressed, 'H. Trower, Esqre Unsted Wood Godalming.'

[3] Addressed on back:—
 H. Trower Esqre
  Unsted Wood
   near Godalming
 altered into J. H. Slater Esqr
   Newick Park
    Uckfield

munication I am unfortunately called upon to make had not converted it into a painful task, one which I should most unwilling have undertaken if any one of the Gatcomb family had been capable of performing it but the most unexpected death of our much esteemed, (I may say universally esteemed) friend Mr. D. Ricardo has been too great a shock to be easily overcome. You will I dare say be anxious to hear the cause of this misfortune, I will therefore just state the outline of the case. the cold in the ear produced a gathering attended with the most acute pain and so great a degree of consequent inflammation that the bone was injured and the injury communicated to the brain and caused a formation of matter there.

It is some satisfaction to know that everything which the very best medical and surgical skill, and the most unremitted and affectionate attention could do was done to alleviate his sufferings and preserve his life, a life valuable not only to his own family and relations but to his country also. I will not attempt to describe to you the feelings of those who witnessed the event. you may conceive and I doubt not will sympathise with them. I am,

My Dear Sir,
Yours most truly,
ANTHY AUSTIN.

Bradley
    near Wottonunderedge, Septr. 12, 1823

this melancholy event happened yesterday at about noon, and I returned home with Mrs. Austin in the evening. I am in hopes that Mrs. A.'s bodily health has not suffered very materially from her constant attendance on her Poor Father. to time we must leave the cure of her mental sufferings.

APPENDIX

ONLY two documents in Ricardo's handwriting, besides the Letters, have been found in the Trower Manuscripts. We have printed them as they were found, side by side with Trower's contributions to the discussion.

The first (A (2))[1] needs a few words of explanation.

The Bullion Committee submitted its Report and it was ordered by the House of Commons to be printed 8th June 1810. At the end of that year Mr Coutts Trotter published a pamphlet entitled: 'The Principles of Currency and Exchanges applied to the Report from the Select Committee of the House of Commons appointed to inquire into the High Price of Gold Bullion &c. &c.' London (Cadell & Davies) 1810. They had reported 'That there is at present an excess in the paper circulation of this country, of which the most unequivocal symptom is the very high price of bullion, and next to that the low price of continental exchanges. That this excess is to be ascribed to the want of a sufficient check and control in the issues of paper from the Bank of England, and originally to the suspension of cash-payments which removed the natural and true control' (Report, p. 73). Mr. Coutts Trotter denies both statements; the paper, he says, is not in excess, and there exists a sufficient check and control over its issues. In his concluding chapter (p. 69) he says: 'In the present actual state of our foreign exchanges, when a given quantity of gold pays a larger portion of a debt on the Continent than any other

[1] Part of it was printed in the Economic Journal, March, 1896, p. 64.

article in this country of equal value,—a judicious merchant, in examining his stores, would determine to export his stock of the precious metals, and, after benefiting by the present certain increased prices, he would trust to a change of times for an opportunity of replacing it, when the tide of exchanges (as sooner or later it will do) sets in the contrary way, and when gold and silver again drop to the Mint price.'

In the paper now printed (A (2)), Ricardo begins with a criticism of this passage of Trotter and with the comments of Trower upon it. He then deals (p. 224 seq.) with certain other arguments of Trower expressed in the paper (A (1)) which consists of two half sheets (4to) closely written on both sides, and without heading or date. It may have been a purely private communication, made in the days when the acquaintanceship of the two men was slight, and formality was even more regarded than it was afterwards. Trotter's book was published after the Report of the Bullion Committee; therefore the first half of the document (A (2)) falls into the middle of 1810, while the second half may be some months earlier. Trower published his views on Silver as the Standard, in the 2nd of his two Letters to the Morning Chronicle, 14th Sept. and 30th Oct., 1809, signed 'A Friend to Bank Notes but no Bank Director,' and Ricardo answered him in the Chronicle of Nov. 23rd, 1809, incorporating his answer in his well-known pamphlet at the beginning of 1810[1].

In any case the MSS. show that Trower's paper (A (1)) was a '3rd letter,' and that he set about a 4th. These were the days of slow travelling and long letters. We have only a fragment of the friendly debate before us.

The second paper (B) is complete in itself. It consists of a single half-sheet (4to), the obverse in Ricardo's unmistakeable clear handwriting (B (1)), at the foot of which Trower writes 'turn over,' adding his comments (B (2)) in his smaller and more angular hand on the reverse.

[1] The Preface to the pamphlet is dated Dec. 1, 1809, and the pamphlet appeared a few weeks afterwards.

A (1).

1. It is admitted by Mr. Ricardo that Silver would be the measure of value if there did not exist a law prohibiting the coining of Silver Bullion into money, but that, in consequence of this law, Gold must now be the measure of value—

By similar reasoning I may contend, that not Gold but Bank Notes are now the measure of value because there exists a law prohibiting the Bank from paying their Notes in Specie.

I allow, that there is this difference between the two cases, that whereas individuals may, if they choose, take Gold Bullion to the Mint to be coined into money, they cannot do so with silver bullion; but this difference in the two cases can have no effect upon the question between us, that question being, whether Bank Notes represent Gold or Silver.—Now, in point of fact, they *at present* represent neither, the Bank being prohibited from paying their Notes in either. In speaking of Bank Notes, therefore, as the representatives of specie, reference must be made to the period when the restriction imposed upon the Bank will be removed. If at that period of time the law inhibiting the coinage of silver money shall continue in force, in that case undoubtedly Gold must be considered as the measure of value in this Country. But, at present, that Act according to my notion, has no more influence upon the question between us than the restriction bill itself has.—

We are agreed in opinion with respect to the circumstance[s] which constitute the one metal a measure of value, in preference to the other, to those circumstances therefore, and to those only, must we look in order to determine, which is that measure. That circumstance is the low valuation at which one of the metals is rated at the Mint, compared with its market price. It is admitted, that Silver is the metal which is, at present, so circumstanced. Silver, therefore, must now be the measure of value. Indeed if we look to the fact we shall find, that there is at present more silver coin in circulation than Gold coin. And how can it be otherwise when the temptation is so great for carrying off the latter. I confess therefore I do not see the force of the objections urged against Silver being now the measure of value, founded as they are upon the Act prohibiting the coinage of that metal.

2. It is admitted, that if the debased Silver Coin were legal tender the excess of the market price above the mint price of silver bullion would be sufficiently accounted for by that circumstance.

The reply to this observation is, that if the debased Silver Coin were legal tender, *without limitation*, the excess of the market above the mint price of that Bullion would not be merely 8 *pr Ct* but a great deal more, and nearly in proportion to the extent of the debasement of that coin. The restriction imposed upon the debased Silver Coin as legal tender, is the *cause*, therefore, why the difference between the Mint and Market price of that bullion is not greater than it is.

3. It is said, 'that it is known [1], that the debased coin does not pass in circulation according to its intrinsic value, but according to the value of the metal, which it ought to contain.'— This is something like begging the question, for it is asserting the point in dispute, the question between us being whether the debased Silver coin do, or do not, so pass. But in proof of this assertion Mr R. makes use of an argument, which, I confess, I did not expect to see him advance, as it can, with the strictest propriety, be so completely turned against him. He says, 'Compared with the Gold coin, which is undebased, is it not of equal if not of superior value to it?' My answer is, 'you say that Bank notes are 20 p Ct. discount [;] compare them with the Gold coin, which is undebased, are they not of equal value to it?' If there be any truth in your argument, there is equal truth in mine; and I may exclaim with you 'What pre-

---

[1] Cf. Ricardo's Reply to Bosanquet, Works, p. 347.

tence can there be then for saying, that the debased value of Bank Notes is a cause of the increase in the price of commodities?'

The same remarks may be applied to Mr R's supposed case of a Merchant with his Warehouse full of Goods, desirous of purchasing silver bullion for the purpose of exportation. Mr R. says 'that if the Merchant could sell his goods, at once, for heavy silver coin, and melt it, he would obtain 8 p Ct. more silver than if with the money he purchased Silver bullion.' This I deny, for I contend, that if the heavy silver coin were in circulation, instead of the light, the present difference between the market and mint price of silver bullion would not exist. The cause for that difference being removed, the effect would necessarily cease.

Again, Mr R. observes, that the fact is 'that £1000 in such debased Silver will purchase precisely as much silver bullion as £1000 in gold coin': to this I may reply, with equal propriety, that the fact is, that £1000 in Bank Notes will purchase precisely as much silver Bullion as £1000 in Gold coin. The argument here employed by Mr R. will serve my cause equally well with his own. Mr R. must therefore either *abandon* this *argument* by which he attempts to prove, that the debased silver coin passes in circulation according to the value of the metal which it ought to contain, or he must entirely *abandon* the *question* between us. For it is quite as strong to prove, that Bank Notes are not at a discount, as it is to prove, that our Silver coins are not [at] a discount, or, in other words, if it be sufficient to shew, that the debased Silver coin is not a cause of the increase in the price of commodities, it is equally sufficient to shew, that the amount of Bank Notes in circulation is not a cause of that increase.

I have now observed upon Mr R's remarks as far as they relate to this point, and wait his reply.

A (2).

[REPLY OF RICARDO TO TROTTER AND TROWER.]

What does Mr. Trotter mean [1] by saying that it may be more advantageous to discharge a foreign debt by the exportation of a dear than of a cheap article;—by the exportation of gold which is dearer than by commodities which are cheaper here than abroad? This is evidently impossible;—it implies a contradiction and needs no argument to prove its absurdity. If he means that the exportation of all other commodities will be attended with so much expense as to make it more advantageous to export gold,—then gold cannot be said to be dearer here than abroad because it is under all circumstances the cheapest exportable commodity. When we say that gold is dearer here than abroad and that commodities are not, we must include the expences attending their transportation to the foreign market, otherwise they are not fair subjects of comparison. If Mr. Trotter means that nothing but gold will be accepted in payment of our debt notwithstanding its relative price,—then there is an end of all comparison between gold and other things,— we have contracted to pay gold and nothing but gold will absolve us from our engagements. But it is not with Trotter's; it is with Mr. Trower's observations that I have now to deal.

He observes that if it could be admitted that a foreign merchant would import gold at a loss, it would follow that merchants were bartering two commodities *on one of which they both lose* (this one I suppose is bullion)[;] their profits then, he says, must be taken out of the other article. The seller must add to the price of the article (of wheat for example) the loss sustained upon the bullion he receives in payment; the buyer must afterwards add to the price of the article (wheat) over and above his profit the loss he

---

[1] See Coutts Trotter's 'Principles of Currency,' &c., 2nd ed., Dec. 1, 1810, pp. 47, 48.

sustains upon the bullion in which he pays for it. In the first place this is not a fair answer to Mr. Trotter,—he supposes a debt already contracted and which can only be discharged by money;—his argument has no reference to any new contract which may take place between the exporter of wheat from the continent and the exporter of bullion or of money from England, and in which contract the consideration of the value of these articles must necessarily enter. His case is this, an importer of wheat into England has engaged to pay a sum of money, a certain weight of bullion, and the time is arrived at which his creditor will accept of nothing else.

Secondly, if we admit that the argument is fairly applied, we are not told on whose account the transaction took place; was it on account of the foreign or of the English merchant? We are led to suppose indeed that it is on account of both, and that they have both an interest in the value of bullion because they are both to add to the price of the wheat to compensate them for the loss on the Bullion,—one of them is to do so because bullion is cheap and the other because bullion is dear. If it be said that the importation of the wheat into England is on account of the English merchant only, then the transaction was complete as far as regarded the foreign merchant at the moment he sold the wheat. He bought it in France for a sum of French currency and sold it for a sum of French currency which was to be paid him either by means of a bill of exchange or by the actual transit of bullion of an equal value,—he has therefore no other interest but to take care to receive his payment, and his profit if any should attach to it. It is probable that he might have only been an agent and have no other interest but his commission for his trouble. If then the transaction be on account of the English merchant what possible inducement will he have to import the wheat if the bullion which he has engaged to give in return for it, be dearer in England than in France, that is to say if he cannot sell it for more money than he has purchased it for.

If he can do so, does it not prove that bullion is cheaper in England than in France? that with the commodity wheat more bullion may be bought in England than in France? As far as those commodities are concerned, what greater evidence can we possess of bullion being dearer in France than in England? Is it a satisfactory answer to say, no; it is the wheat that is dearer in England;—dearer for what? why, for bullion. This I conceive is but another way of saying that bullion is cheaper in England and dearer in France. How are we to distinguish then whether the profit has been obtained by the sale of the money or by the purchase of the wheat, seeing that they precisely express the same thing?

In the supposed case then, of the exportation of bullion, notwithstanding its being dearer in the exporting country, in return for wheat, the fact that wheat is cheaper in the importing country is necessarily involved;—how then can there be any remedy against the disadvantage of exporting bullion by raising the price of the wheat? It is saying, because wheat is cheaper here than abroad,—I will add to the quantity by importing more and will at the same time increase its price. The same argument may be used if the whole transaction were on account of the foreign merchant [1].

'Now, in point of fact,' says Mr. Trower, 'Bank notes, at present, represent neither gold [n]or silver, the Bank being prohibited from paying their notes in either.' The dispute between Mr. Trower and myself, as I understood it, was, whether a bank note was an obligation to pay either. It is true that the bank is by law exempted from fulfilling its obligations, but that fact does not prevent us from ascertaining what their engagement is, and in what manner they would be obliged to perform it if the law were repealed. Here then is the difference in our view of the subject.

[1] Half a page is left blank at this point; the rest is begun on a fresh sheet, and may have been written sooner than the foregoing.

Mr. Trower contends that if the Bank were suddenly obliged to fulfill their engagements they could and would pay in silver coin it being their interest so to do; I on the contrary maintain that if so called upon they would be obliged to pay in gold coin,—that the silver coin is insufficient for the purpose and that by an express law there can be no silver coined. I admit that if silver could be coined that [1] metal would be preferred because it could be obtained at the least expence,—but that, whilst there is a law against the coinage of silver it is in fact reducing us to the use of gold only. The full extent of what I am contending for is allowed by Mr. Trower when he says, 'If at that period of time' (when the restriction on the bank shall be removed) 'the law inhibiting the coinage of silver money should continue in force, in that case undoubtedly gold must be considered as the measure of value in this country.' Is it fair that Mr. T should not argue on things as they are, but on those which he supposes may take place at some future period? The act prohibiting the coinage of silver may be repealed, and when that happens Mr. Trower may be right, silver may then become the standard measure of value, but whilst the law continues in force gold must necessarily be that measure, and the value of bank notes therefore must be estimated by their comparative value with gold coin or bullion.

The fact of there being more silver coin in circulation than gold can be easily accounted for; in the first place there are no bank notes of less amount than one pound [;] hence a necessity for the use of silver in small payments. Secondly, Bank notes being a substitute for gold coins there is absolutely no use for guineas, this joined to their high value compared with their substitute sufficiently accounts for their disappearing from circulation, and lastly the gold coin having retained its standard weight whilst the silver coin is debased 40 p ct. renders it advantageous to melt guineas and to retain the silver in circulation.

---

[1] In original 'that that.'

With respect to the second point in dispute, the effect on the prices of commodities, and of gold and silver bullion, which Mr. Trower supposes to have been produced by the debased state of the silver coins. Why, I would ask, if such be the fact was not the same effect produced on the market prices of those metals before the restriction on the Bank in 1797?

It will not be a satisfactory answer to say, because gold coin was then the standard measure, and, *that* coin not being debased no such effects followed. I say this would not be satisfactory because gold was the measure of value, only as it would more advantageously discharge a debt than standard silver coin;—but we are not now speaking of the standard silver coin but of the debased silver coin. The debased silver would then, as well as now[,] have been comparatively cheaper than the gold coin and could then, if it can now, have been more advantageously employed for the discharge of a debt; but no such effects followed then; gold bullion was steadily under its mint price and silver bullion was only above it because of the inaccurate determination of the mint proportions [1]. Perhaps a little further consideration will make this more clear. In 1797 the silver coin was debased 24 p ct.; at the same time the proportionate value of gold and silver was, in the market, as $14\frac{3}{4}$ to 1 whilst in the coin they were estimated as 15 to 1, gold was therefore the measure of value if the standard metals be compared;—but gold compared with the debased coin was as 19 to 1, there were therefore the same reasons then as there are now for gold bullion being above the mint price, as far as the debasement of silver was concerned; therefore I contend, that if as Mr. Trower supposes the price of commodities be now affected by the debased state of the silver coin, they must for the same reason have been equally so in 1797 and for many years before it. Will Mr. Trower explain why no such effect followed, Gold

---

[1] Cf. High Price of Bullion, Works, pp. 271-3; Reply to Bosanquet, *ib.* 316.

having been before 1797 for 23 years under its mint price?

I have said 'Compare the debased silver coin with the gold coin which is undebased, is it not of equal value to it?' Mr. Trower answers 'You say that Bank notes are 20 p.c. disct [;] compare them with the gold coin which is undebased, are they not of equal value to it?' Mr. Trower in another place observes that if the fact be as I state that £1000 in debased silver coin will purchase precisely as much gold or silver bullion as £1000 in gold coin, so is it also a fact that £1000 in Bank notes will do the same. If then it be admitted that at this time £1000 either in gold coin, in debased silver coin, or in Bank notes are precisely of the same value when used in the purchase of commodities, what is the cause that neither of these will purchase as much gold or silver bullion as they did in 1797 previously to the Bank restriction bill? And, tho' they may be of the same value in circulation here at home, is this agreement in their value forced or natural?

It must be evident that it is not by the value of the undebased gold coin, that the values of the bank notes and of debased silver are at present regulated. If they were so, gold would not be above its mint price because Mr. Trower has always agreed that no one would give more than an ounce of gold for an ounce of gold, gold could not therefore be at £4-10/ or £4-13/ per oz, if the value of the circulating medium were generally equal to that of the gold coin. It necessarily follows that the value of the gold coin is brought down to that of the debased silver, or to the Bank notes. But I have already remarked that the debased silver was always previously to 1797 brought up (because it was always moderate in its quantity) to the value of the gold coins, and that altho' it was legal tender to a certain amount, it was neither sufficiently abundant nor sufficiently current to raise the price of gold bullion above its mint price. Not an instance has occurred of a purchaser of gold bullion having paid a penny an ounce more for it in consequence of his wish of paying in debased silver coin.

If then gold and silver coins be of the same value and at the same time are depreciated in their exchangeable value to ⅘ of their true value; to the value in short of the Bank notes which are in circulation with them, to what can we attribute this phenomenon but to the depreciation of Bank notes? Let us suppose the law against the exportation of guineas repealed, Mr. Trower would not then contend that gold coin, silver coin and bank notes would be of equal value, because he has already admitted that more than an ounce of gold would not be given for an ounce of gold; but under those circumstances gold would continue to sell for £4 - 10/ or £4 - 13/ for bank notes or for debased shillings, but for gold coin it would not be higher than £3 - 17 - 10½ pr oz.

The present value at which gold coin passes in circulation is a forced value; its natural value is 15 p.c. above its forced value, but repeal the law, withdraw the force by which it is kept down, and it will immediately recover its natural value. If then I were to yield the first point in dispute and allow that Bank notes were obligations to pay silver and not gold coin, it would be evident that no other effect could be produced on the prices of gold or silver bullion, or on any other commodities from the debasement of the silver coin but the trifling one occasioned by a very small proportion of the debased silver coin being considered legal tender.

Before the recoinage of the gold coin in the year 1774, gold bullion, as I have already observed, was at £4 pr oz, being 2/1½ above the mint price. The debasement of the gold coin must have had a similar effect in raising the prices of all other commodities. This is a principle no longer disputed. Immediately on the recoinage gold fell under its mint price [1].

Whilst the gold coin was thus debased a guinea fresh from the mint and consequently undebased or any other which had been hoarded and had not partaken of the debase-

---

[1] Cf. High Price of Bullion, Works, p. 273, note.

ment, would have purchased no more goods than a worn and debased guinea, but it would not thence be argued that the debased and the new guinea were of equal value, it being manifest that the prices of all commodities were regulated, not by the quantity of gold in the new guineas, but by the quantity actually contained in the old.

In like manner, now, though a few guineas may be in circulation and may pass in the purchase of commodities for no more than an equal amount in Bank notes, the prices of commodities are regulated not by the quantity of gold which the guineas contain, but by the quantity which the Bank notes will purchase. These two quantities must, if the coin be undebased, and the bank notes not depreciated, be always nearly equal.

The fact of gold coin having been for near a century the principal measure of value is I think placed beyond dispute by the arguments of Lord Liverpool. They are briefly as follows. The debasement of the silver coin has not during that period caused any excess of the market above the mint price of either gold or silver bullion;—neither has it produced any effect on the exchanges with foreign countries, whereas the debasement of the gold coin which occurred during a part of the century never failed to produce a rise in the market price of gold and silver bullion and a corresponding effect on the rate of exchange; that immediately on the gold coin being brought to its present state of perfection the price of bullion fell under its mint price and the foreign exchanges were at par, if not favorable to us.

Lord Liverpool has clearly proved this fact, but has not given any satisfactory reasons why gold should be the standard measure of value in preference to silver.

It appears to me that gold *must* be the principal measure, if not the only measure of value, whilst the relative value of gold and silver is less in the market than the relative value of those metals in the coins, according to the mint regulations.

Gold and silver coins are equally by law legal tender for all sums if of their legal weight.

By the regulations of the mint gold is $15\frac{9}{131}$ times the value of silver. In the market up to the period when Lord Liverpool wrote, gold was only $14\frac{3}{4}$ times, on an average of a very long period, more valuable than silver. It became therefore the interest of every debtor to pay his debt in the gold coin and also the interest of every person, as well as the bank, who carried bullion to the mint to be coined, to carry gold and not silver for that purpose. Thus, if I were a merchant having my warehouses well stocked with goods and was in debt £1000—I could purchase as much gold bullion as is contained in a thousand pounds with less goods than I should be obliged to part with to obtain the quantity of silver bullion contained in a [sic] £1000,—this would determine me to purchase the gold and not the silver, and to carry the gold and not the silver to the mint to be coined. Whilst gold was only $14\frac{3}{4}$ the value of silver, the price of silver bullion would be always *above its mint price*, there would be a loss therefore to the bank in purchasing silver bullion to be coined,—whereas there would be no such loss in purchasing gold bullion for that purpose. *It appears therefore evident that it is only whilst gold is less valuable in the market compared with silver, than it is by the mint regulations, that it will be the only measure of value.* Bank notes will whilst this continues be the representatives of the gold coin, because the bank will always pay in the coin which can be coined at the least expence to them.

But, if in the course of time, *as it appears lately to have done, gold should become more valuable,* and be in the market at a greater proportion to silver than it is in the coins,—if it should be $15\frac{1}{2}$ or 16 times the value of silver, gold would be above its mint price and silver would be at or below its mint value. Gold could then be profitably melted and silver could be profitably coined; *silver would therefore become the standard of value; the bank would pay its notes in silver and consequently bank notes would become the representatives of the silver and not the gold coin. Indeed this is Mr. Trower's argument.* The high price of gold bullion [1], he justly contends, is no proof of the depreciation of bank notes because gold bullion may rise above its mint value from an alteration in its relative value to silver, tho' a bank note were not in existence. It will be seen by what I have already said that *I unequivocally admit the truth of this position.*

But if a high price of gold bullion proceeded from this cause the price of silver bullion would never whilst the coins of full weight only were legal tender, be above the mint price. No one contended when the price of silver bullion was above its mint price and the gold bullion was at or below its mint value (and this was the case generally previous to 1797) that bank notes were depreciated; and, if the price of gold bullion were 20 p.c. above its mint price, and silver bullion were at its mint price, I should allow that bank notes were not at a discount;—but when the prices of both the metals are above the mint prices it is proof conclusive of bank notes being at a discount.

Mr. Trower wishes to account for this from the acknowledged fact of the silver currency being debased.—If this debased currency were legal tender I should not dispute the point with him,—but it is acknowledged by him that it is not;—the debasement of the silver therefore cannot be the cause of the high price of silver bullion.

I shall now answer a few of the observations of Mr. Trower on my last letter in the Chronicle [2].

I quoted the price of silver at 5/9½ without any view of making my argument better or worse [3]. The price of 5/7 was not I believe mentioned by Mr. Trower at the time he wrote, nor did I reflect that it was on that price that his calculations were made; but as he observes, it is for principles we are contending, therefore 5/7 will suit my purpose just as well as 5/9½.

To Mr. Trower there appear inconsistencies in my saying that, if silver be the standard of currency Bank notes were

---

[1] Being that of only one sort of bullion.
[2] 23rd Nov. 1809. The others appeared on 29th Aug. and 20th Sept.
[3] High Price of Bullion, Works, p. 281, foot.

in 1797 at a prem^m of 24 p. c. and are now at a prem^m of 14; this is on the supposition of the debased silver currency being the standard, because £100 in bank notes would purchase in 1797 24 p. c. more silver bullion than what was contained in £100 in the debased silver currency and would now at its present price purchase 14 p. c. more. I have said too that 'if we estimate the value of Bank notes by silver bullion they will be found to be 12 p. c. dis^t.' and in another place 'if silver be the standard currency Bank notes are at a disc^t. of 11 p. c.' I am called upon to explain these passages. I meant that if our silver currency was perfectly of its mint weight and consequently as good as an equal quantity of bullion, Bank notes would if estimated by such a medium be 12 p. c. dis^t.,—but, as our currency is not thus pure, as by law in large paym^{ts} a creditor may be forced to accept as much as £25 in debased currency, bank notes were if estimated by our silver currency at a discount of 11 p. c.

In the calculations made by Mr. Trower he attributes all the excess of the market above the mint price of gold to the debasement of the silver coin, except that part of it which is occasioned by an alteration in the relative value of the two metals. He is correct in estimating the alteration in the relative value of gold and silver (at the price he quotes, £4 - 13/ and 5/7) at 11. 7. 2 pr ct, but he jumps to the conclusion in attributing the balance of the rise of gold above bank notes viz. 8. 1. 3 to the debasement of the silver currency,—he takes for granted that which is the subject of dispute and does not explain to us his data. By the same rule if he were to take the present prices of gold and silver bullion viz. £4. 10/ and 5/9½, he must for the effects of the debasement of the silver coin calculate on no less than 12 p. c. Now he will not say that the debasement of the silver coin has increased since this discussion commenced, therefore he must find out some other cause for the difference between £8. 1. 3 and £12.—

Mr. Trower says that if one metal only were in circulation the market would exceed the mint price in exact proportion to the debasement of the coin, but when it consists of two metals it does not follow that the bullion should be paid for in the depreciated currency. From what has already been said, though we have two metals in circulation one must necessarily be driven from circulation;—and as the depreciated silver is not legal tender no value can be estimated by it.

I am accused of stating an impossible case and it is asked 'what confidence can be placed upon such an hypothesis? it is a mode of reasoning as unusual as it is unavailing.' But is it an impossible case to suppose that my debtor should pay me in silver coin? I am contending with this gentleman that Bank notes are at discount, and in proof of my position I state that if my debtor were to pay me his debt in silver he would by law be obliged to pay me as much as would be equal in value to £1120 in Bank notes. Is not this a fair argument to prove that the silver contained in a £1000 is more valuable than £1000 in bank notes? That it is impossible that any man should so pay me whilst the law allows him to pay me in a piece of paper which is called £1000 indeed, but can command as much silver as is contained in £900 only, is the injury of which I complain, and the fact of its being worth no more which is not denied is a proof of the injury.

I agree with Mr. Trower that silver is a legal tender to any amount as well as gold if it be of its mint weight, but this admission on his part is fatal to his argument. With 62 standard shillings which he admits to be a pound of silver I can always purchase a pound of silver bullion. This he does not deny. It is expressly allowed by him that if silver coin be not debased silver bullion paid for in silver cannot exceed its mint price.

But with 62/ in Bank notes I cannot purchase a pound of silver; I am obliged to give £3. 7 in that medium for a pound of silver or a premium of £8 - 1 - 3. With what consistency can it be maintained that 62 standard shillings, such as are legal tender, are of no more value than £3 - 2 in bank notes?

If the regulations of our mint had been such that every shilling weighed an ounce,—whilst the shillings were of full weight silver could never rise above a shilling an ounce, and tho' the currency were debased and every shilling should come to weigh only half an ounce silver would not rise above one shilling an ounce whilst the law protected the seller of bullion from being paid in the debased coin. 'It is true' he would say 'I have sold you silver at a shilling an ounce but the shilling you tender me is not full weight, you must therefore pay me by weight at the mint price of a shilling.['] The seller would therefore ultimately receive two debased shillings tho' he had sold his silver for one. That such was the state of the silver bullion market we have the experience of near a century. Silver bullion was rarely much above its mint price and the excess which did exist was attributable to the alteration in the relative value of gold and silver. It was paid for in gold, and therefore gold was at its mint value [1].

B (1). [RICARDO.]

A., B., and C. each lay out £100 p^r ann. in corn, when its price is 40/ pr quarter, they each buy 50 quarters. But Government imposes a tax of 10/- pr quarter on corn, and consequently the price of corn rises from 40 to 50 shillings, and the whole 150 quarters consumed will cost £375, instead of £300. In consequence however of the additional price, A., B., and C. can[,] each, only purchase 40 quarters, instead of 50;—and therefore they will together purchase 120 quarters instead of 150. There will remain 30 quarters to be disposed of[,] which will be purchased by Government at the market price of 50/- and therefore for £75. This sum of £75 is precisely the sum which Government has raised by the tax of 10/- on 150 quarters, I think therefore I have shewn that although it is true that 150 quarters of corn will be disposed of for £375 instead of for £300 no

[1] Compare with the whole paper the chapter (xxvii) on Currency and Banks in Ricardo's Pol. Econ. and Taxation, Works, especially pp. 221-225, also High Price of Bullion, Works, 261-290. The last is by no means a simple reproduction of the Letters to the Chronicle.

additional quantity of money will be required for the purpose of purchasing it[1].

B (2).   [TROWER.]

No additional money is required to purchase it, because although more money is *paid* for the corn in consequence of the Tax, yet the cost of production of the corn, its natural price, is not increased. And the seller of the corn pays over to Government the extra price he receives in consequence of the Tax. This money, so paid to Government is given to other persons, by whom that portion of the Corn is purchased, which used to be bought by the taxpayers before the Tax was imposed.

So that the same £300 purchases the Corn whose price is raised by the Tax to £375. And it is enabled to do this in consequence of the *increased ratio* of its circulation, which the imposition of the tax occasions. Before the tax was imposed the 300 purchased 150 quarters of Corn for 300, now it first purchases 120 quarters at 50/ amounting to 300; and then afterwards, that portion of it which was paid for the tax, vz^t 75, purchases the remaining 30 quarters at 50/ amounting to 75. So that that portion circulates twice where before the Tax was imposed it only circulated once.

Thus the only effect of the Tax is to take from the payers of it the power of purchasing 30 quarters of Corn, and to transfer that power to other person[s]; and this is effected by causing the money to pass through the hands of the seller of the Corn to Government and from Government to these other persons. The increase in the ratio of circulation is equal to the amount of the Tax—vz^t 25 pr. C^t.

[1] This is the argument of the note on p. 127 of Works (Political Economy and Taxation, Ch. xv, Taxes on Profits.) The note does not occur in the 1st edition of Political Economy and Taxation, 1817, nor in the 2nd, 1819, but in the 3rd, 1821. The discussion with Trower may perhaps be responsible for it, and be referred to 1819 or 1820.

Compare also Letter XXXIV, p. 104, above, and Works, p. 99, note: 'It may be doubted whether commodities raised in price merely by taxation would require any more money for their circulation. I believe they would not.' This note also occurs first in the third edition.

INDEX

'Abraham Tudela,' 144.
Abstract Pound Sterling, theory of, 74.
Agricultural Reports. 168, 186. *See* Agriculture.
Agriculture, relation to capital and interest, 4 seq.; depression of, 13; Western's motion on, 19; Greenough on, 23; on the Continent, 35; influence of debt reduction on, 97, 98; improvements in, 114; Parliamentary Committee on, 148-50, 155, 161, 182-3, 186; condition of, 170-1, 174, 176, 179, 198, 208.
Althorp, Lord, 189.
America, 50, 51, 58.
Annual Obituary, 53.
Annual Register, 4, 53, 151.
Annual Review, 47.
Annuities, 181, 183.
Antwerp, 34, 36.
'Arena for capital,' 4.
Attwood, Thos., 33, 34, 149, 174.
Austin, A., 16 n.; letters from, 214-5.

Bain, Prof. A., 1, 10, 80.
Balance of powers, 69.
Bank of England, Ricardo on, 8, 72-4; restriction, 9; Bank Court meeting, 11, 14; notes of, 11, 145, &c.; treasure of, 17; Turner on, 19; Sinclair on, 33; stock and capital of, 75-7; directors of, 83; Government debt to, 95; policy of, 169, 182.
Banks, country, 11, 15, 181.
Banks, Mr., 182.
Baring, Alex., 18, 109, 144, 202.
Basevi, George, 206.
Bath Provident Institution, 18.
Bebb, John, 4.

Bennet, Grey, 178.
Bentham, Jeremy, in correspondence with Ricardo, 1; entertaining Mill, 1, 10; views on reform, 51-2, 54 5; aids Ricardo, 72; writing on reform, 80; 'Plan' of, 100.
Berkeley, Colonel, 45.
Birkbeck, Morris, 50 1.
'Birmingham School,' 34.
Black, John, 191.
Blake, Francis, 206.
Bouverie, W. P., 14.
British Review, 43, 48, 50.
Broglie, Duc de, 55, 194-5, 197.
Brougham, Lord, 55, 177, 179-80. 189.
Bullion, price of, 12, 83, 110; controversy, 46.
Bullionists, error of, 12.
Burdett, 54, 55, 200.
Burke, quoted, 52.

Cannan, E., 40, 72, 80, 209.
Canning, George, 103, 169.
Capital, 'arena for employment' of, 4; agricultural and manufacturing, 5; distribution of, 13, 128, 133. *See also* Profits.
Caroline, Queen, 112, 123, 134, 142, 146, 156, 163.
Catholic Claims, 30, 135, 145, 147 8.
Cato Street Conspiracy, 107.
Champion, 168.
Charity, 24, 48.
Chetwynd's Vagrant Bill, 187.
Children's Employment, 30.
Christianity in India, 3, 4. 11.
Chronicle, vi, vii, 42, 191-2, 231.
Clutterbuck, Thomas, 14, 16, 20.
Cobbett, William, 99, 149, 169, 171, 174-6, 182, 199, 202.

Cockerell, Mr., 16.
Colquhoun, 18.
Consols, 75, 96-7, 102, 156-7.
Constancio, translation of Ricardo, 38, 71.
Continent, Ricardo's tour on, 189, 193-7; letters from, 197.
Corn Law, Ricardo's proposed, 187-8; McCulloch on, 190. *See* Agriculture.
Courtenay, Peregrine, 203.
Crespigny, Sir William de, 80.
Critical Review, 4.
Currency, variation in value, 11-2, 51; parliamentary inquiry concerning, 72-3; paper preferred, 110, 144; effects of depreciation, 160, 168-9, 171, 174, 176, 179 80, 198; amount in circulation, 192.
Curtis, W., 108.

Debt, National, effect of, 13, 51, 83; payment by direct assessment, 96, 100, 102, 111; growth of, 102; effect of resumption upon, 110.
Distribution of capital, 13, 128, 133.
Dumont, 194 et seq.

East India Company and Missions, 3.
'Economical and Secure Currency,' 8, 11, 14, 17, 38, 73, 182, 192.
Edgeworth, Miss, 20, 24.
Edinburgh Magazine, 66.
Edinburgh Review, on Indian Missions, 4; on Napoleon, 9; on Ricardo, 39-40, 57; on Bentham, 52; on plan of direct assessment, 99; on free trade, 109; on Godwin, 173, &c.
Elwin, H., 18, 20, 32, 36, 75.
Encyclopaedia Britannica, 82, 96, 111, 139, &c.
Epsom, county meeting at, 175, 177-8.

Fitzwilliam, Lord, 94.
Folkestone, Lord, 200.
Food, supply of, 119-23, 124-7, 128 seq.
Forgery, of bank-notes, 145.
Free trade, 154, 161-2.
Funding system, 13, 96-7, 111.

Ganilh, 197.
Garnier, 196-7.
Gentleman's Magazine, 4.
Godwin, William, 139, 147, 165, 173.

Gold, price of, vi, vii, 12, 78; resolutions as to bullion, 73; as a measure of value, 224 et seq.
Goldsmid, Isaac Lyon, letter to, 204.
Greenough, G. B., letters quoted, 3, 23-4.
Grenfell, P., 17, 72.
Grenside, John, 179.
Grenville, Lord, on sinking fund, 15; on Ricardo, 43-4, 50, 72, 101; on currency, 202.
Grote, G., 204.
Grote, Mrs., 196.
Guise, Sir B. W., 53.

Haileybury College, 18.
Haldimand, W., 108.
Hall, Webb, 171, 177.
Hamilton, Dr., 82, 90-1, 97, 140.
Hansard, passim.
Heathfield, R., letter to, 96-8, 99.
Hereford, dinner to Hume at, 166-7; county meeting at, 198-9, 202-3.
Hobhouse, 200.
Hodgson, D., 149.
Hume, David, on reduction of debt by direct assessment, 99.
Hume, Joseph, on savings banks, 18; election petition, 116; dinner to at Hereford, 167-8; on Sir R. Wilson, 169; on Irish tithe system, 172.
Huskisson, 72, 149, 155, 182, 183, 189, 202, 209.
Hutcheson, Archibald, 99-100.

'Imlac' on Public Credit, 100.
Income tax, 95, 104.
India, missions in, 2, 4, 11; Mill's History of, 10, 44, 48.
Investment of capital, 157 8, 164-5.
Ireland, 21, 145, 148-9, 171-2, 207-8.

Jacob, on corn laws, 162.
Jews, disabilities of, 204.

Kent, Duke of, 79, 81.
King, Lord, 109.

Labour, supply of, 119-23, 124-7, 128 seq.
'Laicus,' letters of, 2-4.
Landholder, taxation of, 145.
Lauderdale, 78.
Liverpool, Lord, 201-2, 229.
Llandaff, Bishop of, 52, 142.
Lockhart, J. G., 94.

Index

Machinery, effects of, 43, 105.
Mackintosh, J., 103.
Macleod, H. D., 20.
Malthus, on capital and its 'arena,' 4; discussion with Ricardo, 8–9; preparing new edition of Essay, 5 n., 10, 19; difficulties at Haileybury, 18; criticisms of Essay, 18, 21, 37, 42, 43, 85; criticizes Ricardo, 38, 39, 40, 113 seq., 119; his Political Economy, 44, 46, 201; first acquaintance with Ricardo, 46; aversion to controversy, 46; reviews of, 46–7; opinions on reform, 69; doctrines in relation to Owen's plans, 79; omits taxation, 93; on 'the main hinge,' 130; Ricardo's 'Notes' on, 136 seq., 151; criticism of Torrens, 163; review of Godwin, 165; on measure of value, 201, 210–2.
Malthus, Miss M. C. H., 141; other relatives of T. R. Malthus, 143.
Marcet, Mrs., 108, 168.
Marriage and pauperism, 27; Royal Marriage Act, 42.
Martineau, Harriet, 4, 54, 84, 94.
Marx, Karl, 105.
Maxwell, Sir M., 54.
McCulloch, J. R., reviews Ricardo, 40, 43, 50, 57, 66; the wrong McCulloch, 61; reproduces misprints, 97; on Heathfield, 99; on Ricardo's constituents, 107; writings of, 109, 173; on Ricardo's 'Notes,' 140; visit to London, 205–6; on measure of value, 206, 212.
Merchants' Petition, 109.
Mill, James, relations with Bentham, 1, 10; with Ricardo, 1, 46, 56; History of India of, 10, 44; on Ricardo's dispute with Torrens, 39; on McCulloch's review of Ricardo, 59; at India House, 80; induces Ricardo to write for Napier, 82; to judge between Ricardo and Place, 90; activities of, 107; with Ricardo, 117; opinion on 'Notes,' 140; 'Political Economy,' 147, 163, 168, 173; on measure of value, 206; visits Gatcomb, 211.
Murray, John, 36, 71.
Mushet, Robert, 157.

Napier, Macvey, 82, 97; letter to, 111.
Napoleon, estimate of his character, 9; effects of 1815 on price of gold, 12 and note.
O'Meara, 198.
Optimism of Ricardo, 22, 34 n.
Owen, Robert, 37, 41, 47, 50, 79 81, 108, 125, 207.
Oxley, Mr., 36.

Palgrave, H. R. I., 1 n.
Palmer, General, speech of, 98.
Palmer, Horsley, 99.
Parliament, Ricardo's seat in, 51–3, 65, 72; reform in, 51–2, 54–5, 59–65, 66–70, 101, 199–200; Ricardo's constituents, 107; general election, 108; questions before, 170.
Parliamentary papers, supply of, 29, 74, 150.
Parnell, Sir H., on sinking fund, 181.
Payne's 'Family of Malthus,' 141, 143.
Peel, 19, 145, 169; Currency Act of, 168, 193, 199.
Peterloo, 84.
Pitt, sinking fund of, 86–7; India Bill of, 49.
Place, Francis, 34, 84; letters to, 85, 90.
Plunket, Mr., 145.
Political Economy, general scope of, 93; few masters in, 106; the right principles of, 108–9; not a panacea, 133.
Political Economy Club, 206.
Poor Laws, 23–9, 42–4, 47, 74, 191.
Population, 18, 21, 25–6, 37.
Price, Richard, 140.
Price, Uvedale, 167.
'Principles of Political Economy and Taxation,' 30, 36; second edition, 71, 96, 104, 123, 141.
Profits, determination of, 128 seq.; tax on, 104–5.

Quakers, and savings banks, 18.
Quarterly Review, 46 7, 58, 78, 168, 170.

Reform, *see* Parliament.
Rent, 113 seq., 121.
Resumption of cash payments, Turner on, 19; Sinclair on, 33; Ricardo before Committee on, 73; Resolutions of Committee, 73, 95.
Ricardo, David, passim.
— his daughters, 16, 70.
— Ralph, 7.
— Samson, 99.

Ricardo, Osman, 117.
Robinson, F. J., 169, 201.
Romilly, Sir S., 54. 71.
Rose, George, 18, 26-8.
Rossi, 197.
Russell, Lord John, 173.

Savings banks, Ricardo's views on, 14, 15, 18; Southwark, 18; Westminster, 22; City, 22, 23; Rose's clause, 26-7; relation to pauperism, 28-9; limit of deposits, 31-2; Gloucester, 44; popular prejudices against, 44; Trower's plan, 40.
Say, J. B., 38, 71, 128, 133, 137, 173, 196-7.
Say, Louis, 197.
Scarlett's Bill, 191.
Scotch Establishment, 145.
Scotsman, 43, 50, 65.
Scott, Sir Walter, 78, 106-7.
Senior, N. W., 206.
Sharp, Richard, 53, 108.
Sheriff-ship, Ricardo's, 45, 49, 56, 60, 95; Trower's, 103, 109
Sidmouth, Lord, 169.
Silver, vii, 78; as a measure of value, 219-21, 224-34; as standard of currency, Append. A.
Sinclair, Sir John, letters to, 6, 33, 110, 150, 174.
Sinking Fund, savings bank of the nation, 15; reduced, 51; not respected, 74-5; Hamilton on, 82; from taxes and from loans, 85-91; Ricardo's objection to, 95, 186, 201; essay on, 96-7, 111, 139; reversion of, 181, 183-5.
Sismondi, 84, 195, 197.
'Six Acts,' 101.
Smith, Adam, 9, 30, 40, 43, 46, 152, 196.
Smith, Sydney, xiv, 165-6.
Smithies, Mr., 203.
South Sea Plan, 191.
Southey, 46-7.
Stael, Mme. de, 55, 195.
Stock Exchange, 6-7, 75.
Stourton, Lord, 163.
Sumner, J. B., 47.
Surrey, county meeting, 200.

Taxation, of property, 19; increase of, 51, 75; need of study of, 83, 163; direct and indirect, 98; effects on price, 105, 234-6; effect on production, 105-6; relation to agriculture, 170-1, 175-6, 178-98; Trower's plan of assessed, 180, 183-5.
Tierney, Geo., 51, 101.
Timber duties, 150.
Times, 3-4, 37, 41, 144, 146.
Times, New, 79.
Tithes, as investments, 157-8, 164-5; in Ireland, 172.
Toleration, Ricardo on, 204.
Tooke, Thomas, 109, 149, 161, 208.
Torrens, Major, 37-40, 66, 80, 108, 162, 206.
Trade, competition in, 35.
Trotter, Coutts, pamphlet of, 217-8; Ricardo's criticism of, 222-4.
Trower, Hutches, passim.
— John, vi, 3.
— Walter, xiii, 3.
— Miss Frances, viii seq., 24, 37, 94.
Turner, Samuel, 19, 78-9, 83, 190.

Value, measure of, 39, 151 seq., 206, 210-2, 219-21, 224-34; distinguished from price, 57-8; real and exchangeable, 162.
Vansittart, N., Attwood's letter to, 33; Stock Notes of, 51; Sinking Fund of, 87-8; successor of, 169.

Wages, 24-5, 119-20.
Wakefield, E., 18.
Wallas, G., 34, 84-5.
Walpole, Spencer, 151.
Warburton, 206.
Wars, continental, 201, 209, 213.
Wellesley, Lord, 172.
West, Edward, 58.
Western, 19, 193.
Weyland, J., 21, 47.
Wheatley, J., letter to, 159.
Whitmore, 183.
Wilberforce, W., 18.
Wilson, Sir R., 164, 169.
Wodehouse, 183.

THE END

19/10\99

Clarendon Press, Oxford.

SELECT LIST OF STANDARD WORKS.

DICTIONARIES	page 1
LAW	„ 2
HISTORY, BIOGRAPHY, ETC. . . .	„ 4
PHILOSOPHY, LOGIC, ETC.	„ 6
PHYSICAL SCIENCE, ETC.	„ 7

1. DICTIONARIES.

A NEW ENGLISH DICTIONARY
ON HISTORICAL PRINCIPLES,

Founded mainly on the materials collected by the Philological Society.

Imperial 4to.

EDITED BY DR. MURRAY.

PRESENT STATE OF THE WORK.

			£ s. d.
Vol. I. { A / B } By Dr. MURRAY	Half-morocco		2 12 6
Vol. II. C By Dr. MURRAY	Half-morocco		2 12 6
Vol. III. { D } By Dr. MURRAY / { E } By Mr. HENRY BRADLEY	. . . Half-morocco		2 12 6
Vol. IV. { F } By Mr. HENRY / { G } BRADLEY	F-Field		0 7 6
	Field-Frankish		0 12 6
	Franklaw-Glass-cloth		0 12 6
	Germano-Glass-cloth		0 2 6
Vol. V. H—K By Dr. MURRAY.	H-Hod		0 12 6
	Hod-Horizontal		0 2 6
	Horizontality-Hywe		0 5 0
	I-Iu		0 5 0

☞ *The remainder of the work, to the end of the alphabet, is in an advanced state of preparation.*

*** *The Dictionary is also, as heretofore, issued in the original Parts—*

Series I.	Parts I-IX.	A—Distrustful . . . . each	0 12 6
Series I.	Part X.	Distrustfully—Dziggetai	0 7 6
Series II.	Parts I-IV.	E—Glass-cloth . . . . each	0 12 6
Series III.	Part I.	H—Hod	0 12 6
Series III.	Part II.	Hod—Hywe	0 7 6

Oxford: Clarendon Press. London: HENRY FROWDE, Amen Corner, E.C.

A Hebrew and English Lexicon of the Old Testament, with an Appendix containing the Biblical Aramaic, based on the Thesaurus and Lexicon of Gesenius, by Francis Brown, D.D., S. R. Driver, D.D., and C. A. Briggs, D.D. Parts I–VII. Small 4to, 2s. 6d. each.

Thesaurus Syriacus: collegerunt Quatremère, Bernstein, Lorsbach, Arnoldi, Agrell, Field, Roediger: edidit R. Payne Smith, S.T.P. Vol. I, containing Fasciculi I–V, sm. fol., 5l. 5s.

*** *The First Five Fasciculi may also be had separately.*

Fasc. VI. 1l. 1s.; VII. 1l. 11s. 6d.; VIII. 1l. 16s.; IX. 1l. 5s.; X. Pars. I. 1l. 16s.

A Compendious Syriac Dictionary, founded upon the above. Edited by Mrs. Margoliouth. Parts I and II. Small 4to, 8s. 6d. net each.

*** *The Work will be completed in Four Parts.*

A Sanskrit-English Dictionary. Etymologically and Philologically arranged. By Sir M. Monier-Williams, D.C.L. 4to. 2l. 2s.

A Greek-English Lexicon. By H. G. Liddell, D.D., and Robert Scott, D.D. *Eighth Edition, Revised.* 4to. 1l. 16s.

An Etymological Dictionary of the English Language, arranged on an Historical Basis. By W. W. Skeat, Litt.D. *Third Edition.* 4to. 2l. 4s.

A Middle-English Dictionary. By F. H. Stratmann. A new edition, by H. Bradley, M.A. 4to, half-morocco, 1l. 11s. 6d.

The Student's Dictionary of Anglo-Saxon. By H. Sweet, M.A., Ph.D., LL.D. Small 4to, 8s. 6d. *net.*

An Anglo-Saxon Dictionary, based on the MS. collections of the late Joseph Bosworth, D.D. Edited and enlarged by Prof. T. N. Toller, M.A. Parts I–III. A–SÁR. 4to, stiff covers, 15s. each. Part IV, § 1, SÁR–SWÍÐRIAN. Stiff covers, 8s. 6d. Part IV, § 2, SWÍÞ-SNEL-ÝTMEST, 18s. 6d.

*** *A Supplement, which will complete the Work, is in active preparation.*

An Icelandic-English Dictionary, based on the MS. collections of the late Richard Cleasby. Enlarged and completed by G. Vigfússon, M.A. 4to. 3l. 7s.

2. LAW.

Anson. *Principles of the English Law of Contract, and of Agency in its Relation to Contract.* By Sir W. R. Anson, D.C.L. *Ninth Edition.* 8vo. 10s. 6d.

—— *Law and Custom of the Constitution.* 2 vols. 8vo.
Part I. Parliament. *Third Edition.* 12s. 6d.
Part II. The Crown. *Second Edition.* 14s.

Baden-Powell. *Land-Systems of British India;* being a Manual of the Land-Tenures, and of the Systems of Land-Revenue Administration prevalent in the several Provinces. By B. H. Baden-Powell, C.I.E. 3 vols. 8vo. 3l. 3s.

Digby. *An Introduction to the History of the Law of Real Property.* By Sir Kenelm E. Digby, M.A. *Fifth Edition.* 8vo. 12s. 6d.

Oxford: Clarendon Press.

Grueber. *Lex Aquilia.* By Erwin Grueber, Dr. Jur., M.A. 8vo. 10s. 6d.

Hall. *International Law.* By W. E. Hall, M.A. *Fourth Edition.* 8vo. 22s. 6d.

—— *A Treatise on the Foreign Powers and Jurisdiction of the British Crown.* By W. E. Hall, M.A. 8vo. 10s. 6d.

Holland. *Elements of Jurisprudence.* By T. E. Holland, D.C.L. *Eighth Edition.* 8vo. 10s. 6d.

—— *The European Concert in the Eastern Question;* a Collection of Treaties and other Public Acts. Edited, with Introductions and Notes, by T. E. Holland, D.C.L. 8vo. 12s. 6d.

—— *Studies in International Law.* By T. E. Holland, D.C.L. 8vo. 10s. 6d.

—— *Gentilis, Alberici, De Iure Belli Libri Tres.* Edidit T. E. Holland, I.C.D. Small 4to, half-morocco, 21s.

—— *The Institutes of Justinian,* edited as a recension of the Institutes of Gaius, by T. E. Holland, D.C.L. *Second Edition.* Extra fcap. 8vo. 5s.

Holland and Shadwell. *Select Titles from the Digest of Justinian.* By T. E. Holland, D.C.L., and C. L. Shadwell, D.C.L. 8vo. 14s.

Also sold in Parts, in paper covers—
Part I. Introductory Titles. 2s. 6d.
Part II. Family Law. 1s.
Part III. Property Law. 2s. 6d.
Part IV. Law of Obligations (No. 1), 3s. 6d. (No. 2), 4s. 6d.

Ilbert. *The Government of India.* Being a Digest of the Statute Law relating thereto. With Historical Introduction and Illustrative Documents. By Sir Courtenay Ilbert, K.C.S.I. 8vo, half-roan. 21s.

Jenks. *Modern Land Law.* By Edward Jenks, M.A. 8vo. 15s.

Markby. *Elements of Law considered with reference to Principles of General Jurisprudence.* By Sir William Markby, D.C.L. *Fifth Edition.* 8vo. 12s. 6d.

Moyle. *Imperatoris Iustiniani Institutionum Libri Quattuor;* with Introductions, Commentary, Excursus and Translation. By J. B. Moyle, D.C.L. *Third Edition.* 2 vols. 8vo. Vol. I. 16s. Vol. II. 6s.

—— *Contract of Sale in the Civil Law.* 8vo. 10s. 6d.

Pollock and Wright. *An Essay on Possession in the Common Law.* By Sir F. Pollock, Bart., M.A., and Sir R. S. Wright, B.C.L. 8vo. 8s. 6d.

Poste. *Gaii Institutionum Juris Civilis Commentarii Quattuor;* or, Elements of Roman Law by Gaius. With a Translation and Commentary by Edward Poste, M.A. *Third Edition.* 8vo. 18s.

Raleigh. *An Outline of the Law of Property.* By Thos. Raleigh, D.C.L. 8vo. 7s. 6d.

Sohm. *Institutes of Roman Law.* By Rudolph Sohm. Translated by J. C. Ledlie, B.C.L. With an Introductory Essay by Erwin Grueber, Dr. Jur., M.A. 8vo. 18s.

Stokes. *The Anglo-Indian Codes.* By Whitley Stokes, LL.D.
Vol. I. Substantive Law. 8vo. 30s.
Vol. II. Adjective Law. 8vo. 35s.
First and Second Supplements to the above, 1887-1891. 8vo. 6s. 6d. Separately, No. 1, 2s. 6d.; No. 2, 4s. 6d.

3. HISTORY, BIOGRAPHY, ETC.

Adamnani *Vita S. Columbae.* Ed. J. T. Fowler, D.C.L. Crown 8vo, half-bound, 8s. 6d. *net* (with translation, 9s. 6d. *net*).

Aubrey. '*Brief Lives,*' *chiefly of Contemporaries, set down by John Aubrey, between the Years* 1669 *and* 1696. Edited from the Author's MSS., by Andrew Clark, M.A., LL.D. With Facsimiles. 2 vols. 8vo. 25s.

Baedae *Historia Ecclesiastica,* etc. Edited by C. Plummer, M.A. 2 vols. Crown 8vo, 21s. *net*.

Bedford (W.K.R.). *The Blazon of Episcopacy.* Being the Arms borne by, or attributed to, the Archbishops and Bishops of England and Wales. With an Ordinary of the Coats described and of other Episcopal Arms. *Second Edition, Revised and Enlarged.* With One Thousand Illustrations. Sm. 4to, buckram, 31s. 6d. *net*.

Boswell's *Life of Samuel Johnson, LL.D.* Edited by G. Birkbeck Hill, D.C.L. In six volumes, medium 8vo. With Portraits and Facsimiles. Half-bound, 3*l.* 3s.

Bright. *Chapters of Early English Church History.* By W. Bright, D.D. *Third Edition. Revised and Enlarged.* With a Map. 8vo. 12s.

Casaubon (Isaac). 1559-1614. By Mark Pattison. 8vo. 16s.

Clarendon's *History of the Rebellion and Civil Wars in England.* Re-edited from a fresh collation of the original MS. in the Bodleian Library, with marginal dates and occasional notes, by W. Dunn Macray, M.A., F.S.A. 6 vols. Crown 8vo. 2*l.* 5s.

Hewins. *The Whitefoord Papers.* Being the Correspondence and other Manuscripts of Colonel CHARLES WHITEFOORD and CALEB WHITEFOORD, from 1739 to 1810. Edited, with Introduction and Notes, by W. A. S. Hewins, M.A. 8vo. 12. 6d.

Earle. *Handbook to the Land-Charters, and other Saxonic Documents.* By John Earle, M.A. Crown 8vo. 16s.

Freeman. *The History of Sicily from the Earliest Times.*
Vols. I and II. 8vo, cloth, 2*l.* 2s.
Vol. III. The Athenian and Carthaginian Invasions. 24s.
Vol. IV. From the Tyranny of Dionysios to the Death of Agathokles. Edited by Arthur J. Evans, M.A. 21s.

Freeman. *The Reign of William Rufus and the Accession of Henry the First.* By E. A. Freeman, D.C.L. 2 vols. 8vo. 1*l.* 16s.

Gardiner. *The Constitutional Documents of the Puritan Revolution,* 1628-1660. Selected and Edited by Samuel Rawson Gardiner, D.C.L. *Second Edition.* Crown 8vo. 10s. 6d.

Gross. *The Gild Merchant;* a Contribution to British Municipal History. By Charles Gross, Ph.D. 2 vols. 8vo. 24s.

Hastings. *Hastings and the Rohilla War.* By Sir John Strachey, G.C.S.I. 8vo, cloth, 10s. 6d.

Hill. *Sources for Greek History between the Persian and Peloponnesian Wars.* Collected and arranged by G. F. Hill, M.A. 8vo. 10s. 6d.

Hodgkin. *Italy and her Invaders.* With Plates & Maps. 8 vols. 8vo. By T. Hodgkin, D.C.L.
Vols. I-II. *Second Edition.* 42s.
Vols. III-IV. *Second Edition.* 36s.
Vols. V-VI. 36s.
Vol. VII-VIII (*completing the work*). 24s.

HISTORY, BIOGRAPHY, ETC.

Payne. *History of the New World called America.* By E. J. Payne, M.A. 8vo.
   Vol. I, containing Book I, *The Discovery*; Book II, Part I, *Aboriginal America*, 18s.
   Vol. II, containing Book II, *Aboriginal America* (concluded), 14s.

Johnson. *Letters of Samuel Johnson, LL.D.* Collected and Edited by G. Birkbeck Hill, D.C.L. 2 vols. half-roan, 28s.

—— *Johnsonian Miscellanies.* By the same Editor. 2 vols. Medium 8vo, half-roan, 28s.

Kitchin. *A History of France.* With Numerous Maps, Plans, and Tables. By G. W. Kitchin, D.D. In three Volumes. New Edition. Crown 8vo, each 10s. 6d.
   Vol. I. to 1453. Vol. II. 1453–1624. Vol. III. 1624–1793.

Lewis (*Sir G. Cornewall*). *An Essay on the Government of Dependencies.* Edited by C. P. Lucas, B.A. 8vo, half-roan. 14s.

Lucas. *Introduction to a Historical Geography of the British Colonies.* By C. P. Lucas, B.A. With Eight Maps. Crown 8vo. 4s. 6d.

—— *Historical Geography of the British Colonies:*
   Vol. I. The Mediterranean and Eastern Colonies (exclusive of India). With Eleven Maps. Crown 8vo. 5s.
   Vol. II. The West Indian Colonies. With Twelve Maps. Crown 8vo. 7s. 6d.
   Vol. III. West Africa. With Five Maps. Crown 8vo. 7s. 6d.
   Vol. IV. South and East Africa. Historical and Geographical. With Ten Maps. Crown 8vo. 9s. 6d.
   Also Vol. IV in two Parts—
   Part I. Historical, 6s. 6d.
   Part II. Geographical, 3s. 6d.

Ludlow. *The Memoirs of Edmund Ludlow, Lieutenant-General of the Horse in the Army of the Commonwealth of England, 1625–1672.* Edited by C. H. Firth, M.A. 2 vols. 8vo. 1l. 16s.

Machiavelli. *Il Principe.* Edited by L. Arthur Burd, M.A. With an Introduction by Lord Acton. 8vo. 14s.

Prothero. *Select Statutes and other Constitutional Documents, illustrative of the Reigns of Elizabeth and James I.* Edited by G. W. Prothero, M.A. Crown 8vo. Second Edition. 10s. 6d.

—— *Select Statutes and other Documents bearing on the Constitutional History of England, from* A.D. 1307 *to* 1558. By the same Editor. [*In Preparation.*]

Ramsay (Sir J. H.). *Lancaster and York.* A Century of English History (A.D. 1399–1485). 2 vols. 8vo. With Index, 37s. 6d.

Ramsay (W. M.). *The Cities and Bishoprics of Phrygia.* By W. M. Ramsay, D.C.L., LL.D.
   Vol. I. Part I. The Lycos Valley and South-Western Phrygia. Royal 8vo. 18s. net.
   Vol. I. Part II. West and West-Central Phrygia. 21s. net.

Ranke. *A History of England, principally in the Seventeenth Century.* By L. von Ranke. Translated under the superintendence of G. W. Kitchin, D.D., and C. W. Boase, M.A. 6 vols. 8vo. 63s.
   Revised Index, separately, 1s.

Rashdall. *The Universities of Europe in the Middle Ages.* By Hastings Rashdall, M.A. 2 vols. (in 3 Parts) 8vo. With Maps. 2l. 5s., net.

London: HENRY FROWDE, Amen Corner, E.C.

Smith's *Lectures on Justice,*
Police, Revenue and Arms. Edited,
with Introduction and Notes, by
Edwin Cannan. 8vo. 10s. 6d. net.

—— *Wealth of Nations.*
With Notes, by J. E. Thorold Rogers,
M.A. 2 vols. 8vo. 21s.

Stephens. *The Principal Speeches of the Statesmen and Orators of the French Revolution, 1789–1795.*
By H. Morse Stephens. 2 vols.
Crown 8vo. 21s.

Stubbs. *Select Charters and other Illustrations of English Constitutional History, from the Earliest Times to the Reign of Edward I.* Arranged and edited by W. Stubbs, D.D., Lord Bishop of Oxford. *Eighth Edition.* Crown 8vo. 8s. 6d.

—— *The Constitutional History of England, in its Origin and Development. Library Edition.* 3 vols. Demy 8vo. 2l. 8s.

Also in 3 vols. crown 8vo, price 12s. each.

Stubbs. *Seventeen Lectures on the Study of Mediaeval and Modern History.* Crown 8vo. 8s. 6d.

—— *Registrum Sacrum Anglicanum.* An attempt to exhibit the course of Episcopal Succession in England. By W. Stubbs, D.D. Small 4to. *Second Edition.* 10s. 6d.

Swift (F. D.). *The Life and Times of James the First of Aragon.* By F. D. Swift, B.A. 8vo. 12s. 6d.

Vinogradoff. *Villainage in England.* Essays in English Mediaeval History. By Paul Vinogradoff, Professor in the University of Moscow. 8vo, half-bound. 16s.

Woodhouse. *Aetolia; its Geography, Topography, and Antiquities.* By William J. Woodhouse, M.A., F.R.G.S. With Maps and Illustrations. Royal 8vo. price 21s. net.

4. PHILOSOPHY, LOGIC, ETC.

Bacon. *Novum Organum.*
Edited, with Introduction, Notes, &c., by T. Fowler, D.D. *Second Edition.* 8vo. 15s.

Berkeley. *The Works of George Berkeley, D.D., formerly Bishop of Cloyne;* including many of his writings hitherto unpublished. With Prefaces, Annotations, and an Account of his Life and Philosophy. By A. Campbell Fraser, Hon. D.C.L., LL.D. 4 vols. 8vo. 2l. 18s.

The Life, Letters, &c., separately, 16s.

Bosanquet. *Logic; or, the Morphology of Knowledge.* By B. Bosanquet, M.A. 8vo. 21s.

Butler. *The Works of Joseph Butler, D.C.L.,* sometime Lord Bishop of Durham. Divided into sections, with sectional headings, an index to each volume, and some occasional notes; also prefatory matter. Edited by the Right Hon. W. E. Gladstone. 2 vols. Medium 8vo. 14s. each.

Fowler. *The Elements of Deductive Logic,* designed mainly for the use of Junior Students in the Universities. By T. Fowler, D.D. *Tenth Edition,* with a Collection of Examples. Extra fcap. 8vo. 3s. 6d.

—— *The Elements of Inductive Logic,* designed mainly for the use of Students in the Universities. By the same Author. *Sixth Edition.* Extra fcap. 8vo. 6s.

—— *Logic;* Deductive and Inductive, combined in a single volume. Extra fcap. 8vo. 7s. 6d.

Fowler and Wilson. *The Principles of Morals.* By T. Fowler, D.D., and J. M. Wilson, B.D. 8vo, cloth, 14s.

Green. *Prolegomena to Ethics.* By T. H. Green, M.A. Edited by A. C. Bradley, M.A. *Fourth Edition.* Crown 8vo. 7s. 6d.

Hegel. *The Logic of Hegel.* Translated from the Encyclopaedia of the Philosophical Sciences. With Prolegomena to the Study of Hegel's Logic and Philosophy. By W. Wallace, M.A. *Second Edition, Revised and Augmented.* 2 vols. Crown 8vo. 10s. 6d. each.

Hegel's *Philosophy of Mind.* Translated from the Encyclopaedia of the Philosophical Sciences. With Five Introductory Essays. By William Wallace, M.A., LL.D. Crown 8vo. 10s. 6d.

Hume's *Treatise of Human Nature.* Edited, with Analytical Index, by L. A. Selby-Bigge, M.A. *Second Edition.* Crown 8vo. 8s.

—— *Enquiry concerning the Human Understanding, and an Enquiry concerning the Principles of Morals.* Edited by L. A. Selby-Bigge, M.A. Crown 8vo. 7s. 6d.

Leibniz. *The Monadology and other Philosophical Writings.* Translated, with Introduction and Notes, by Robert Latta, M.A., D.Phil. Crown 8vo. 8s. 6d.

Locke. *An Essay Concerning Human Understanding.* By John Locke. Collated and Annotated, with Prolegomena, Biographical, Critical, and Historic, by A. Campbell Fraser, Hon. D.C.L., LL.D. 2 vols. 8vo. 1l. 12s.

Lotze's *Logic,* in Three Books; of Thought, of Investigation, and of Knowledge. English Translation; edited by B. Bosanquet. M.A. *Second Edition.* 2 vols. Cr. 8vo. 12s.

—— *Metaphysic,* in Three Books; Ontology, Cosmology, and Psychology. English Translation; edited by B. Bosanquet, M.A. *Second Edition.* 2 vols. Cr. 8vo. 12s.

Martineau. *Types of Ethical Theory.* By James Martineau, D.D. *Third Edition.* 2 vols. Cr. 8vo. 15s.

—— *A Study of Religion:* its Sources and Contents. *Second Edition.* 2 vols. Cr. 8vo. 15s.

Selby-Bigge. *British Moralists.* Selections from Writers principally of the Eighteenth Century. Edited by L. A. Selby-Bigge, M.A. 2 vols. Crown 8vo. 18s.

Wallace. *Lectures and Essays on Natural Theology and Ethics.* By William Wallace, M.A., LL.D. Edited, with a Biographical Introduction by Edward Caird, M.A., Hon. D.C.L. 8vo, with a Portrait. 12s. 6d.

5. PHYSICAL SCIENCE, ETC.

Balfour. *The Natural History of the Musical Bow.* A Chapter in the Developmental History of Stringed Instruments of Music. Part I, Primitive Types. By Henry Balfour, M.A. Royal 8vo, paper covers. 4s. 6d.

Chambers. *A Handbook of Descriptive and Practical Astronomy.* By G. F. Chambers, F.R.A.S. *Fourth Edition,* in 3 vols. Demy 8vo.
Vol. I. The Sun, Planets, and Comets. 21s.
Vol. II. Instruments and Practical Astronomy. 21s.
Vol. III. The Starry Heavens. 14s.

De Bary. *Comparative Anatomy of the Vegetative Organs of the Phanerogams and Ferns.* By Dr. A. de Bary. Translated by F. O. Bower, M.A., and D. H. Scott, M.A. Royal 8vo. 1*l*. 2*s*. 6*d*.

—— *Comparative Morphology and Biology of Fungi, Mycetozoa and Bacteria.* By Dr. A. de Bary. Translated by H. E. F. Garnsey, M.A. Revised by Isaac Bayley Balfour, M.A., M.D., F.R.S. Royal 8vo, half-morocco, 1*l*. 2*s*. 6*d*.

—— *Lectures on Bacteria.* By Dr. A. de Bary. *Second Improved Edition.* Translated by H. E. F. Garnsey, M.A. Revised by Isaac Bayley Balfour, M.A., M.D., F.R.S. Crown 8vo. 6*s*.

Druce. *The Flora of Berkshire.* Being a Topographical and Historical Account of the Flowering Plants and Ferns found in the County, with short Biographical Notices. By G. C. Druce, Hon. M.A. Oxon. Crown 8vo, 16*s*. net.

Elliott. *An Introduction to the Algebra of Quantics.* By E. B. Elliott, M.A. 8vo. 15*s*.

Goebel. *Outlines of Classification and Special Morphology of Plants.* By Dr. K. Goebel. Translated by H. E. F. Garnsey, M.A. Revised by Isaac Bayley Balfour, M.A., M.D., F.R.S. Royal 8vo, half-morocco, 1*l*. 1*s*.

Johnston. *An Elementary Treatise on Analytical Geometry,* with Numerous Examples. By W. J. Johnston, M.A. (R.U.I.) Crown 8vo. 6*s*.

Prestwich. *Geology, Chemical, Physical, and Stratigraphical.* By Sir Joseph Prestwich, M.A., F.R.S. In two Volumes. 3*l*. 1*s*.

Price. *A Treatise on the Measurement of Electrical Resistance.* By W. A. Price, M.A., A.M.I.C.E. 8vo. 14*s*.

Sachs. *A History of Botany.* Translated by H. E. F. Garnsey, M.A. Revised by I. Bayley Balfour, M.A., M.D., F.R.S. Crown 8vo. 10*s*.

Solms-Laubach. *Fossil Botany.* Being an Introduction to Palaeophytology from the Standpoint of the Botanist. By H. Graf zu Solms-Laubach. Translated by H. E. F. Garnsey, M.A. Revised by I. Bayley Balfour, M.A., M.D., F.R.S. Royal 8vo, half-morocco, 18*s*.

Biological Series.

I. *The Physiology of Nerve, of Muscle, and of the Electrical Organ.* Edited by Sir J. Burdon Sanderson, Bart., M.D., F.R.SS. L.&E. Medium 8vo. 1*l*. 1*s*.

II. *The Anatomy of the Frog.* By Dr. Alexander Ecker, Professor in the University of Freiburg. Translated, with numerous Annotations and Additions, by G. Haslam, M.D. Medium 8vo. 21*s*.

IV. *Essays upon Heredity and Kindred Biological Problems.* By Dr. A. Weismann. Authorized Translation. Crown 8vo.
Vol. I. Edited by E. B. Poulton, S. Schönland, and A. E. Shipley. *Second Edition.* 7*s*. 6*d*.
Vol. II. Edited by E. B. Poulton, and A. E. Shipley. 5*s*.

Oxford
AT THE CLARENDON PRESS

London, Edinburgh, and New York

HENRY FROWDE

www.ingramcontent.com/pod-product-compliance
Lightning Source LLC
Chambersburg PA
CBHW031957230426
43672CB00010B/2186